Also by Jasper White

Lobster at Home

Jasper White's Cooking from New England

50 Chowders

ONE-POT MEALS—CLAM, CORN & BEYOND

Jasper White

PHOTOGRAPHS BY GENTL & HYERS, ILLUSTRATIONS BY GLENN WOLFF

SCRIBNER

NEW YORK LONDON TORONTO SYDNEY SINGAPORE

Scribner
1230 Avenue of the Americas
New York, NY 10020

Designed by Britta Steinbrecht

Set in Frutiger and Letter Gothic

Manufactured in the United States of America
3   5   7   9   10   8   6   4

Library of Congress Cataloging-in-Publication Data
White, Jasper.
50 Chowders : one pot meals, clam, corn & beyond / Jasper White ; photographs by Gentl & Hyers ;
illustrations by Glenn Wolff.
p. cm.
1. Soups. 2. Stews. I. Title: Fifty chowders. II. Title.
TX757 . W45 2000
641.8'13—dc21
00-025242
ISBN 0-684-85034-6

For my mother, **Mary**

Contents

Acknowledgments

I would like to express my love and gratitude to all my family, friends, and associates, especially:

Nancy White, my wife, and our children J.P. (Jasper Paul), Mariel, and Hayley, who ate more chowder last summer than anyone in America! You were such good sports and great eaters. I love you dearly and I'm grateful for all you add to my life.

Mom, Dad, Nat, Trevor, Muriel, Fiona, Rick, Michael, Hillary, Matt, Annie, Julie, Billie, Jamie, and all my nieces and nephews.

Maria Guarnaschelli, my editor and writing mentor, who requires that I give each book my all because she does. You're the best!

Doe Coover, my literary agent, advisor, and friend, who believed in my simple idea for this book.

Patrick Lyons and Ed Sparks, my partners at Summer Shack.

M. C. Hald for her meticulous attention to detail. Judith Sutton, copy editor, who put the finishing touches on each page. Beth Wareham, Anne Kemper, John Fontana, and all the talented staff at Scribner.

Britta Steinbrecht for her brilliant design.

Glenn Wolff, illustrator, whose splendid art has enhanced yet another of my books.

Andrea Gentl and Marty Hyers, photographers, who brought my chowders to life and made their images alluring!

Michael Pederson, food stylist, who "gets" chowder and was a joy to cook with, and his assistant, Tracy Harlor.

Helen Crowther, prop stylist, whose many bowls were just waiting for chowder!

Chef Bob Redmond, who taught me how good a real Yankee fish chowder can be.

The many authors whose books provided an understanding of traditional chowders and inspiration for modern adaptations, especially John Thorne, Richard Hooker, and Cap'n Phil Schwind.

The fishermen, aquaculturists, and farmers who do the hard part of chowder making.

A List of the Recipes

8. Chowder Companions

Introduction

chowder (chou'dẽr), **n.** [<Fr. *chaudière,* pot],
a dish consisting of fresh fish, clams, etc., stewed
with vegetables, often in milk
—*Webster's New World Dictionary*

Webster's rightfully omits the word *soup* in its definition—chowder is "a dish" unique unto itself. In order to understand chowder, you must move away from the image of the pasty-white clam chowder many restaurants serve in a small cup with a bag of crackers. Visualize instead a large shallow bowl with big slices of potato and onion and thick flakes of fresh haddock heaped in the middle of a steaming aromatic liquid. Crisp pork cracklings and chopped chives top the creamy broth dotted with black pepper, chopped thyme, and droplets of melted butter. Next to this feast is a basket holding golden brown corn fritters and toasted buttery common crackers. This is the real thing—New England Fish Chowder—but it is only one of the dozens of home-style chowders you can make from this book. Once you discover the diversity of ingredients you can cook into a chowder and see the scope of styles and colors open to you, I think you will wonder, as I still do, how people ever came to think there were only one or two chowders in the world.

I grew up at the New Jersey Shore, where many fish houses served chowder, usually red (tomato) clam chowder, in cups. A few places offered New England (white) clam chowder, and I remember having corn chowder once or twice. My perspective on chowder was typical of many Americans outside of New England, for whom the commercialization ("howard-johnsonization") of chowder had obscured the essence of this dish, leaving only the puzzle of the odd word *chowder,* which I thought meant soup. But everything changed when I moved to Boston in 1979, to work as sous-chef at the Copley Plaza Hotel. The executive chef, Bob Redmond, was a dyed-in-the-wool Yankee cook who took pride in the regional dishes he put on the menu. He was especially passionate about his fish chowder, which featured chunks of haddock the size of your fist. Made with a potent fish stock and a generous quantity of fish, Chef Redmond's chowder was a blockbuster: it tasted more like fish than fish. I also took note of how popular it was as a main course, especially at lunch. I was beginning to perceive that chowder was much more than a soup.

For many New Englanders, as well as Canadians from New Brunswick, Nova Scotia,

Prince Edward Island, and Newfoundland, chowder is a connection to their history, made by fifteen generations of their ancestors. With a few staples like lean salt pork or bacon, onions, potatoes, and a couple of herbs, a home cook can make a great-tasting chowder with whatever the sea or the farm provides. Like the fishing communities where it originated, chowder is unpretentious. It celebrates the excellence of local ingredients in their seasons, especially in "found foods" like clams and fish, which could be gathered or caught by locals. Another basic characteristic of chowder is its ease of preparation—even chowders that take more than an hour to make don't require anything more than keeping an eye on the pot. Precision cutting, constant stirring, and anxious attention are not part of the Zen of chowder making.

Certain types or styles of chowders are entrenched in certain regions: white chowder in New England, clear chowder in Rhode Island, red chowder in New York, brown chowder in Bermuda. For clam chowder, soft-shell clams are preferred in Maine, quahogs in Cape Cod, and geoducks in the Pacific Northwest. As a result, chauvinism is part of the culture of chowder making, sometimes to a fault. By insisting that only a certain type of clam, fish, dairy product, or vegetable makes the "true" or "best" chowder, the same people who carry on the legacy of chowder have also limited its scope. The reality is that cooks have improvised chowders continuously for about three hundred years, and there was never one true chowder.

Boston, New Bedford, Mystic, and other busy New England ports were points of departure for sailors, fishermen, whalers, and adventurers, who spread their fondness (and probably their recipes) for chowder throughout North America: New York, Maryland, Virginia, Louisiana, California, and the Pacific Northwest, and Bermuda and the Caribbean. Farmhouse chowders, made without seafood, brought chowder making to landlocked areas, where excellent country cooks added their own magic.

Chowders can assume many profiles in menu planning. Some are ideal as a starter before a light meal, but most are special and satisfying enough to be the main course. A big pot of chowder is perfect for a large gathering of friends and family, and because chowder truly is best when made ahead, you'll have plenty of time to enjoy your company. It also makes a quick and easy weeknight supper, if you make the chowder over the weekend. All you need to do is toss a garden salad and warm the chowder—in less than twenty minutes, you'll be enjoying a first-class meal. If you're serving a creamy chowder, ripe melon or other fresh fruit is the ideal dessert. Avoid serving creamy chowders on hot days. There are plenty of lighter chowders that are more appropriate. The color of chowder can be yellow, red, pink, white, beige, or chocolate; a chowder can be thick and opaque or thin and clear; some chowders are monochromatic, others are multicolored. Flavors and styles change with the ingredients you add. All have the ability to inspire new versions—and that's what makes the art of making chowder so much fun!

Last August, I caught a fat striped bass on the rocks in front of my wife, Nancy's, family summer house at Warren's Point in Little Compton, Rhode Island. At low tide, my kids—J.P., Mariel, and Hayley—gathered small wild mussels from those same rocks. That night, I made a broth with white wine and garlic, onions, peppers, and tomatoes bought from Walker's Farm, just down the road. I filleted the bass and cut it into thick pieces, which I arranged in a large baking dish with the mussels and very thin slices of potato. I also added slices of Portuguese sausage that were left over from a barbecue we had the night before. I covered it all with the broth and placed it in the oven to bake. With the sound of crashing waves as our dinner music, our family sat down to a beautiful baked chowder made with food that we were very connected to. Putting the meal together was second nature to me—there was no planning, it just happened. And although I was in the middle of writing this book on chowder, I gave no thought to creating a recipe. How could I list the ingredients? Three beautiful smiling faces of my beloved children as they harvested mussels, . . . one striper I caught myself in a place that I know intimately, . . . breezy, chilly, briny ocean air to taste? No, this was not a recipe for my book. It was, however, the essence of chowder—the reason I wrote this book. And it is my hope that by cooking the recipes in this book, you will master the essentials of chowder making, and when the karma is right, a chowder will just happen in your kitchen.

Chapter 1

The Folklore and History of Chowder

Throughout this book, I inject bits and pieces of the folklore and history of chowder as it pertains to the recipe or subject at hand. This time line is intended to put those bits and pieces in order, to give you a clearer idea of the evolution of chowder. Chowder-like seafood stews and dishes occurred simultaneously in many parts of the world, but this book is about a specific dish—North American chowder, and the variations that derived from it. The early history of chowder, prior to 1751, is shrouded in a lack of written information, but from that point forward, the story unfolds in cookbooks and other published writings. Recipes tell the story of different ingredients and how chowders changed as certain foods became abundant and fashionable. It should be noted, however, that those recipes are often a reflection of changes that occurred years before. Other written material, letters, periodicals, and books, help give us an idea of the cultural importance of chowder, especially along the Atlantic coast. The information I used to piece this history together came from dozens of wonderful books, but three in particular were invaluable: Sandra L. Oliver's *Saltwater Foodways,* Richard J. Hooker's *Book of Chowder,* and John Thorne's *Down East Chowder.* The complete list can be found in the bibliography on page 237. I apologize, in advance, for digressing into a somewhat personal overview in the last thirty years of the time line that follows, but this was my era, I lived and breathed it, so I wanted to relate my own experience of it.

1700–1750

Although it is certain that chowder comes into existence at some point during this period, everything else is speculation, of which there is no shortage. The French word for cauldron, *chaudière* or *chaudron,* is often referred to as a point of origin for the name, but the word *jowter,* meaning fishmonger, and its dialect variations, *chowter* and *chowder,* were being used in Cornwall and Devonshire, England, in the sixteenth century. Two seafood stews, *faire la chaudière,* from the fishing villages of Brittany, and *chaudrée de Fouras,* from the Fouras region of France, are frequently mentioned by food writers as a possible predecessor to chowder, while others point to the English crusted *pye,* layered with salt pork and fish. French settlers in Canada, French fishermen, Channel Islander (English) settlers in Massachusetts, English fishermen, and Native Americans from the Micmac tribe are all among the list of suspects who may have cooked the original chowders. Others speculate that it was the mixture of French and English fishermen, possibly in the fishing camps along the Newfoundland coast, that gave rise to the creation of chowder. The basic staples carried aboard most fishing vessels in the early 1700s—salt pork, hardtack (ship's biscuit), and fresh fish—make it easy to believe that chowder originated at sea. As John Thorne points out in his book *Down East Chowder,* given the limited staples aboard fishing boats during this period, one would "come to wonder not how chowder came into existence but what else they ever found to eat." Whether of French or English origin, or a combination of the two, chowder is not claimed by either culture. And although the English seem well aware of chowder during the eighteenth century, it all but disappears from their repertoire soon afterward. It is in Newfoundland, Nova Scotia, New Brunswick, and New England that chowder making flourishes and where chowder becomes an integral part of the diet and culture.

1732
Benjamin Lynde, a New Englander, mentions in his diary that he had "dined on a fine chowdered cod"—the first written reference to North American chowder.

1751
On September 23, the *Boston Evening Post* publishes the oldest-known printed recipe for fish chowder:

> First lay some Onions to keep the Pork from burning,
> Because in Chouder there can be no turning:
> Then lay some Pork in Slices very thin,
> Thus you in Chouder always must begin.
> Then season well with Pepper, Salt and Spice;
> Parsley, Sweet-Marjoram, Savory and Thyme,
> Then Biscuit next which must be soak'd some Time.
> Thus your Foundation laid, you will be able
> To raise a Chouder, high as Tower of Babel:
> For by repeating o're the Same again,
> You may make Chouder for a thousand Men,
> Last Bottle of Claret, with Water eno' to smother 'em
> You'l have a Mess which some call *Omnium gather 'em.*

These directions teach us the method of layering chowder ingredients, which is how all chowders are made at the time. A few New England cooks make chowder using the layering technique to this day. The fact that the onions are used to prevent the "pork from burning" tells us that the salt pork of the time is very lean. Also take note of the bold use of herbs and spices, a practice that would die out in the early 1800s. Red wine is used in this chowder, but it most likely speaks of affluent Bostonians; it is unlikely that average working people could afford to season their chowder with a bottle of red wine.

1763

Hannah Glasse publishes the recipe "To Make Chouder, a Sea Dish" in the eighth English edition of her *Art of Cookery*. Her chowder is similar to other layered chowders, with "pickled pork," onions, herbs, biscuit, and cod, but the recipe departs from tradition with its optional "oysters, or truffles or morels." The reference to the sea in the title gives credence to the speculation of chowder's maritime origins. This cookbook was first published in England, but Glasse's is one of the last chowder recipes to appear in an English cookbook.

1792

John Pearson opens America's first commercial bakery in Newburyport, Massachusetts, producing Pilot Bread, a refined version of hardtack, also called ship's biscuit, an important chowder ingredient. Pearson's bakery business would eventually evolve into what became the National Biscuit Company, better known as Nabisco. Under the name Crown Pilot crackers, Nabisco produces Pearson's version of hardtack to this day. Hardtack was used in the earliest chowders. Aboard ships, it may have been the only source of carbohydrates. It is unlikely that hardtack was added to enhance chowder: Chowder was, more likely, a means to make hardtack more palatable.

1796

The first American cookbook, *American Cookery*, by Amelia Simmons, is published. Her first edition does not include a chowder recipe, but the second edition, published in 1800, does contain one. Amelia Simmons's Chouder is made with bass, and although no potatoes are called for in her recipe, she suggests it be served with "potatoes, pickles, applesauce or mangoes." This is the first mention of potatoes in a chowder recipe.

1824

Two different chowder recipes are published. Thomas Cooper, a distinguished educator, uses anchovy sauce as well as mushroom ketchup to flavor his cod chowder in (get this) *A Treatise of Domestic Medicine . . . to Which Is Added, a Practical System of Domestic Cookery.* The other recipe, by Mary Randolph, in her book *The Virginia Housewife,* uses "any kind of firm fish" along with the usual salt pork, onions, and crackers, but her chowder removes the fish from the pot and thickens "the gravy with flour and butter" before pouring it back over the fish. It sounds very thick and heavy, with a small amount of broth, which is typical of early fish chowders. The tradition of little broth or liquid in early chowders is probably reflective of the fact that aboard ships, fresh water was one of the most precious ingredients.

1828
The common cracker, which, along with Crown Pilot crackers, has become the quintessential chowder cracker, is produced commercially in Vermont for the first time (as stated on the bag of the Vermont Country Store's common crackers). These round, puffed, hard crackers were first known as Boston crackers and most likely originated in that bustling seaport.

1833
Lydia Maria Child publishes the twelfth edition of *The American Frugal Housewife*. In a section simply called Fish, she explains how to layer salt pork, onions, crackers, and fish to make a chowder in typical New England fashion, but she mentions lemons and beer as possible additions and, of even greater significance, she states that "tomato catchup is very excellent" and "a few clams are a pleasant addition." The tomato is just beginning to gain acceptance among Americans, who, until just a few years prior, still considered it to be poisonous. This recipe includes the first written reference to using clams in chowder, even though they are not the main ingredient. Four years later, Eliza Leslie, from Philadelphia, would write in her *Directions for Cookery* that "chowder may be made of clams"; she also becomes an early advocate of the potato as a chowder ingredient, suggesting "a layer of sliced potatoes."

1842
Famous statesman and chowder maker Daniel Webster records his method for making fish chowder, calling for a combination of the head of a cod and fillets of haddock cooked in a "sufficient quantity of water." He also uses "good Irish potatoes" and just "a few of the largest Boston crackers" in what seems to be the first modern, brothy chowder. From this time forward, potatoes become more popular and important in chowder, as the use of hardtack and crackers in the chowder itself decreases, eventually becoming food that is served alongside chowder.

1850–1860
Several chowder recipes using clams and tomatoes appear. Clam chowders are becoming accepted as a suitable substitute for fish chowders, but it will be another fifty years before they become widely popular. Tomatoes are becoming a popular food, but are used sparingly in chowders, especially those from Cape Cod and to the north. Tomatoes have not yet fallen vic-

tim to the New England versus Manhattan rivalry; in fact, one Boston recipe from 1851 from *The American Matron* includes tomatoes and milk. Milk, cream, and butter are beginning to appear in a few recipes—an 1860 fish chowder recipe from the archives of the Shaker Museum in Old Chatham, New York, includes two cups of cream and three tablespoons of butter.

1860–1880

Milk, cream, and butter steadily gain acceptance as chowder ingredients, especially in northern New England, somewhat less so in Rhode Island, Connecticut, and to the south. Potatoes, on the other hand, are becoming common in chowders up and down the Atlantic coast. Recipes for the first farmhouse chowders, made with chicken or veal, and one made exclusively with potatoes, appear on the Massachusetts islands of Nantucket and Martha's Vineyard, as documented in *Nantucket Receipts* (1874). Chowder is no longer a simple dish of fish or clams: it has become a genre, a way to make dinner. Now deeply ingrained in the culture of New England, it is reaching its all-time high in popularity. Chowder parties, as they are called, are becoming a happy summer pastime along the New England coast. Families pack up a kettle, dishes, flatware, and ingredients for chowder making, as well as cold foods, watermelons, and dessert, and head to the beach for a picnic with chowder as the main event. A fire is built above the high tide line, a tripod set up, and the kettle hung over the embers. The key ingredient, usually a big bluefish or bass, fish that feed close to the shore, is freshly caught out of the surf. Making the chowder is part of the entertainment, and as these parties grow to become events that include seventy or more people, sometimes affiliated with a church, business, or political party, the "chowder master" becomes an important position, much like the "bake master" at a clambake. Clambakes are also popular during this time.

1884

Mary J. Lincoln, the first principal of the famous Boston Cooking School and predecessor to Fannie Merritt Farmer, the second and more famous principal, writes a beautifully descriptive recipe for fish chowder in *Mrs. Lincoln's Boston Cook Book,* taking the reader carefully through every step and variation of the fish chowder process. But two other even more important factors make this book a classic. First, Mrs. Lincoln lists measured ingredients separately from the instructions, a format that is still used today. Second, she includes the first-known recipe for corn chowder, a dish that would become the king of farmhouse chowders, quite possibly the most popular chowder ever! Over the next twenty years, there would be a flurry of corn chowder recipes, all quite similar, printed in books and periodicals from Maine to California.

1886

A recipe by Sarah T. Rorer, appearing in *Mrs. Rorer's Philadelphia Cook Book,* uses bacon, the first chowder recipe I've seen up to this point in chowder's history that does not include salt pork. Salt pork would remain an important chowder ingredient, but bacon would become even more popular during the next century, as dependence on salt pork declined and good-quality salt pork became more difficult to procure.

1894

Charles Ranhoffer, the former chef of Delmonico's, New York City's finest and America's most famous restaurant, publishes his tome *The Epicurean,* which includes a tomato-based clam chowder, which may possibly be the point of origin, at least for the name, of Manhattan Clam Chowder. This also begins the era of chowder as a menu item in restaurants. Both tomatoes and clams have become an industry on Long Island, so the combination seems inevitable— summer hotels in Coney Island serve so much chowder they are referred to as chowder mills. Another theory of the origin of Manhattan Clam Chowder credits the Neapolitan immigrants, who adapted their *zuppa di vongole* (clam soup) for American palates.

1896

Fannie Merritt Farmer includes five different chowders, including a Lobster Chowder, in the first edition of her *Boston Cooking School Cookbook,* a book that would go through dozens of revisions and reprints and is still in print today, as the *Fannie Farmer Cookbook.* There is nothing revolutionary about her recipes, which are very similar to her mentor Mary J. Lincoln's, but the inclusion of a variety of chowders marks the start of chowder as a category in New England cookbooks.

1900–1950

By the beginning of the twentieth century, chowder has become well established as a genre in American cooking. The style of chowder is more brothy than its nineteenth-century pre-decessor; almost all include potatoes, and crackers are served on the side. The use of salt pork or bacon remains a constant. Regional styles and preferences begin to take hold, cre-ating rivalries, at least in the minds of food writers. In Maine, cooks prefer soft-shell clams, while on Cape Cod, quahogs are the shellfish of choice. All of northern New England abhors the tomato-based chowders from Connecticut and New York, while in Rhode Island, cooks add neither milk nor tomatoes to their chowders. In other regions, like the Chesapeake Bay and New Orleans, chowder is just one of many seafood stews in the repertoire of seafood dishes. In San Francisco and other places on the Pacific coast, chowders, especially clam, abalone, and salmon, are quite popular. Farmhouse chowders of every description, made from beans, parsnips, eggs, turnips, mushrooms, mixed vegetables, and chicken, are offered as recipes in a multitude of cookbooks (which are becoming an industry in their own right). Famous chefs like Alexander Filippini, Louis P. DeGouy, and Dione Lucas join ranks with Charles Ranhoffer, adding their magic to the legacy of chowder, with the use of rich stocks and the reintroduction of herbs and spices.

1948
Codfish Chowder, Newfoundland Style, a recipe printed in *The Gold Cook Book,* by Louis P. DeGouy, serves as a reminder that chowder, which may have originated in Atlantic Canada, is still an integral part of that region's cuisine. The story of chowder in Canada (to my knowledge) has yet to be written, but in my discussions with friends who hail from New Brunswick, Nova Scotia, and the other Maritime Provinces, I've learned that chowder making has remained a steadfast tradition throughout the centuries.

1950–1960
In terms of America's culinary history, we are now entering the dark ages. Economic boom and a passion for all things modern fuel an era where strip malls, fast food chains, and convenience foods capture the hearts of Americans. Chowder making in many homes begins with a can opener, and in the hands of professional cooks of questionable ability, chowder is quickly being degraded to a soup-like paste, with pathetic bits of rubber-like clams and tasteless potatoes.

1960–1980
I respectfully call these the "Jackie O. years." With her great style and love of French cuisine, this widely imitated public figure sparks a period of intense francophilia in America's restaurant culture that lasts well beyond her years in the White House. True American cooking during this period is found almost solely in the homes of those few who are passionate about their culinary heritage and in obscure roadhouses. Fine dining means French or "Continental-style" cuisine, much of which is phony or second-rate, an embarrassment to lovers of real French cuisine. Of the food media, only a few strong voices, most notably those of James Beard and Evan Jones, speak and write with pride about American food.

Note: I began my career in the early seventies, when, as a student at the Culinary Institute of America, American food was taught in conjunction with cafeteria feeding. (Corn chowder was part of that curriculum.) The only restaurant at the school in those years was the Escoffier Room, where we learned the basics of classical French cuisine—excellent training, but a reinforcement of the perception of American food as inferior. In the first eight years of my career, I never worked in a restaurant where the menu was written in English! Even at the Parker House in Boston, America's oldest continually operating hotel dining room, Boston scrod was listed as "Schrod de Boston."

In this environment, which is quietly accepted by the food service industry, chowder continues to decline in quality and prestige.

1980–1999

For every action there is a reaction, and in the early 1980s, the food media fuels the fire of what is termed the "New American Cuisine." Taking my cues from a handful of bold young American chefs, in 1982 I open the Bostonian Hotel, the first hotel dining room in Boston that, in recent years, presents its menu in English and features regional American dishes, Lobster and Corn Chowder among them. Young American chefs are suddenly being commended for breaking the barriers imposed by the definition of fine dining in the past. Many of us are exploring our American roots, looking for inspiration to create new dishes loosely based on a combination of cooking styles from different regions across the United States, as well as France (with which we are more than familiar), the Mediterranean, and Asia. Chowder is not exactly redefined during this era, but it is given a new lease on life and a second look by chefs and food writers; in 1985, a lobster and corn chowder even makes the cover of *Food & Wine* magazine. There are enough new variations of chowder to change at least some food lovers' perception of chowder as a lifeless, dull, pasty soup. The New American Cuisine results in a hodgepodge of cooking styles that range from brilliant to bizarre, but although it is short-lived, it levels the playing field, legitimizing not only American food, but many other indigenous cuisines from around the world as well. "Fine dining" no longer exclusively means French dining, although some of the greatest food is still being cooked by young French chefs in America—a few of whom have been known to make their own excellent versions of chowder.

In the high-tech, fast-paced culture of America at the turn of the twenty-first century, the appreciation of good food has increased, not declined. However, our ability to find the time to cook, especially on workdays, is becoming a thing of the past. But since chowder only improves when it is made ahead, and will keep for at least three days if properly refrigerated, it provides an opportunity for a very quick and satisfying meal at the end of a busy day. It is my opinion that chowder, in some form or other, will endure, as it has for more than two hundred and fifty years, as sustenance and pleasurable eating in the new century.

2000

50 Chowders, by Jasper White, the first hardcover book of contemporary chowders, is published.

Chapter 2

Chowder Ingredients

"If you are very careful," Garp wrote,
"if you use good ingredients, and you don't take shortcuts,
then you can usually cook something
very good. Sometimes it is the only worthwhile
product you can salvage from a day."
—John Irving, THE WORLD ACCORDING TO GARP

Chowder is greater than the sum of its parts. As in many slow-cooked dishes, the aroma and flavor of the various ingredients combine to create something new and unique. When you eat fish chowder, you won't experience flavor bursts of separate ingredients as you would with a quick-cooked Asian soup. Although you will be able to distinguish the individual textures and some of the flavors of the fish, onions, potatoes, salt pork, cream, and herbs in New England Fish Chowder, it is the singular flavor created by the combination of these foods that will dominate. Because of this, every ingredient is important: four great ingredients and one mediocre one can make chowder mediocre.

Chowder, however, cannot really be defined by its ingredients. When most of us think of chowder, New England–style fish or clam chowder is what comes to mind: made from seafood, salt pork or bacon, onions, potatoes, stock, milk or cream, herbs, and spices. But there are twenty chowders in this book alone that do not contain any seafood at all. A few don't feature salt pork or bacon, and there are no potatoes in Shaker Fresh Cranberry Bean Chowder (page 180). Some cooks use water or milk instead of stock. Certain chowders, especially those made with tomatoes, contain no milk or cream. And herbs and spices vary from recipe to recipe. Onions, on the other hand, are a constant, as they are in most soups, but they are not the defining ingredient. I would not call any dish that didn't contain at least some of the above ingredients, especially potatoes and salt pork or bacon, a true chowder, but when the day is done, I believe a chowder is more easily defined by the style, spirit, and techniques we use when putting it together than by a set list of ingredients.

Although I do call for many different ingredients in my chowder recipes, some reappear quite often. In this chapter, I provide general advice and points of interest on those most commonly used. I've devoted the largest section to fish. Shellfish is so diverse that I give it general mention here, and then supply specific details in the recipes. Stocks and broths are not included here, because they are initial preparations and so important to my way of making chowder that I devote an entire chapter to them. In the early history of chowder making, ship's biscuit (also called hardtack) and common crackers were among the most important ingredients. Before potatoes were available, cooks added crumbled or powdered ship's biscuit to their simmering chowders. Hardtack, an important source of carbohydrates (sometimes the only source at sea), was made palatable by chowder and, in turn, thickened it. Although some New Englanders still cook dry biscuits or crackers in their chowders, most (including me) eat them alongside. See pages 204–208 for a discussion of ship's biscuit, hardtack, Pilot crackers, and common crackers.

Fish

The first written mention of chowder appeared in 1732, in the diary of Benjamin Lynde, a New Englander who noted that he had "dined on a fine chowdered cod." I passed over this historical tidbit at least a dozen times before I grasped its significance. Reading the earliest recipes for chowders, you could easily assume that cod, haddock, and bass, called for in most recipes, were the preferred fish for the dish, but that is backward. With his use of *chowder* as a verb, Benjamin Lynde provides an important insight: the cod was primary, chowder was how you cooked it. With nothing more than a kettle, a tripod to hang it from, and an open fire, eighteenth-century cooks figured out how to make the best dish possible with the fish that was available. Chowder originated and evolved in response to the ingredients and technology available at the time.

The nineteenth century brought about many changes in ingredients, but it also saw the revolutionary transition from cooking over an open fire to cooking over a wood- or coal-fired stove. The transition, which took place in homes and on fishing vessels, would span the better part of the century. As with most new technologies, the urban affluent were first to enjoy it. Before the stove came into existence, chowders were prepared by layering slices of salt pork and onions, crumbled or shaved ship's biscuit (hardtack), and large pieces of fish in a kettle. Descriptions in old chowder recipes of how the fish was prepared—"cut it in pieces six inches long," or "cut it in pieces the size of your hand"—leave the impression that filleting and boning fish was not a common practice during the early years of chowder making. The layers of pork, onions, and fish were seasoned with herbs and spices and then a liquid, usually water, wine, beer, or cider, was added. The kettle was tightly covered and hung over the open fire. Obviously, the cook had little control over the temperature the chowder cooked at, other than to remove it from the heat. I imagine the results were not something that you or I would enjoy—the flavor might have been quite good, but the texture was probably mushy and porridge-like from a combination of soggy hardtack and overcooked fish. It was not until the advent of cast-iron stoves in the early 1800s that cooks had enough control over the heat to be able to sauté the salt pork and onions and then to add other ingredients in stages, resulting in chowders with richer flavor and a more pleasing texture. And as commercially manufactured stoves continued to be improved, it became easier to successfully cook chowders made with more delicate items, like fish fillets and shellfish.

Over the years, it's likely that locals living along coastal areas of North America have added almost every edible sea creature to the chowder pot. While investigating chowder recipes in the course of writing this book, I counted no fewer than twenty-four different species of fish and shellfish from the Atlantic Ocean, the Caribbean, the Gulf of Mexico, and the Pacific Ocean that result in chowders good enough to record for posterity. This leaves little excuse for not making a seafood chowder, because substituting one fish or shellfish for another less easily found is central to the tradition of chowder making! Cod, haddock, and bass are still my first choice for most fish chowders, possibly because these fish, which were incredibly abundant at one time, are why chowder was created in the first place: their lean and flaky texture balances beautifully with the richness of chowder. I'm crazy about bluefish in chowders too. If you have a favorite local fish, you can substitute it, by weight, in any fish chowder recipe. Below, I describe the characteristics of the most commonly used chowder fish and tell you how to cut them up for chowder. If at all possible, use the fish I recommend the first time you make one of my recipes—it will provide a standard, a point of reference, of how the recipe ought to taste.

Chowder Fish 101

If you want to learn how to fillet fish at home, you need to buy a whole fish. You can use the head and frame (bones) to make a rich stock, and, another plus, you can appraise a whole fish for freshness more easily. Look at its general appearance: rigor mortis (stiffness) is the ultimate sign of a recently caught fish. Fresh fish has a bright sheen and the color of its skin will be brilliant, not dull. Slime is another sign of freshness, except when it appears on the gills. Since gills are one of the first parts of the fish to deteriorate, firm red gills that are not slimy and smell clean are a sign of quality. Look for bright clear eyes. The fish should feel firm and be free of bruises or cuts.

When buying fillets, look at the flesh—it should be moist and shiny, almost translucent, and the color should be brilliant, whether white, pink, or orange. The fillets should have a clean ocean smell that is faint, like salty air in the evening, never a pronounced fishy smell. Extremely fresh fish has a fragrance that sometimes reminds me of cucumbers. The meat should feel firm, not mushy, and the fillets should be smooth not cracked. And don't forget to buy a head and frame, from the same species as the fillet when possible, so you can make a rich stock for the chowder.

At the market, fresh fish, whole or fillets, should be stored on ice. Whole fish can be kept directly in ice because the skin protects the meat. Fillets should either be sitting on ice or wrapped tightly in plastic wrap and buried in ice. In both cases, the ice should be in a drain pan that allows the melting ice to run off so the fish is never in water. Temperature control is the single most important factor in storing fish. A good vendor will keep the fish at close to freezing (32° to 36°F) at all times, and you should too. One hour at room temperature ages the fish a day! I keep a cooler in my car trunk to transport seafood (and cold beer) from the market to my house. If you can't do that, make the fish market your last stop and rush the fish home to your refrigerator. Usually the back of the bottom refrigerator shelf is the coldest place. It should be 38°F or less—if it isn't, readjust the temperature gauge.

Get to know your fish vendor. Seafood is a tricky business, and it is always a safer bet to deal with specialists. In general, an independent fish market is the most reliable place to buy seafood. With a few exceptions, large supermarkets are rarely able to focus on and maintain a quality seafood program. Seek out a seafood market that does a brisk business: the busier it is, the fresher the fish; the fresher the fish, the busier it is. Talk to your fish vendor. You can learn a lot. Let him or her get to know you and your high standards as well as your passion for good seafood.

Most of the fish that are best for chowder have a similar bone structure; they are called round fish by fish cutters. Cod, haddock, bass, bluefish, salmon, and tautog are just a few of the many "round" species that, although not identical, are close enough so that the filleting technique is similar. If you are buying fillets, you still need to remove any pinbones that are present. Round fish all have a line of pinbones running laterally down the fillet, starting from behind the head. Each species is a little different in terms of length and direction, but the bones are easy to feel by running your finger lengthwise over the fillet. For chowder, there is no need to pull out the pinbones one by one as for other dishes. Simply make what fish cutters call a V cut (see How to Fillet Round Fish, page 31), and you will remove the pinbones in thirty seconds. Flatfish such as flounder and sole are not very good in chowder because their soft flesh falls apart and dissolves during cooking. And since halibut, a species of flatfish that happens to make a splendid chowder, is too large to buy whole, I have not outlined the cutting technique for flatfish.

Last, the species of fish and the size of the particular fish you are using determine how you cut the fillets for chowder. Cutting the pieces of fish is easily done. All you need is a sharp knife. I use a French knife, but almost any knife will do. The idea is to end up with bite-sized pieces. The firmer the fillet, the smaller you cut it; less-firm fish are cut into larger pieces, because they will break up into bite-sized pieces during cooking. You should cut the firmest types, such as monkfish and swordfish, into pieces about 1 to 2 inches square. Medium-firm fish, such salmon, bluefish, striped bass, halibut, tautog, and wolffish, should be cut into 3- to 4-inch pieces. Cod, haddock, pollack, hake, and black sea bass fillets, which are naturally flaky, need no cutting at all. After they have cooked in the chowder, they will break up on their own. Cut large fillets lengthwise in half, then cut into the desired-size squares. If the fish fillets are thin (less than 1 inch thick), cut the squares on the large side of the recommended size. Conversely, if they are very thick (more than 1 inch), cut them on the small side of the recommended size. Don't worry about being too precise. Once the pieces are cooked in the chowder, they will break up a little and be somewhat uneven in size. That's okay—the best homemade chowder looks this way!

How to Fillet Round Fish

If the fish has not been gutted, make an incision from under the throat down to the bottom of the belly. Remove all the entrails; if there is any roe, wrap about 1 tablespoon of it (to add to the chowder) and store in the refrigerator. Since you will not be using the skin in chowder, there is no need to remove the scales from the fish. Fish fillet knives are long, thin, and flexible and should be very sharp. Some fish cutters prefer different shapes, sizes, and thickness; some chefs even use small French knives instead of fillet knives. It is a matter of personal preference, but for the beginner, I would recommend a fish fillet knife made of medium-hard steel, not overly flexible, because firmer knives give you a little more control.

Make a diagonal incision behind the head of the fish. You will see the large backbone. Keeping the tip of the knife pressed firmly against that bone, without letting the tip extend past the center, and holding the knife flat, cut down the top of the fish. Fold the flesh back as you go so you can see where you are. Now, starting at the head again, hold the knife at a slight downward angle as you cut the bottom half of the fillet away from the rib bones. When you reach the end of the belly, about two thirds of the way down, hold your knife flat again and finish removing the fillet. Turn the fish over and repeat on the other side. Save the head and frame for stock.

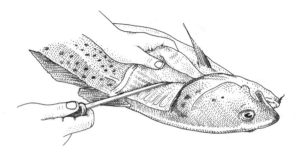

How to Remove the Skin from a Fillet

Place the fillet skin side down on the cutting board. Make an incision near the tail end, positioning your knife between the meat and the skin. Hold the skin firmly with one hand as you slide the knife forward, separating the meat from the skin in one motion while keeping your knife at a slight (10-degree) angle to the cutting board.

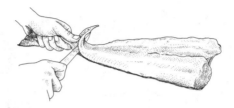

How to Bone a Fillet

Lay the fish fillet skin (or skinned) side down on the cutting board. Trim away any visible bones or cartilage. With your fingers, locate the row of pinbones that starts at the head end of the fillet, slightly off center toward the thickest part of the fillet. With a sharp knife, make a cut along one side of the bones down the length of the row, staying as close as possible to the bones. Do the same on the other side of the bones, then remove the row of bones. This is called a V cut.

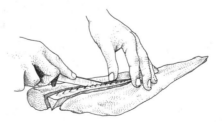

Fish Species

I've provided a list of the kinds of fish I think are best for chowder. If you would like to use a fish I haven't listed, try to match it with the qualities of a fish on my list, and choose a recipe that is appropriate for that type of fish. I have omitted freshwater fish because what is sold is farm-raised (mostly trout, tilapia, and catfish) and has a bland and unexciting flavor. I have also left out small ocean fish like porgies, alewives, herring, and the like because it is too much work to remove all the bones. Although chowder made with these fish would be tasty, that much preparation is contrary to the idea of chowder making, which is typically fun and easy. The fish are listed in the order that reflects my personal favorites.

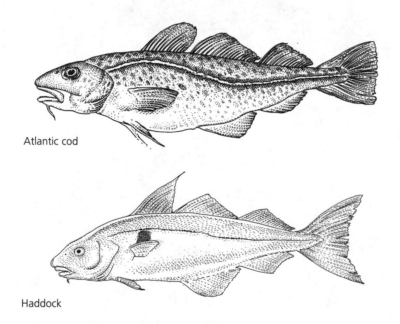

Atlantic cod

Haddock

Atlantic Cod and Haddock Along with bass, these closely related species are the finest chowder fish. (Pacific cod is not related to Atlantic cod; it is not a true cod.) For years, haddock was more expensive than cod, considered by most Boston chowder makers to be slightly superior in flavor and texture. In recent years, the prices have fluctuated because of the shortage of cod and they are now about equally priced. I still have a slight prejudice toward large haddock, because it is a bit firmer than cod, resulting in beautiful large flakes. I also think its flavor is slightly richer than cod's. For chowder, I buy cod and haddock fillets with the skin on so I am sure I'm getting those species. Cod has light brown spotted skin; haddock has silver-blue spotted skin with a black lateral stripe. Skin them, but leave the fillets whole or in as large pieces as possible. Even though they will break up a bit during cooking, they will still be in delectable large pieces when you serve the chowder. These two fish are excellent in any fish chowder because they are very lean and flaky. Their flavor is full, but not as pronounced as that of fattier fish, making them appealing to most enthusiastic eaters. Their heads are very full-flavored and should be used for stock. Cod or haddock is essential for making authentic New England Fish Chowder (page 79).

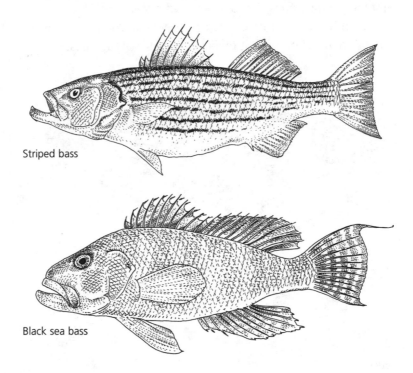

Striped bass

Black sea bass

Striped Bass and Black Sea Bass The once-endangered wild striped bass (known as rockfish south of Delaware) has made a marvelous comeback on the eastern seaboard. The season is limited to a few months a year for sport fishermen and is even shorter for commercial fishing, so be on the lookout for it during the summer months. Striped bass is one of the very best fish for chowder because of its full flavor and firm, meaty texture. Black sea bass is also a superb fish with rich flavorful white meat, but the supply is spotty. Large sea bass (over 4 pounds) are excellent for chowder; the smaller ones are also good, but the flakes are not as big. Both striped and black bass fillets need to be skinned. Black bass can be left whole; striped bass should be cut into 2- to 4-inch squares. They will break up during cooking but will still be in luscious large pieces when the chowder is served. Bass is terrific in just about any fish chowder. My Savory Summer Fish Chowder (page 96) was created especially to celebrate summer fish like striped bass and bluefish.

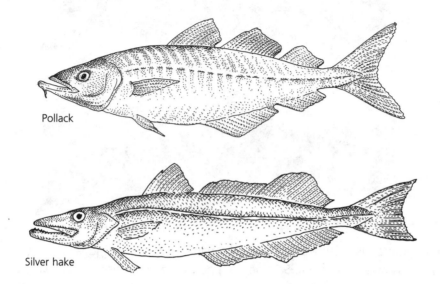

Pollack

Silver hake

Pollack and Silver Hake These fish are close cousins to cod and haddock, with a similar flaky texture, lean white meat, and a full but not overly powerful flavor. Under optimal conditions, pollack can be excellent in chowder. Unfortunately, pollack is often caught by commercial gill netters and suffers any number of batterings before it is sold for a cheap price at market. Silver hake, also known as whiting, makes terrific chowder. It is actually the preferred species of New England fishermen of Sicilian and Portuguese heritage, because hake, found on both sides of the Atlantic, was a favorite long before these ethnic groups arrived in America. Look for hake with shiny silver skin, to avoid confusion with another fish called red hake (fishermen call it "mud" hake), which has a mushy texture that isn't suitable for chowder. Pollack is popular in Maine chowders, like Church Supper Fish Chowder (page 83), and hake is especially good in South Coast Portuguese Fish Chowder (page 90). The fillets should be skinned and added whole to the chowder, where they will break up beautifully during the cooking.

Bluefish and Salmon These rich, fatty fish produce a chowder with robust flavor. In addition to skinning and boning them, you need to trim away the dark blood lines. Cut the fillets into large 3- to 4-inch pieces. As they cook and are stirred, they will break up into bite-sized pieces. Because their taste is so pronounced, they can hold their own against bold flavors and spicy seasonings. Bluefish especially makes a distinctive and savory chowder. I consider it a

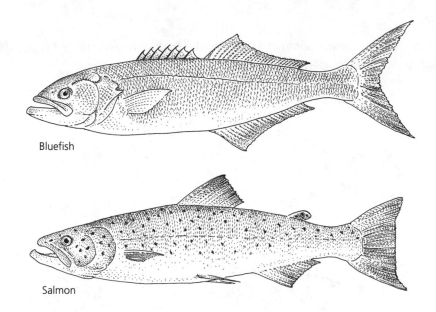

Bluefish

Salmon

must for Bermuda Fish Chowder with Crab (page 102) and an ideal choice for Savory Summer Fish Chowder (page 96). Salmon is a popular chowder fish on the West Coast; see my Pacific Northwest Salmon Chowder (page 105).

Halibut, Tautog, and Wolffish Except for the fact that their flesh is white and they all impart a delicious sweet taste to chowder, these fish are very different from one another. Thin halibut (called chicken halibut) fillets can be left whole; thicker pieces should be cut into 3- to 4-inch pieces. Be careful not to overcook halibut, or its flesh will turn soft and mealy. Tautog, also known as blackfish, is a popular chowder fish in southern New England, where it is plentiful and can be caught close to shore. Wolffish is also known as ocean catfish, although it is no relation to catfish; it has large fangs for cracking open shellfish, which is why its flesh tastes so sweet

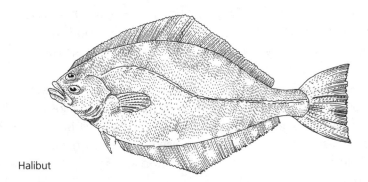

Halibut

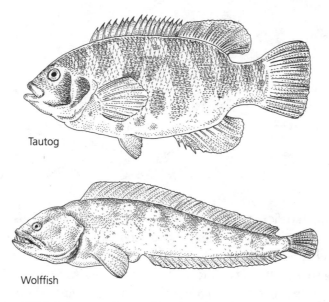

Tautog

Wolffish

and delicious. And wolffish is inexpensive, making it quite a bargain, considering its great flavor. Like large halibut, tautog and wolffish should be skinned and cut into 3- to 4-inch pieces. They will break up into bite-sized pieces as they cook and are stirred in the chowder. All three species are very good in New England Fish Chowder (page 79) and in Church Supper Fish Chowder (page 83), where the mild flavor of the creamy chowder helps to showcase their sweetness.

Monkfish and Swordfish These two fish have very firm flesh that actually becomes even more dense as they cook . . . up to a point. If they are overcooked, they will become mushy. The fish themselves are very flavorful, but because of the density of the flesh, their flavors don't integrate with chowder ingredients as well as flakier fish do. The heavy membrane that surrounds the monkfish tail must be well trimmed, then the fillet cut into 1- to 2-inch pieces.

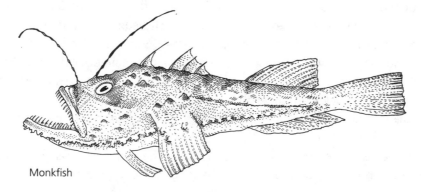

Monkfish

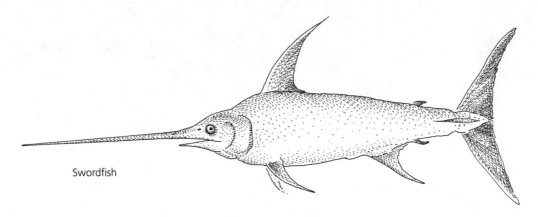

Swordfish

Monkfish has a sweet, delicious flavor, and when the fillets are added just after the chowder is removed from the heat, it can be exceptionally good. Chowder made with swordfish is bound to make swordfish lovers (and there are many) very happy. Cut away the dark meat (blood line) of the swordfish and cut into 1- to 2-inch pieces. As for monkfish, add the cubes just after the chowder is removed from the heat. You can substitute these fish in any fish chowder recipe except Layered Fish Chowder (page 86).

Shellfish

The term *shellfish* covers a wide range of sea animals from different families (genus) and different types (species) within those families. Because they have few similarities to each other, they are difficult to talk about in general terms. Crabs and lobsters share some characteristics, but not enough to make them interchangeable in recipes. Shrimp pair well with the same flavors that are good with crab and lobster, but they need to be handled differently. Scallops, oysters, clams, and mussels are all bivalves that share many physical likenesses, but their flavors are quite different and the weight of the shell compared to the amount of meat each kind yields is different for each, making it impossible to supply a ratio for substituting one for the other. Conch and squid benefit from long slow cooking in chowder. Scallops and shrimp would be ruined by the same process. Clams, from 1-inch steamers to 2-foot geoducks, with different sizes and shapes in between, are vastly different. Some are hard-shell; some are soft-shell. One thing they all have in common: each makes a dynamite bowl of chowder.

This doesn't mean that you can't substitute ingredients or ideas in shellfish chowders, but you do need to develop an understanding of the different shellfish before you experiment and make changes in the recipes. For that reason, I provide specific guidelines in all the recipes that call for shellfish.

Buying shellfish is not unlike buying finfish (see page 29). As always, you need to find a purveyor you can trust. Choosing a reliable seafood market and getting to know the staff is the most important step in creating successful shellfish chowders. Shellfish needs to be held under strict temperature control, preferably between 34° and 38°F; it should never be exposed to warm temperatures. One big difference between shellfish and fish is that many types, including lobsters, crabs, clams, oysters, and mussels, are alive when you buy them. Freshness takes on a new meaning. As long as shellfish are alive, they are good to cook with, but lobsters and crabs that have been away too long from their natural habitat can lose their unique flavor. If bivalves (clams, oysters, and mussels) are out of the water too long, they will give off less broth, resulting in a weaker chowder. Live shellfish can die when exposed to freshwater, so if ice is used for chilling, it is important that it drain very well.

Salt Pork and Bacon

In the Early American kitchen, chowder began with salt pork. Every household had one or more pork barrels with enough preserved pork to (hopefully) provide protein throughout the lean winter months. In colonial America, salt pork was made from the entire pig except the head and innards, and it was cured in a liquid brine, not with a dry salt rub, as it is today. Precious grains were not usually fed to pigs, whose diet consisted of kitchen scraps, like apple cores, and whatever they could forage. So, in contrast to the fatty salt-cured pork belly that is prevalent today, salt pork in colonial times was fairly lean, resembling something similar to corned beef.

Before the early 1900s, Americans believed that seafood protein was inferior to meat protein. Therefore, salt pork was added to enrich and give substance to seafood chowders and it was used in greater proportions than today. Out of necessity, early maritime cooks created the classic flavor combination of pork and seafood that has mustered the test of time. We no longer need the pork barrel to endure the winter. And we have proof that animal protein is not superior to fish protein. But salt pork, which is not smoked, and the more recent alternative, bacon, which is smoked, have survived in our chowder recipes because the combination of pork and seafood is irrefutably delicious.

Good-quality salt pork is characterized by streaks of pink meat and clear white fat, with a hefty proportion of meat to fat (40 percent or more). Any yellow or brown discoloration in the fat is a sign of age and should be avoided. The reliable brands that I use are Gwaltney's from Virginia and Farmland from Missouri (see sources for others, page 231). If you live near an Italian market or specialty store, pancetta (unsmoked Italian bacon) is a first-rate substitute.

As the use of salt pork declined in American cooking, bacon became a very popular replacement. Although bacon is a late-twentieth-century addition to chowder, the smoky flavor it imparts isn't. The first chowders were cooked over open hearths in the colonial kitchen, smoky ships' stoves, or driftwood embers at beach chowder parties, all of which imparted the flavor of smoke. So a chowder made with bacon tastes similar to the early chowders made with salt pork. I recommend country-style slab (unsliced) bacon for chowder, like Harrington's from Vermont or Hatfield from Virginia (see sources, page 231).

My preference for salt pork or bacon varies according to recipe. I use salt pork in my Steamer Clam Chowder (page 114) and bacon in my New England Clam (Quahog) Chowder (page 112). I prefer salt pork for New England Fish Chowder (page 79), bacon for Lobster and Corn Chowder (page 170). I love the way the flavors of smoky bacon and sweet lobster combine. Once you understand their characteristics, you can freely substitute salt pork for bacon or vice versa (by weight) in any recipe to suit your personal preference.

Salt pork and slab bacon keep best in the freezer. I find that if I defrost salt pork or bacon for about twenty minutes before I dice it, the partially frozen meat is much easier to cut than if completely thawed. The first step before dicing is to trim off the rind with your knife. Save the rind; you can use it to flavor the stock.

When you're cooking salt pork, it's best if the diced pork (cracklings) are removed from the pot once they are browned. The fat remains in the pot to flavor the chowder and the cracklings are reheated to be sprinkled on top as a garnish at the end. Some cooks use this technique when using bacon as well, but I don't. When cooking bacon, I remove most of the fat after it is browned, and I leave the diced bacon in the pot to simmer. The result is a deeper yet milder smokiness that doesn't overpower the other chowder ingredients. I save the bacon fat and use it to flavor Skillet Corn Bread (page 219) or Sweet Corn Fritters (page 222); both are superb served alongside chowder. When cooking either salt pork or bacon, start with a low heat, then increase the heat as soon as there is enough liquid fat to prevent scorching.

Substitutions

Because I pour off most of the bacon fat but leave the fat from the salt pork in the pot, my recipes with bacon contain 2 tablespoons more butter than the recipes that use salt pork. So if you substitute bacon for salt pork, increase the amount of butter by 2 tablespoons. Conversely, if you substitute salt pork for bacon, reduce the amount of butter by 2 tablespoons.

If you don't have a religious objection to pork, you owe it to yourself to add it to chowder. However, if you wish to omit the salt pork or bacon, you can substitute butter or your choice of olive or vegetable oil. Since good-quality salt pork or bacon is about 50 percent lean, you should substitute half the weight in butter or oil. In other words, if a recipe calls for 4 ounces salt pork or bacon, substitute 2 ounces (4 tablespoons) butter or 2 ounces (liquid measure) oil.

Other Meat and Poultry

Salt pork and bacon are not the only meats found in chowder. All over America, cooks who understood the technique and karma of making chowder had no problem adapting it when confronted with a lack of seafood or a need to use other ingredients. This spawned what today we call "farmhouse chowders"—dishes, like the original fish chowders, that were based on what cooks found locally. In addition to corn, beans, and other vegetables, veal, game, and poultry all found their place in the chowder pot.

Veal chowder (page 190) originated in Nantucket and was popular on Martha's Vineyard as well. It sounds improbable, but the light taste of veal makes a lovely chowder. Red meats like beef and lamb are not suitable for chowder; they are too rich and overpowering. Beef broth or stock, however, is a key ingredient in Bermuda Fish Chowder with Crab (page 102) and produces one of the most intensely flavored chowders of all. You can use a stewing chicken to make a good chicken chowder (page 195), but tender young chickens will make a better one (page 193). Leftover turkey can be turned into Leftover Turkey Chowder with Sage (page 197), and even game birds produce an interesting chowder (Pheasant and Cabbage Chowder, page 201). Chowders made from veal and poultry are prepared in much the same way as those made with seafood—you make a strong broth from the main ingredient, then make chowder with it. Since there is only a handful of these types of chowders in this book, I have supplied the needed information for each specific meat or poultry item directly in the specific recipe.

Potatoes

Before potatoes became common in chowder, ship's biscuit, or hardtack (see page 206), was cooked in chowder, providing what was often the only form of carbohydrate, but resulting in a very thick concoction. Potatoes began gaining acceptance in the early 1800s. The process was a slow one, as many people still feared they were poisonous, but by the end of the Civil War, potatoes had become a standard ingredient in most chowders. As John Thorne points out in his excellent treatise *Down East Chowder*, "It might be argued that [the potato's] arrival ushered chowder into the modern age, since it was its presence that turned chowder from a near-pudding into a stew." The potato made chowder lighter. The potato can play a pivotal role in a chowder, in fact, adding its own flavor, contributing substance, and, best of all, thickening it in a way that creates a light body while helping to suspend the overall flavor of all the ingredients. In contrast, flour-thickened clam chowder, the one many people think of as the standard, uses the potato as a mere garnish, which is why it is my least favorite type of chowder.

Types of Potatoes

Potatoes are found in almost every chowder recipe except those made with beans or, even more rarely, sweet potatoes. The best potatoes for chowder have a medium starch content. High-starch potatoes like the Russet Burbank (Idaho being the most famous) or Russet

Arcadia will turn to mush or even completely dissolve in chowder. Low-starch waxy potatoes like Red La Soda and Red La Rouge (both called new potatoes), as well as Lady Fingers and Ruby Crescents (both called fingerlings) and any variety of firm-textured potato that is harvested when under one inch in diameter (and called creamers) have limited use in chowder. Low-starch potatoes can be used in flour-thickened chowders or in specialty chowders like Egg Chowder with Bacon and New Potatoes (page 188), but for most chowders, their lack of starch and firm texture prevents them from becoming an integral part of the chowder. They remain a garnish, never really melding with the other ingredients.

So we return to the perfect chowder potato, the medium-starch, "all-purpose" potato. Generic all-purpose potatoes are sometimes referred to as chef's potatoes. Superior and Kennebec are the most common all-purpose varieties. Kennebec is grown extensively in Maine and on Prince Edward Island in Canada. In New England, we call them either Maine or PEI potatoes accordingly. The Green Mountain is also a terrific potato variety for chowder. A fairly new variety, but one that is now found in almost every supermarket, is the yellow-fleshed Yukon Gold. Developed in Canada a few years ago, the Yukon Gold has full flavor, a lovely color, and the perfect starch content for chowder. It has become one of my favorites.

Dicing, Slicing, and Cooking Potatoes

Once you choose the right potato, you need to know how to put it to work! My ideal chowder is lightly thickened by the natural starch of potato, with chunks of potato still firm enough to hold together but soft enough that they fall apart when you bite into them. There are several ways to accomplish this. Different recipes call for different-sized slices or dices. Stay close to the recommended size, but don't worry if there is some irregularity, because the smaller pieces will melt into the chowder while the larger ones retain their shape. One old New England cut called "thick-thin" is made by cutting wedges around the outside of the potato as you go, creating triangular shapes that are thick on one end, thin on the other. This type of cutting is foreign to my professional mind-set because it is inefficient, but you may wish to try it for recipes that call for sliced potatoes. Last, I usually recommend vigorous cooking at the stage the potato is added (after the onion is sautéed). This releases the starch from the outside of the potato chunks or slices, leaving the center intact. Once the potatoes are done, the heat should be turned down, and from that point on the chowder should never be cooked above a slow simmer. Look closely at the texture of the broth when the potatoes are almost fully cooked. This is when you can smash a few potato pieces along the side of the pot with a slotted spoon or thick wooden spoon if you want to make the chowder a little thicker.

The size of the dice or slices of potato is really a matter of personal taste. But I like the size of the main ingredient and the potato to be consistent with one another. For example, I use a large dice for the lobster in lobster chowder and specify a similar dice for the potatoes and onions. In most fish chowders, where the fish flakes into large, somewhat flat pieces, I use potato slices of a similar size. For quahog chowder, the potato is cut into medium dice to reflect the dice of the clam. There are exceptions: corn chowder, for instance, where the main ingredient is too small to replicate. However, although there is an overall logic in the cuts of potatoes called for in my recipes, you may change the size to suit your preference, as long as you cook the potatoes for the length of time appropriate to their size.

The technique for dicing is the same no matter what the size is. First peel the potato, then cut a thin lengthwise slice from one side. This gives the potato a flat bottom, so it cannot roll as you cut it, making slicing safer and easier. Next, slice the potato lengthwise into the desired thickness. Then cut the slices lengthwise into long sticks of the same thickness. To finish, cut them across into cubes of the same thickness, creating a uniform dice. Remember that perfection is not the goal here; you just need the majority of the diced pieces to be of similar size—some irregular cutting is desirable, in fact.

When slicing potatoes, their size and shape will be a factor. Start by peeling the potato, then cut lengthwise in half. Now you can cut it crosswise into slices or, if the slices would be too wide, cut the potato halves lengthwise in half again before slicing. For most chowders, I cut potatoes into slices about 1/3 inch thick.

Since the starch of the potatoes is so important to chowder making, I do not recommend preparing them ahead and holding them in water to prevent discoloring. That common practice will result in a loss of starch. It's better if you have all the ingredients except the potatoes ready when you begin making your chowder; that way, you can prepare the potatoes while the pork is rendering and the vegetables are cooking. Don't worry, you'll have plenty of time!

Onions and Family

You can't make a chowder without onions or some member of the onion family. In fact, onions are the only ingredient found in every chowder recipe in this book. In terms of flavor, they are not the defining factor, but they play a strong supporting role, adding sweetness and pungency while rounding out the overall taste of the chowder.

Types of Onions

The standard yellow Spanish onion, available year-round in nearly every supermarket, is the onion of choice for most chowders. Choose ones that are firm with no discoloring or mushy, soft spots. Medium to large onions (8 ounces or more) are easiest to cut into uniform dice; small onions are harder to work with, and they tend to have a stronger flavor as well. At certain times, because of seasonal factors or improper storage, onions will be particularly pungent or bitter. Your nose will tell you as soon as you cut into one. When this is the case, place the onions in cold water after you dice them, then drain them very well before cooking. Another alternative is to simply cut back on the quantity of onions you add to the chowder.

Specialty onions, like Florida Sweets, Vidalia, and Maui, which are delicious raw or marinated, are so mild in flavor when cooked that the chowder may taste bland. Red onions give the right flavor to chowder but discolor with the long cooking, imparting an unappetizing gray hue. Shallots give good flavor too and can be used in a pinch, but because of their small size, they are not the best choice (most of the chowders in this book call for onions cut into medium or large dice). Leeks are not commonly used, but they do yield a very fine chowder. I feature them in both my Oyster and Leek Chowder (page 141) and Mushroom and Leek Chowder (page 183), but wouldn't hesitate to substitute them in other chowders. Because neither scallions nor chives benefit from extended cooking, they are better when finely chopped and sprinkled over certain chowders as a garnish.

Dicing Onions

Most chowder recipes call for diced onions. The technique is the same for all sizes of dice. First cut the stem and opposite end off, then peel off the skin. Next slice the onion lengthwise in half. Place each half flat on the cutting board and place the palm of one hand on top of the onion. Depending on the desired size of dice, make 3 to 6 parallel slices down the length of the onion, stopping at the stem end so the onion doesn't fall apart. Then make a series of equally spaced horizontal cuts, again stopping at the stem end so the onion doesn't fall apart. Last, cut across the horizontal cuts at the desired dimension of the dice. Lay the remaining piece of onion (where you did not cut all the way through) down on the board and cut it into the desired size. As you work, remember to always keep your fingers curled in and let the knife rest against your knuckles; it is impossible to cut yourself with this age-old technique. Because of the structure of an onion, you will never achieve a perfectly uniform dice. That's all right. As long as you cut the approximate size, it will not affect the success of your chowder.

Garlic

Garlic is used in some of these chowders, especially the bold-flavored ones like Bermuda Fish Chowder with Crab (page 102), South Coast Portuguese Fish Chowder (page 90), and Manhattan Red Clam Chowder (page 133). It is also added in smaller quantities to a few of the others, like my New England Clam (Quahog) Chowder (page 112). Please pay special attention to the quantity called for in the recipes. In most cases, my intention is to impart the slightest whisper of garlic. If you add too much, it will ruin the overall taste.

Celery

You will find small amounts of celery in most clam chowder recipes and in many other chowders as well. I do not find big pieces of celery appealing in chowder. Since it is the flavor of celery that I want, I cut it into small dice (⅓ inch) so it nearly dissolves into the chowder. I don't ask you to peel the celery, because that kind of tedious detail is contrary to the spirit of chowder making: it's better if you just use the tender inner stalks. If, however, you do use the tough outer stalks, it wouldn't hurt to gently run a potato peeler lengthwise down the outside of the stalk to remove the stringy part.

Corn

Corn chowder is the indisputable king of farmhouse chowders. The flavor of corn combines so naturally and beautifully with other chowder ingredients, it is little wonder that this staple of the American kitchen has found its way into hundreds of chowder recipes. The essence of chowder is making something special out of what is at hand, and for many people, especially those away from the coast, corn fits that criterion. In addition to playing the leading role in Corn Chowder (page 175), it performs wonderfully as a supporting ingredient in Lobster and Corn Chowder (page 170), Savory Summer Fish Chowder (page 96), Chicken Chowder with Corn (page 196), and several others.

Canned corn has been around for more than a hundred and fifty years, and its use in corn chowder is probably just as old. I do not use canned corn, but you can substitute canned or frozen niblets by volume in any of the recipes that call for fresh corn. Canned creamed corn has an artificial flavor I dislike, and I do not recommend it. My style of cooking cele-

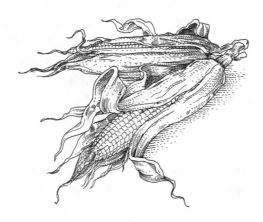

brates fresh ingredients, and I don't like to use foods that are not in season. Since chowder doesn't call for or need the most tender delicate types of summer corn (trucked-in cellophane-wrapped supermarket corn works fine), I am content to make good corn chowders from fresh corn for eight or nine months of the year.

Types of Corn

The best types of sweet corn for chowder are the hearty yellow or bicolor varieties. Most of the corn in the market today is one of the sugar-enhanced hybrids. Unlike the old-fashioned varieties that need to be rushed from the field to the pot, these maintain their sweetness for long periods. Because of the extended cooking corn receives in chowder, texture is not a factor. When you choose corn for chowder at the supermarket, you most likely won't have a lot of choice, but any of it will most likely be right for chowder. At the farm stand, keep in mind that tender young freshly picked white corn like Silver Queen, which is an ethereal experience when eaten on the cob with butter and salt, is not nearly as tasty when cooked in chowder. Look for large ears, preferably of yellow corn; bicolor is the second choice. And it is fine to save a few pennies and buy yesterday's corn. Some of the best varieties of yellow corn are Earlivee, Kandy Kwik, Sugar Buns, and Tuxedo. Among the most flavorful varieties of bicolor corn are Athos, Double Gem, Delectable, and Clockwork.

I have come across early chowder recipes that call for dried corn, but I'm sure these were driven by necessity, not choice. Sweet corn is a vegetable; dried corn is a starch. Adding it to a chowder would produce something more akin to porridge than chowder.

Cutting Corn from the Cob

To prepare corn for chowder, husk it, then carefully remove the silk. Wiping the ear with a dry towel will remove any recalcitrant silk. Stand the ear with the tapered end up on the cutting board. Using a sharp knife, cut from top to bottom, keeping the knife close to the cob but not cutting into it. Then use the back of the knife to scrape away the remaining moist bits of corn still attached to the cob—what I call the "milk." The cobs can be broken in half and added to any stock that is intended for a corn chowder; if you add the cobs to the stock, don't scrape them, just leave the milky bits on for flavor.

Tomatoes

Despite the unnecessary New England–New York rivalry concerning red and white chowders, the fact remains that since tomatoes became popular in America in the middle of the nineteenth century, they have been used in chowder. Prior to the early 1800s, many Americans thought that tomatoes were poisonous! But even in New England, where chowder is supposed to be white, tomatoes were called for as early as 1851 in chowder recipes from Boston and Cape Cod. My theory is that the New England tradition of disparaging red chowders, i.e., tomato hating, stems from the Red Sox–Yankees rivalry, which began in 1919, after Boston sold Babe Ruth to the Yankees. It must have some such origin, because it's hard to deny that the flavor of tomatoes with clams and other seafood is exquisite.

Tomatoes are mostly associated with Manhattan Red Clam Chowder (page 133), but they are, in fact, used in many classic chowders, including South Coast Portuguese Fish Chowder (page 90), Bermuda Fish Chowder with Crab (page 102), Bahamian Conch Chowder (page 156), and several others. Some chowders call for a large amount of canned tomatoes and their liquid; others use them sparingly. I strongly suggest that you stay with the amounts specified in my recipes the first time you make a red chowder. Afterward, you can alter the proportions to suit your preference.

I recommend using whole canned tomatoes packed in their juice. Since tomatoes for chowder are diced, you'll need to remove the tomatoes from their liquid, dice them as specified, and then combine them and their liquid before you measure them. Or, if you can find them, you can use good-quality diced tomatoes in juice, a relatively new product, in any recipe that calls for diced tomatoes. Do not use crushed tomatoes. Any good-quality whole tomatoes would be appropriate, but I have always preferred the flavor of canned plum tomatoes, whether domestic or imported. Fresh tomatoes have a hard time competing against canned tomatoes in chowder. Unless they are truly sun-ripened tomatoes, available only for a short period in the summer, they lack flavor. And they also need to be firm enough to stay together over the long cooking. Some of the best eating varieties become mealy when subjected to heat and disintegrate in chowder. Again, I have had my best results with plum tomatoes. Since I do not pretend to know the characteristics of the infinite varieties of tomatoes available across the United States, my recipes simply call for peeled diced canned or fresh tomatoes (and their juice).

Peeling and Dicing Tomatoes

If using fresh tomatoes, begin by scoring an X in the bottom of each tomato with a paring knife. Dip them into boiling water for about 30 seconds, then transfer to an ice water bath. As soon as they are chilled, the skins will peel off easily. Next, cut each tomato lengthwise in half and gently squeeze the juice from the tomato into a small bowl; reserve the juice. The tomatoes are now ready to be diced. The juice can be strained if you object to the seeds; I don't bother unless the tomatoes are particularly seedy. Combine the diced tomatoes with the juice before measuring.

If using canned tomatoes, pour the juice into a small bowl and reserve. Holding it over the bowl to catch the juices, carefully slice each tomato lengthwise in half with a paring knife. The tomatoes are now ready to be diced. The juice can be strained if you object to the seeds.

Cooking Tomatoes in Chowder

The acid in tomatoes causes raw potatoes to form a very thin, almost unnoticeable skin, which prevents them from releasing their starch. Therefore, I add tomatoes to chowder only after the potatoes are fully cooked. The exception is Bermuda Fish Chowder with Crab (page 102), where finely diced potatoes cook for 2 hours with the tomatoes.

Milk, Cream, Butter, and Cheese

New England is rich in seafood, dairy products, and orchard fruits. It is the Normandy (France) of America! And, as in Normandy's cuisine, the marriage of seafood and dairy in New England cooking was a product of circumstance, of creating dishes from local ingredients. Since the mid-1800s, New England chowders have almost always been made with milk or cream, sometimes a combination of the two. Butter is often used when starting to cook the chowder, and dyed-in-the-wool New England chowder cooks often add a small dollop of cold butter to each bowl as they are dishing up. A few recipes even recommend adding a bit of Cheddar cheese to flavor the broth! There is no denying the greatness of the seafood-dairy combination, even if it flies in the face of the current craze for Mediterranean-inspired dishes. Although I enjoy many of the nondairy chowders immensely, often for their more robust flavors, it is the taste of a simple buttery, slightly creamy, briny chowder that is my gold standard.

Most of the milk, cream, and butter available to us doesn't have a unique taste. Dairy products are processed in such large quantities nowadays that it would be hard to detect any characteristic that would make them special. This is viewed by some as a great achievement in agriculture, providing more consistent quality to more people (most of whom are unaware of how extraordinary milk, cream, and butter can taste). I can't argue with this logic, but I can point out that there are dairy products available that are sweeter and richer, with more complex flavors, than commercial milk, cream, and butter. In New England, a few small dairies (some organic) still dot the map, and their products are noticeably better. If you have access to a small local dairy, or if your supermarket carries specialty butters and other dairy products, give them a try. They will make your chowder taste even better!

If you are lactose-intolerant or are avoiding dairy products altogether, you will find plenty of chowders in this book that are not based on milk or cream. And if you want to make a certain recipe that contains dairy, you can omit the milk or cream, substituting equal

amounts of stock or broth. Olive oil or other vegetable oils can be substituted for butter in any recipe. Of course, in either case, the flavor of the dish will be changed as well.

Milk Versus Cream

Like me, you may remember when cream clogged the neck of milk bottles. You don't see it that often these days; milk just isn't as rich as it was in the past. That is one of the reasons I prefer using stock finished with cream in my chowders, rather than milk. Only two recipes in this book use milk: Church Supper Fish Chowder (page 83), a good recipe that serves as a point of reference, and Rhode Island Clear Clam Chowder (page 130), which is served with a pitcher of warm milk on the side. Milk-based chowders are authentic; they are what native New England cooks make at home, but I am not a home cook, and I think using a strong stock finished with cream provides superior results. First of all, milk-based chowders are just that—milk with very little broth or stock. The milk does a decent job of soaking up the flavors, but it rarely produces the intense flavor of a chowder cooked in stock, then finished with a little heavy cream. Along the New England coast, there is a "secret" technique (known to most local people) of soaking lobster bodies (carcasses) in milk overnight for use in chowder or lobster stew the next day. I have tried it and this method does impart some lobster flavor, but it does not match a chowder made with a rich stock and finished with cream. A chowder finished with the right amount of cream is only slightly richer than one made with milk, and it resembles chowder made with the rich milk of the past.

Another reason I prefer chowders made with heavy cream is that they don't curdle or separate, not ever! When making chowder with milk, you have to be very careful, because it may curdle if you boil it. And every now and then, it will still curdle for no apparent reason. The safest way to use milk in chowder is to make a white sauce (béchamel) before you add it, but then you wind up with a pasty kind of chowder. I believe there is a direct correlation between butterfat content and the likelihood of curdling. With nonfat or 1 percent or 2 percent milk, curdling is inevitable. Whole milk (4 percent butterfat content) decreases the chances of curdling, and as you travel through the hierarchy (each with a higher content of butterfat) from milk to half-and-half to light cream to whipping cream to heavy cream, the chance of curdling decreases, finally disappearing with heavy cream. It's true that chowders with milk don't curdle that often, but as a professional, with no tolerance for waste or disaster, I choose heavy cream and I urge you to. And just because the dairy product is richer, it doesn't mean the chowder has to be. You need only a cup of cream per each pint of half-and-half or 3 cups of milk. Too much cream can make the chowder excessively rich and cloying while muting the flavor.

Evaporated Milk

In parts of New England, especially Maine, some cooks prefer to use condensed or evaporated milk in their chowders. This custom obviously grew from necessity, especially for local people living on islands or in other remote places, where a constant supply of fresh dairy products wasn't a birthright. It is also a favorite with Down East campers, who make chowder with freshly caught fish. I have tried evaporated milk in chowder and found the texture and sweetness to be unpleasant. But I know that people who grew up on a diet of condensed or evaporated milk have a great fondness for it and prefer it even when fresh milk and cream are easily had. It can be substituted in equal amounts for cream in any of my recipes.

Butter

I prefer sweet (unsalted) butter to salted because it gives me complete control over the salt level in the food I prepare. Yankee cooks have a wonderfully old wicked habit of putting a dollop of butter on each bowl of chowder after it has been dished up. If the chowder is already seasoned to your liking, the extra butter, if salted, may make it too salty. I also have a sneaking suspicion that the best butter is usually packed as sweet, but I have never been able to confirm that. There is an interesting selection of butters available at the market these days. My local market carries Kate's Butter from Old Orchard Beach, Maine, a local treat with delicious flavor. A great many markets carry organic butter, and specialty markets carry exquisite imported butters from France and Ireland. With the current high prices of ordinary butter, specialty butters, at less than a dollar more a pound, have become more popular. It is money well spent.

Cheese

The use of cheese in chowder is rare. I first heard of it from a Maine cook, who worked in a restaurant where they added Cheddar to fish chowder. I've also seen it in a few old New England cookbooks. Vermont or other white Cheddar can be used sparingly, to add distinction, possibly recapturing some of the missing nuances achieved with milk from small dairies. In larger quantities, cheese lightly thickens the chowder while adding a bold flavor. I like the idea, but use it with a light hand because most chowders are already rich enough. I do feature cheese in my Potato Chowder with Cheddar Cheese (page 186) and offer it in a variation of my Chesapeake Crab Chowder (page 167). The cooking is simple: gently stir in the grated cheese when you add the cream. You can add cheese to several other chowders in this book, but don't overdo it—stay with white chowders other than clam. Often it's better to leave well enough alone!

Spices and Herbs

Chowder has suffered a bit of fatigue over the last hundred years (like a lot of New England cooking). Until recently, the use of herbs and spices in New England cooking could be described as minimalist—in chowders, almost nonexistent. But that wasn't always the case. The first published chowder recipe in North America (printed in the *Boston Evening Post* in 1751) called for pepper, sweet marjoram, savory, thyme, and parsley. Other chowder recipes from the 1700s and 1800s called for mace, cloves, nutmeg, curry powder, paprika, cayenne pepper, chives, and flavorings like lemon peel or Worcestershire sauce. Some recipes simply called for "herbs and spices," leaving it to the discretion of the cook. Dried herbs and spices from India, China, Europe, and the Caribbean were very popular in Boston, where clipper ships were constantly bringing in new supplies of exotic ingredients. Maybe the use of spices declined with the ending of the clipper ship trading days, I'm not sure. By 1896, when Fannie Merritt Farmer published her *Boston Cooking School Cookbook,* pepper was the only spice remaining in her recipe for fish chowder.

Spices

Pepper has always been important in chowder. Although past recipes did not list specific amounts of pepper, most recommended being generous. My recipes leave the quantity of pepper to the cook, but I specify ample amounts of whole black peppercorns in my stocks and broths. I like a substantial amount of ground pepper in my chowder, and I prefer black pepper over white because it has a more robust flavor. Who cares about the black specks? I *like* the way they look!

In the spirit of the original chowders, you will find many other spices in the recipes throughout this book—including cloves in Bermuda Fish Chowder with Crab (page 102), nutmeg in Bahamian Conch Chowder (page 156), a curry mixture in Lightly Curried Mussel Chowder (page 147), and Hungarian paprika in Lobster and Corn Chowder (page 170). I bring out the flavor of dried spices by cooking them in fat, so in most recipes they are added with the onions, sautéed, and then simmered, cooking the entire time of the recipe. This technique brings out the flavor in the spices and allows them to mellow and integrate with the chowder. Stay with the recommended amount of spice in each recipe, at least the first time you make it.

I call for dried bay leaves in many chowders. Their average size is about 1½ inches, but I have seen them from 1 to 3 inches long; assume the recipe is using average-sized bay leaves and adjust accordingly. If you must substitute fresh bay (laurel) leaves for dried, use with caution because they can be overpowering—they are at least five times stronger than dried and can ruin a chowder.

Remember to date all your dried spices and herbs. They lose flavor over time, and most should be replaced after a year.

Herbs

With few exceptions, I prefer to cook with fresh herbs. Fresh thyme, parsley, chives, and basil are sold almost everywhere these days, so I call for them in many of my recipes. Other fresh herbs, such as tarragon, chervil, and savory, are not always easily found, so whenever a recipe calls for them, I provide an option. Dried herbs are best handled like dried spices, their flavor expanded by sautéeing them with the onions, then simmering them in the chowder.

There are two ways to use fresh herbs in chowder. To extract the most flavor from aromatic herbs like thyme, rosemary, and savory, give them a long cooking time, like dried herbs. Tender herbs like parsley, chives, chervil, and cilantro are best added during the last minute of cooking, or even sprinkled over the chowder after it is plated. Remember, when picking off the leaves of thyme, parsley, or other herbs for chopping, save the stems to add extra flavor to your stock.

Spices and herbs can add dimension, contrast, and wonderful tastes to chowder, but it is important that they complement, never dominate, the overall flavor. Tender fresh clams possess their own herbaceous quality. When making chowder with them, I use very small amounts of herbs so the ocean flavor is not overwhelmed. In contrast, when making chowder with large bluefish, for example, I try to match the bold taste of the fish with more assertive seasonings.

Chapter 3

Stocks and Broths:
The Essence of Chowder

If one's stock is good, what remains of the work is easy.
—Auguste Escoffier, LE GUIDE CULINAIRE, 1903

Traditionally, the preparation of rich stocks and broths was not an essential pre-condition for making chowder. You can make a good enough fish chowder with water. This book, however, is not about chowders that are good enough. It is about chowders that are memorable, chowders that will astound. If you want a chowder with robust aroma and taste, as well as great texture and lingering flavors, in almost every case, you *must* use stock or broth, preferably homemade. The recipes in this chapter show you how easy and inexpensive it is to make wonderful homemade stocks and broths right in your own kitchen.

The Lingo

Stocks and broths are infusions, like tea. In the context of meat and poultry, stocks are made with bones and broths are made with meat, sometimes in combination with bones. In the case of seafood, the words *stock* and *broth* could be used interchangeably, but they are not. Fish stock is made with fish frames (bones) and sometimes heads. Lobster and crab stocks are usually made with carcasses and shells. There is some meat in the carcass, but a lot of the flavor comes from the shells, so we chefs usually call the result stock. Clams and mussels release a "broth," because so much of the flavor in the liquid comes from the actual body (meat) and the juices inside the shell.

Store-Bought Stocks and Broths

If you use canned or other commercially prepared stocks or broths, carefully read the list of ingredients on the can, bottle, or package before you bring one home. Brands that usually have the best and most natural flavor have the cleanest ingredients (the least amount of preservatives). Good-quality canned chicken stock is made from chicken bones, vegetables, spices, and very little salt (look for low-sodium brands). The best clam juice or clam broth comes in small bottles and contains only one ingredient: the juice of fresh clams. There are some very acceptable "gourmet" stocks, broths, and reductions available in upscale markets, but these will cost you dearly and still won't taste as good as any you make yourself.

Substituting Stocks and Broths

Many of my chowder recipes call for the stocks and broths in this chapter. Others are made with their own special stock or broth. In either case, if you stay with the specified quantity of stock or broth called for in the recipe, you can substitute store-bought stocks or broths (chicken for chicken, clam for clam) with no problem and with decent results. You can also substitute water or a combination of water and stock or broth (homemade or commercial), but the result will be less potent than if the chowder is made with all stock or broth. You can also substitute light chicken stock or clam broth for fish stock, but the character of the resulting chowder will be changed. Chicken stock is fairly neutral and blends surprisingly well with many seafoods. But bottled clam broth can affect the taste of a chowder that doesn't contain clams, muddling or overpowering the flavors that were intended to dominate.

Guidelines for Making Stocks and Broths

Making stock and broth is not an art form: it is a simple skill that anyone who follows my directions can master. You only need to keep in mind a few important points:

The quantities in the recipes for stocks and broths can and should be used as a guideline. Unlike the chowder recipes here, I don't give exact weights for vegetables, because a few ounces more or less of onion, celery, or carrot will make little difference (you can substitute leeks for onions in any stock recipe). If you happen to have a little extra onion, celery, or carrot around, by all means add it to your stockpot. Likewise, if a recipe calls for 2½ pounds of bones and you have 3, use all of them. It is the technique and the ratio of water to bones that is most important. As long as you adhere closely to my recommended amounts, you can be confident that your stock will turn out superbly. For herbs and spices, stay with my recommended amounts, because their potent flavors are meant to complement, not dominate.

The ratio of water to bones is very important. I recommend a 6- to 8-quart stockpot for most recipes. Most pots are similar in shape, but the way your chicken carcass and bones, lobster shells, or fish frames fit into a particular pot can vary, affecting the amount of water you will need. Although the recipes in the book give specific amounts for water and bones, the important thing to be aware of is that there should be *just enough water to cover the ingredients.* By using a minimal amount of water, you are certain to create a full-flavored stock or broth. If by chance the stock or broth cooks down below the ingredients, simply add more water as necessary during the cooking. Make your stocks and broths as concentrated as possible, knowing that if you don't have enough to make a specific chowder recipe, you can always make up the difference with a little water.

If the chowder recipe calls for fresh thyme leaves, you can save the stems for the stock. If the stock recipe calls for 4 sprigs of thyme, for example, substitute the 4 picked stems and add 1 more whole sprig (with leaves) for good measure.

Don't add any vegetables that are not called for in a stock or broth unless you are using that stock in a particular chowder recipe that would make such additions appropriate. For example, you can add bits of bell pepper to the stock if bell pepper is called for in the chowder recipe. Or you can add corncobs to a stock that is intended for corn chowder. In general, the goal is to make a stock in which the flavor of the main ingredient (chicken, fish, etc.) is pronounced. Other flavors should remain in the background.

To multiply any stock recipe in this book by two or even three, increase all the ingredients *except* the water proportionately. Since larger batches take more time to reduce, you should use about ¼ cup less water (total) for a double batch and ½ cup less (total) for a triple batch. Conversely, when you cut a recipe in half, you should expect to add a little more water during the cooking. Just remember (once again) that there should be just enough water to cover the ingredients. If you add too much water at the beginning, you will end up with a weak-tasting stock. And if you try to salvage it by cooking it longer, you run the risk of making your stock bitter.

With the exception of Strong Fish Stock (page 58) and the broths made from clams (page 62) and mussels (page 65), all my stocks and broths start with combining bones or carcasses with water and bringing the mixture to a boil. As it comes to a boil, I skim the white foam from the top. The foam contains impurities that can harm the flavor of the stock if they are allowed to be cooked back into it. I use a circular swirling motion with a ladle, starting from the center and pushing the foam out to the sides, where I can easily remove it with the ladle. Once all the foam is removed, I turn the stock down to a simmer, add the vegetables, spices, and herbs, and *never let it boil again.* Boiling can bring out bitterness in the bones or carcasses and even spices. Simmering, on the other hand, releases all the desirable qualities of each ingredient.

When making broth from clams and mussels, it is particularly important to use only as much liquid as the recipe calls for. Too much liquid will produce a weak broth. The yield for a broth made by steaming clams or mussels may vary, because the quantity of liquid is determined by what the clams and mussels release, and bivalves start to lose liquid the moment they are harvested. The fresher the clams or mussels, the greater the amount of broth they will give up.

I have given approximate cooking times for the stocks and broths in this chapter, which are as accurate as possible. If you follow the instructions in the recipes you will create the bases for wonderful chowders, but there are variables that make it impossible to prescribe exact times. For example, if you make a stock from the bones of 3-pound chickens, the optimum flavor will be extracted more quickly than if you make the stock with the bones from 4-pounders. The same holds true of a stock made from smaller versus larger lobster carcasses. The temperature at which you simmer the stock or broth also plays a role. With every extraction, once you reach optimum flavor, it is best to strain the stock or broth as soon as possible, because the next stage will be bitterness. My usual technique for determining when a stock or broth is perfectly done starts with lightly salting it toward the end of the cooking. The exceptions are the quick-cooked clam and mussel broths, which bring enough of their own salt. Salting brightens the stock or broth and allows me to taste its true flavor more clearly. I usually start tasting about 30 minutes before the end of the prescribed cooking time. Then I taste at 10-minute intervals. The moment I can't taste an improvement over the previous taste, I remove the stock or broth from the heat and strain it. Thus the actual cooking time may be anywhere between 20 to 30 minutes less, or more, than the recipe calls for.

Because the cooking times for fish stocks are much shorter than for meat and poultry stocks and can therefore be gauged more exactly, tastings are not needed. Nevertheless, I lightly salt my fish stock toward the end of cooking so I can accurately discern its true taste. The salt also inhibits bacterial growth, preserves flavor, and extends the shelf life of the stock or broth.

It is extremely important to chill stock or broth as quickly as possible after it is strained. The sooner it is out of the danger zone (40° to 140°F is ideal for bacterial growth) the better. Chilling the stock quickly preserves flavor and extends its shelf life. One way to chill stock quickly is to strain it into a stainless steel or other nonreactive metallic container and place it in an ice bath, stirring occasionally. *Do not cover the stock until it is out of the danger zone.*

If quickly chilled and covered airtight, most stocks will keep their freshness and taste in the refrigerator for 3 days. All of the strained stocks and broths in this chapter can be frozen with minimal loss of flavor. Freeze them in small containers, premeasured in cups and/or pints. Small amounts freeze faster and enable you to defrost the amount you need without creating any waste. Some home cooks freeze stocks and broths in ice cube trays, then store the cubes in plastic refrigerator bags.

Bacteria grows slowly in the freezer, but it does grow. Ideally, you should use frozen broths and stocks within a few weeks of making them. After 2 months, as a safety precaution, they should be discarded. For this reason, it is very important to date the stocks and broths (and any other homemade foods) when you package them for freezing.

Strong Fish Stock

Julia Child included this recipe in the book from her television series *In Julia's Kitchen with Master Chefs,* which also features my recipe for New England Fish Chowder (page 79). As the name implies, this stock has a concentrated fish flavor, and is therefore a superb choice for any of my fish chowder recipes. Its intense taste limits its use in shellfish chowders, which are better made with the less assertive Traditional Fish Stock (page 60). This recipe uses a technique called "sweating" to extract maximum flavor from every ingredient. Although sweating adds a step, this stock is still effortless to make and takes only five minutes longer to cook than the Traditional Fish Stock.

I begin by sautéing a very thinly sliced mirepoix (onions, celery, and carrots) with herbs and peppercorns. I then layer fish heads and frames (bones) on top of these vegetables, add a little white wine, and cover the pot. As the heads and bones "sweat" (and steam), the proteins are drawn out. If you peek, you will actually see little white droplets of flavorful proteins coagulating on the surface of the bones. After the sweating is completed (about 15 minutes), I cover the bones with water and simmer them briefly. I let the mixture steep for 10 minutes before straining it, producing a stock that is full-flavored and gelatinous. The fish heads are what endow this stock with its marvelous jellied consistency, which in turn gives a luscious mouth feel to the chowder broth.

Cook's Notes

Strong Fish Stock can be used in any fish chowder, using 1 or 2 heads from haddock or cod mixed with any combination of flounder, sole, bass and/or halibut frames (bones).

You can employ the "sweating" method with any fish you use to make a chowder—simply substitute the same amount of heads and bones. Keep in mind, however, that while the heads and bones of salmon, bluefish, and other species of oily fish make a stock that is right for their own chowders, its flavor is too pronounced to be suitable in other chowders or soups.

For equipment, you will need a 7- to 8-quart heavy stockpot with a tight-fitting lid, a wooden spoon, a ladle, and a fine-mesh strainer.

2 tablespoons unsalted butter
2 medium onions, very thinly sliced
4 stalks celery, very thinly sliced

2 medium carrots, very thinly sliced
2 dried bay leaves
¼ cup roughly chopped fresh flat-leaf parsley leaves and stems

6 to 8 sprigs fresh thyme
2 tablespoons black peppercorns
1 large (6 inches long or more) or 2 small
(4 inches long or less) fish heads from
cod or haddock, split lengthwise,
gills removed, and rinsed clean of
any blood

2½ to 3 pounds fish frames (bones) from
sole, flounder, bass, and/or halibut,
cut into 2-inch pieces and rinsed
clean of any blood
¼ cup dry white wine
About 2 quarts very hot or boiling water
Kosher or sea salt

1. Melt the butter in a heavy 7- to 8-quart stockpot over medium heat. Add the onions, celery, carrots, bay leaves, parsley, thyme, and peppercorns and cook, stirring frequently with a wooden spoon, until the vegetables become very soft without browning, about 8 minutes.

2. Place the fish head on the vegetables and stack the fish frames evenly on top. Pour in the wine, cover the pot tightly, and let the bones sweat for 10 to 15 minutes, or until they have turned completely white.

3. Add enough very hot or boiling water to just barely cover the bones. Give the mixture a gentle stir and allow the brew to come to a simmer. Simmer for 10 minutes, uncovered, carefully skimming off any white foam that comes to the surface, trying not to take any herbs, spices, or vegetables with it. (Using a ladle and a circular motion, push the foam from the center to the outside of the pot, where it is easy to remove.)

4. Remove the pot from the stove, stir the stock again, and allow it to steep for 10 minutes. Strain through a fine-mesh strainer and season lightly with salt. If you are not going to be using the stock within the hour, chill it as quickly as possible. Cover the stock *after* it is thoroughly chilled (it will have a light jellied consistency) and keep refrigerated for up to 3 days, or freeze for up to 2 months.

Makes about 2 quarts

Traditional Fish Stock

This stock is even easier to put together than Strong Fish Stock (page 58). It does not require fish heads, only the bones of flat fish—sole, flounder, halibut, or turbot—and it doesn't call for the extra step of sweating the bones. It has a more delicate seafood flavor, and it is not as gelatinous as the Strong Fish Stock, making it very versatile. In addition to chowder and seafood stews like bouillabaisse, you can use this to make fish velouté and delicate French sauces such as Bercy (based on velouté and shallots) or bonne femme.

Cook's Notes

Traditional Fish Stock and Strong Fish Stock (provided the Strong Fish Stock is not made with nontraditional fish like salmon or bluefish), can be used interchangeably in chowder. However, Strong Fish Stock is preferable for fish chowder and Traditional Fish Stock is preferable for chowders that use shellfish or a mixture of different seafoods. The milder Traditional Fish Stock lets the shellfish flavors come through more clearly.

For equipment, you will need a 7- to 8-quart stockpot, a ladle, and a fine-mesh strainer.

4 pounds fish frames (bones) from sole, flounder, halibut, and/or turbot, cut into 2-inch pieces and rinsed clean of any blood
½ cup dry white wine
About 2 quarts water
2 medium onions, very thinly sliced
4 stalks celery, very thinly sliced

2 medium carrots, very thinly sliced
2 dried bay leaves
¼ cup roughly chopped fresh Italian parsley leaves and stems
6 to 8 sprigs fresh thyme
2 tablespoons black peppercorns
Kosher or sea salt

1. In a 7- to 8-quart stockpot, combine the fish bones, white wine, and just enough water to cover (you won't need the full 2 quarts of water here). Bring to a boil, skimming off the white foam from the top of the stock as it approaches boiling, then reduce the heat so the stock simmers. (Using a ladle and a circular motion, push the foam from the center to the outside of the pot, where it is easy to remove.)
2. Add the onions, celery, carrots, bay leaves, parsley, thyme, and peppercorns and stir them into the liquid. If the ingredients are not covered by liquid, add a little more water. Allow the stock to simmer gently for 20 minutes.

3. Remove the stock from the stove, stir it again, and allow it to steep for 10 minutes. Strain through a fine-mesh strainer and season lightly with salt. If you are not going to be using the stock within the hour, chill it as quickly as possible. Cover the stock *after* it has completely cooled and keep refrigerated for up to 3 days, or freeze for up to 2 months.

Makes about 2 quarts

Clam Broth
(Quahogs and Large Cherrystones)

The fragrance of clam broth, the essence of steamed clams, is one of the greatest in all of seafood cooking. Reminiscent of the ocean, only better, this cloudy, steel-colored broth is always served alongside steamers, as a dip to heat and clean the clams, and is traditionally (always, in my case) sipped afterward. Clam broth is also the main ingredient in clam chowder, where it contributes more clam taste than the meat from the clams. Many soup companies and seafood restaurant chains use chopped meat from large sea clams, which are cleaned and rinsed to the point where they have lost all flavor. They only provide the bite of the clam—all the flavor comes from the broth. Imagine how your chowder will taste when you make it with your own broth and use fresh clam meat.

Classic clam chowder is made with freshly shucked quahogs (pronounced "ko-hog") or other clams that are chopped, then simmered in a milky broth with all the other ingredients. It is not always possible to buy freshly shucked clams—very few markets offer them anymore. Since even moderately good shuckers have trouble opening quahogs and large cherrystones, I think it is best to steam open the clams, making it easy to remove the meat from their shells. The meat is reserved, to be diced and added to the chowder at the end of cooking, and you'll be rewarded with a broth that possesses a deep pervading clam flavor, perfect for red, white, or clear clam chowder.

Bottled clam broth is found everywhere. Check the ingredients: the better ones are made only with clams. Some bottled clam juices are almost as good as you can produce in your own kitchen, so I won't tell you not to use them in chowder. However, since you will need clams for their meat anyway and since clams produce their own broth as you steam them open, you will rarely have to use bottled clam juice for my recipes. Bottled broth is often used in chowders that use canned or other processed clams, which I have not included in this book.

I don't embellish clam broth when I use it in chowder. I prefer a broth that tastes only of clam essence and water. If I am eating steamers, I might add a bit of celery, onion, thyme, and pepper to flavor it, but for chowder, I don't need to—I add the other flavorings directly to the chowder. This way, I can savor the complex flavors of the broth itself: robust, clammy, briny, herbaceous, and wonderful all on its own. The tastier the broth, the less seasoning I'll add to the chowder.

Cook's Notes
Many different sizes and species of clams can be used for chowder. This recipe calls for the most popular and practical hard-shell clams—quahogs and large cherrystones, which I call

Cherrystone

Quahog

for in six different clam chowders in this book. Sea clams are not easy to get hold of and don't make particularly good chowder anyway (these are the ones the commercial guys use). Littlenecks make good chowder, but they are expensive and are indubitably at their best when eaten raw. Other small clams (also expensive), such as Manila clams, mahogany clams, and cockles from Europe, also make fine chowder, but they are really best presented on their own in their shells in any number of steamed or stewed dishes. I do, however, use cockles in my Irish Shellfish Chowder (page 150).

Littlenecks, topnecks, cherrystones, and quahogs are all the same species of hard-shell clam *(Artica aslandica).* It is their size that gives them their name, littlenecks being the smallest and quahogs the largest. Quahogs are famous for chowder. They range in size from 10 to 16 ounces; I like the smaller ones (10 to 12 ounces) best because they have less of the soft, mushy belly. Even better, large cherrystones (6 to 9 ounces) make a terrific chowder with sweet clam flavor.

If you want to use any of these small hard-shell clams for chowder, make the clam broth as directed. The yield of broth and clam meat will vary depending on the species and their freshness, but not enough to affect the outcome of your chowder.

Cooking time is simple: as soon as the clams open, they—and the broth—are done.

Soft-shell clams, called steamers or, sometimes, "pisser" clams, make superb broth and therefore excellent chowder. The recipe for their broth is included in the recipe for Steamer Clam Chowder (page 114). Likewise, the techniques for making chowder with geoducks, the remarkable giant clams from the Pacific Northwest (page 123), and razor clams, the beautiful, unusual, and increasingly rare bivalve (page 118), are explained thoroughly in their recipes.

At the fish market, look for clams that are steely gray, not chalky white (the white is a sign of age). If a clam is open, even slightly, push its shells back together; if it doesn't stay closed, discard it. If the shell is cracked, discard it. Feel the clams for weight. If one feels light, it could be dead; if it feels unusually heavy, it may be filled with mud. Try to pry it open and see if you have one of these problems. If you do, discard it.

For equipment, you will need a 7- to 8-quart stockpot with a tight-fitting lid, a wooden spoon, and a fine-mesh strainer.

2 cups water
8 pounds large cherrystone clams or small
quahogs, scrubbed and rinsed clean

1. Put the water in a 7- to 8-quart stockpot and bring to a boil over high heat. Add the clams and cover tightly. After 5 minutes, uncover and stir the clams with a wooden spoon. Quickly cover the pot again and let steam for 5 minutes more, or until most of the clams have opened. Don't wait for them all to open, or they will be overcooked. It should only take a little tug or prying to open the stragglers once they are all removed from the heat. The total cooking time for large cherrystones will be about 10 minutes; quahogs will need as much as 5 minutes longer. (Littlenecks and other small clams will take only 6 to 8 minutes.) While the clams are steaming, the broth becomes foamy and light. It usually spills over a bit just as the clams are cooked and ready.

2. As soon as you remove the clams from the stove, carefully pour as much of the broth as you can into a tall narrow container. Let the broth sit for 10 minutes, then carefully pour through a fine-mesh strainer. You can line the strainer with cheesecloth as an extra precaution, but if you are careful and stop before you pour off all the broth, it is not really necessary. After sitting, 99 percent of the grit will have collected at the bottom of the container. If you are not using the broth within the hour, chill it as quickly as possible and cover it *after* it has completely cooled. Keep refrigerated for up to 3 days, or freeze for up to 2 months.

3. Meanwhile, remove the clams from their shells, cover, and refrigerate until ready to use. (They are easier to dice and hold together better after they are chilled.)

Makes about 1 quart (with 1 pound [2 cups] clam meat)

New England Fish Chowder (page 79) with Toasted Common Crackers

South Coast Portuguese Fish Chowder (page 90)

Pacific Northwest Salmon Chowder
with Peas (page 107)

Top: Manhattan Red Clam Chowder (page 133)
Bottom: Steamer Clam Chowder (page 114) with Crown Pilot Crackers

San Francisco Crab "Meatball" Chowder (page 164)

Shaker Fresh Cranberry Bean Chowder (page 180)
with Christopher Kimball's Buttermilk Baking Powder Biscuits (page 210)

Pheasant and Cabbage
Chowder (page 201)
with Skillet Corn Bread (page 219)

Mussel Broth

Broth made from fresh mussels is not as strong or as salty as clam broth, but it has an assertive and rich taste that holds its own, especially when combined with interesting herbs and spices. The famous Parisian mussel soup, billi bi, for example, uses saffron. I add a small bit of Madras curry powder as a backdrop to the briny shellfish flavor in my mussel chowder (page 147). For some mussel dishes, I might use white wine, garlic, onions, and herbs in the steaming liquid, but for chowder, I prefer not to embellish the mussel broth. I use mussels and water only, then add the seasonings directly to the chowder after I have tasted the broth. It's the pure flavor of the sea I want to dominate in the chowder.

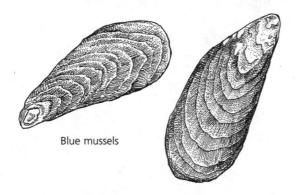

Blue mussels

Cook's Notes

Because mussel shells are light compared to those of clams, they yield more broth and a little more meat per pound. Five pounds of mussels produce as much broth and meat as 8 pounds of clams, making them fairly economical.

On the East Coast, local mussels, both wild and cultivated, are a good deal. Wild mussels are usually less expensive, but they tend to be smaller, yielding less meat per pound. Cultivated mussels, especially those from PEI (Prince Edward Island), are meaty, easy to clean and debeard, and good-tasting to boot. One could argue the merits of cultivated and wild mussels. Wild mussels can have exquisite flavor, but they vary greatly in quality depending on their place of origin. Cultivated mussels are consistently good and very dependable. New Zealand green-lip mussels are available in some markets, but they are expensive and do not make a better broth or chowder than our East Coast mussels. Penn Cove mussels from Puget Sound (Washington State) are bright in flavor and make a superb chowder.

Making the broth is simple and quick; preparing the mussels is more work. First, give the mussels a quick rinse. Then, using a kitchen rag or towel, wipe the shells clean and, if you see one, pull off the beard sticking out from the center of each mussel. Make sure each mussel is closed tight. If it isn't, squeeze the shells together; if it doesn't stay closed, discard it—it is dead. Also discard any mussels with cracked shells.

Mussels open very quickly when steamed or otherwise heated, but unlike clams, they need to cook just a bit longer after they open. If you undercook the mussels, the meat will be soft and hard to store without being damaged.

For equipment, you will need a 7- to 8-quart stockpot with a tight-fitting lid, a wooden spoon, and a fine-mesh strainer.

1 cup water
5 pounds medium mussels, scrubbed,
    debearded, and rinsed

1. Put the water in a 7- to 8-quart stockpot and bring to a boil over high heat. Add the mussels and cover tightly. After 3 minutes, uncover and stir the mussels with a wooden spoon. Quickly cover the pot again and let steam for 3 minutes more, or until most of the mussels have opened. As the mussels are steaming, the broth becomes foamy and light. It usually spills over a bit, just as the mussels are cooked and ready.
2. Remove the mussels from the stove and carefully pour as much of the broth as you can into a tall narrow container. Let the broth sit for 10 minutes, then carefully pour through a strainer. You can line the strainer with cheesecloth as an extra precaution, but if you are careful and stop before you pour off all the broth, it is not really necessary. After sitting, 99 percent of the grit will have collected at the bottom of the container. If you are not using the broth within an hour, cool it as quickly as possible. Cover the broth *after* it has completely cooled and keep refrigerated for up to 3 days, or freeze for up to 2 months.
3. Meanwhile, remove the mussels from their shells, cover, and refrigerate until ready to use.

Makes about 1 quart (with 1 pound [2 cups] mussels)

Lobster Stock

Lobster carcasses, or "bodies," as we call them in New England, make a sublime broth. They can be roasted and simmered with seasonings like tarragon and saffron to make a potent liquid. But those bold flavors would be muddled in chowder. For that purpose, I make a much simpler stock that has a strong lobster flavor but neutral background flavors. I keep it unembellished and add the flavorings directly to the chowder.

Lobster and Corn Chowder (page 170) is made by cooking live lobsters, shucking the meat, and then making a stock with the shells and carcasses. Behind the lobster's face, at the top of its head, is a grain sac, also called the sand sac or head sac. This organ functions as a stomach and holds food (usually bait) in various stages of decomposition, which is the reason why I always split the carcass lengthwise and remove the head sac. If there is any tomalley (green stuff), you can add that to the stock because it adds a round, soft lobster flavor. This is all the preparation required for the lobster. Then you just combine the carcasses and shells with water, vegetables, herbs, and spices and simmer until you produce a flavorful stock. The following recipe is for a plain lobster stock. If you are making lobster and corn chowder, add a few shaved corn cobs (left over from the corn for the chowder) to the stock for more corn flavor.

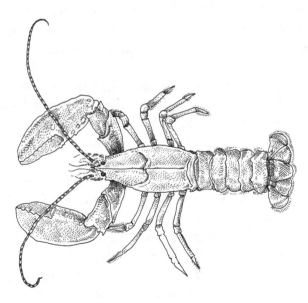

Cook's Notes

To extract the most flavor from lobster carcasses, the stock has to cook somewhere between a simmer and a boil, faster than the slow simmer that is normal for most stocks. This way, the liquid evaporates quickly, until you are left with about half of the original volume. If at any time the stock reduces below the shells, simply add a bit of water. This recipe is designed to work in tandem with the recipe for lobster and corn chowder, so it uses about 2 pounds of carcasses and shells, the amount left over from the lobster cooked for meat in the chowder. If by chance you have any extra lobster carcasses available, add one or two more to this stock for extra lobster flavor.

For equipment, you will need a 6- to 8-quart stockpot, a ladle, and a fine-mesh strainer; I like to use a medium-weight Chinese cleaver when cutting up lobsters, but a large chef's knife will do.

2 pounds lobster carcasses and shells

2 quarts water

1 cup dry white wine

1 cup chopped tomatoes with their juice (fresh or canned)

2 medium onions, thinly sliced

2 stalks celery, thinly sliced

2 small carrots, thinly sliced

4 cloves garlic, crushed

4 sprigs fresh thyme

2 dried bay leaves

¼ teaspoon fennel seeds

1 teaspoon black peppercorns

Kosher or sea salt

1. Split the lobster carcasses lengthwise and remove the head sac from each one. Place the carcasses, shells, and tomalley in a 6- to 8-quart stockpot, cover with the water, and bring to a boil, skimming the white scum from the surface of the stock. (Using a ladle and a circular motion, push the foam from the center to the outside of the pot, where it is easy to remove.) Reduce the heat so the stock is cooking at a fast, steady simmer.

2. Add the wine, tomatoes, onions, celery, carrots, garlic, thyme, bay leaves, fennel seeds, and peppercorns, and let the stock simmer and cook down for about 1 hour. Add a little water if the stock falls below the lobster shells.

3. Season the stock lightly with salt. Taste for a rich flavor. If it seems light, simmer for about 20 minutes longer. Strain the stock with a fine-mesh strainer. If you are not going to be using it within the hour, chill it as quickly as possible. Cover the broth *after* it has completely cooled and keep refrigerated for up to 3 days, or freeze for up to 2 months.

Makes about 1 quart

Crab Stock

Crabs make a distinctly flavored, strong stock that, although limited to use in crab dishes only, is well worth the effort. A crab chowder made with a homemade stock will fill your home with an aroma that will make seafood lovers crave the bowls you are about to serve. I have made stock with blue crabs, the most common crab on the East Coast and the Gulf states; rock crabs, the most common crab in northern New England; and Dungeness crabs, the West Coast crab of great fame and incredible sweetness. Even though the sizes vary, they all behave about the same way in stock, as long as you cut them into pieces about the same size. The stock from Dungeness crabs, though, which are substantially larger than blue and rock crabs, requires an added 20 to 30 minutes cooking time.

There are three different approaches to making crab stock. The first is to buy crabs, cook them, pick out the meat, and then use the picked-over bodies and shells from the legs for stock. But extracting the meat is tedious work and, since good-quality crabmeat is not difficult to find, some cooks prefer to buy crabmeat along with a couple of crabs, then "sacrifice" the whole crabs for the stock. Some seafood markets, especially in blue crab country (south of New York), offer small "soup crabs" at reasonable prices. The third, and least preferable, option is to use a small amount of crab bodies and shells and supplement them with shrimp shells and/or lobster bodies. The following recipe can be adapted to any choice you make.

Cook's Notes

The top shell, called the carapace, of all species of crabs offers little flavor other than that from the greenish brown tomalley you will find tucked in the interior. The head sac attached to the carapace, behind the face of the crab, is inedible and should not be added to stock. So I remove the tomalley to add to the stock for extra flavor and discard the carapace. The body is filled with meat and is excellent added to stock, especially if it is not picked of all its meat. The shells from the legs add good flavor whether they are picked or not.

If you are using picked-over shells, they will already be broken up enough to be used for stock with no further preparation. If you are using whole crabs, pull off the top shell (carapace) and remove and save the tomalley. Discard the carapace. Break off the legs and roughly chop them, in order to extract maximum flavor. Cut the body into 4 or more pieces about an inch in size.

Besides the crab, only a few vegetables, herbs, and spices are needed to make a great stock. More assertive seasonings are best added later, directly to the chowder. The tomatoes called for in this stock can be the centers from the tomatoes prepared for Chesapeake Crab Chowder (page 167). You can also use chopped fresh or canned tomatoes. Use this recipe as a guideline, adding more onions or celery to your taste, but do not increase the amount of thyme or bay leaves.

For equipment, you need a 6- to 8-quart stockpot, a ladle, and a fine-mesh strainer; I like to use a medium-weight Chinese cleaver when chopping up crabs, but a large chef's knife will do.

2 pounds picked-over crab shells (cracked or chopped) and/or crab bodies (cut into 1-inch pieces, carapace discarded; see Cook's Notes), crab tomalley, and, if necessary, shrimp shells or lobster carcasses

2 quarts water

1 medium to large onion, coarsely chopped

1 to 2 stalks celery, coarsely chopped

1½ cups chopped tomatoes (tomato "guts" or canned or fresh; see Cook's Notes)

2 cloves garlic, crushed

2 dried bay leaves

2 teaspoons black peppercorns

4 sprigs fresh thyme

Kosher or sea salt

1. Place the crab bodies, shells, and tomalley (and optional shrimp shells or lobster carcasses) in a 6- to 8-quart stockpot and cover with the water. Bring to a boil, skimming the white foam from the surface of the stock. (Using a ladle and a circular motion, push the foam from the center to the outside of the pot, where it is easy to remove.) Reduce the heat so the stock cooks at a fast, steady simmer.

2. Add the onion, celery, tomatoes, garlic, bay leaves, peppercorns, and thyme, and let the stock simmer and cook down for about 1 hour. The liquid should just cover the crab shells as the stock cooks; if it doesn't, just add a little water.

3. Season the stock lightly with salt. Taste for a rich flavor; if it seems light, simmer for about 20 minutes longer.

4. Strain the stock through a fine-mesh strainer. If you are not going to be using it within the hour, chill it as quickly as possible. Cover the broth *after* it has completely cooled and keep refrigerated for up to 3 days, or freeze for up to 2 months.

Makes about 1 quart

Chicken Stock

Chicken stock is one of the great all-purpose kitchen preparations, and you'll be surprised at how useful it is in chowder making. It is unsurpassed as a vehicle for soups and stews, providing nutrients, a luxuriant texture, and a delicious flavor. I am always amazed at how the flavor of chicken stock melts into other flavors and allows them to come through clearly. That's why it is a staple ingredient in most any culture's soups.

Chicken stock can be used in place of fish stock or clam broth in chowder and seafood recipes. It is a necessity in corn chowder and other farmhouse chowders. It is so useful, in fact, you may want to double the recipe and keep some in the freezer.

Chicken stock is made with chicken bones, vegetables, herbs, and spices. Not all markets cut chicken as frequently as they once did, since the large processor companies have taken over this job, so it is a good idea to call your butcher or supermarket to be sure they save them for you. Typically necks, backs, and wing tips are sold for stock and they work fine, but it helps the stock to have a few carcasses as well. Cut the carcasses into 3 or 4 pieces before using. My wife, Nancy, freezes carcasses from roast chicken dinners. When she gathers enough, she defrosts them and makes a very good stock. You can make stock from raw chicken bones, cooked chicken carcasses, or a combination of both.

Cook's Notes

Leave the skin on the onion; it helps give the stock a lovely golden color.

Follow my recipe, but don't be afraid to add a bit more chicken, onion, carrot, and/or celery. The vegetables for chicken stock can be coarsely chopped, in large pieces—the cooking time is ample to extract all of their flavor.

For equipment, you will need a 7- to 8-quart stockpot, a ladle, and a fine-mesh strainer.

6 pounds chicken bones (backs, necks, carcasses, and/or wing tips)
3 quarts water
2 large onions, unpeeled, coarsely chopped
4 stalks celery, coarsely chopped
3 medium carrots, coarsely chopped

2 cloves garlic, crushed
3 dried bay leaves
8 fresh parsley stems (Italian or curly)
6 sprigs fresh thyme
2 whole cloves
2 teaspoons black peppercorns
Kosher or sea salt

1. Place the chicken bones in a 6- to 8-quart stockpot, add the cold water, and bring to a boil, stirring occasionally with a wooden spoon and skimming the white foam from the top of the stock. (Using a ladle and a circular motion, push the foam from the center to the outside of the pot, where it is easy to remove.) Turn down to a simmer and skim again. It is important to have a clean stock before you add the other ingredients, because the foam is impure and should not be cooked into the stock; if the stock is not clean before you add the herbs and spices, you will wind up skimming them off, altering the flavor of the recipe. However, there is no need to skim the fat; it will flavor the stock during the cooking and can be removed after straining.

2. Add the onions, celery, carrots, garlic, bay leaves, parsley stems, thyme, cloves, and peppercorns and simmer slowly for 3 hours, gently stirring a few times. Top the stock off with water if the level goes below the bones. Toward the end of the cooking time, season the stock lightly with salt and start tasting it for doneness (see page 56).

3. Strain the stock through a fine-mesh sieve. If you are not going to be using it within the hour, chill it as quickly as possible. You can skim the fat while the stock is still warm, but the easiest way is to wait until the fat solidifies on the top of the chilled stock, then just remove it in one piece. Cover the broth *after* it has completely cooled and keep refrigerated for up to 3 days, or freeze for up to 2 months.

Makes about 2¹/₂ quarts

Chicken Broth

Chicken broth can be made with a stewing chicken (a retired egg-laying hen) or even a rooster. Old birds produce a heavy-duty elixir with richness and deep flavor. But the meat, although tender after a long, slow simmering, is uneventful. And a 6-pound stewing chicken gives up a lot of meat, especially if you are making the broth for chowder. So I use a tender 3-pound chicken for chowder and simmer it until the meat is falling from the bones (see Farmer's Chicken Chowder, page 193). I remove the meat from the carcass and throw the bones back in the pot to simmer some more, creating a broth that is almost as memorable as one made from a stewing chicken. If you would like to use a stewing chicken (and I admire you for doing so), go to the recipe on page 195. Chowder made this way will cost no more than fifty cents for a filling bowlful.

Just about the entire world knows of the beneficial effects of chicken broth and soups made from that broth. When I am not feeling 100 percent, clam broth and Rhode Island Clear Clam Chowder (page 130) also do the job of renewing my spirit. Chowder made from chicken broth can also be a restorative, but when making it for that purpose, I omit the bacon and cream.

For the most part, chicken stock and chicken broth are interchangeable. You don't need to make a rich chicken broth for most farmhouse chowders. In Corn Chowder (page 175), for example, the corn should be the predominant flavor, and so a more subtle flavored stock is preferable to a potent broth. Chicken stock can be substituted for fish stock in a few fish chowder recipes, but unless chicken broth is diluted, it could overpower the fish flavor.

Beef Stock or Broth

Yes, beef stock. It is essential in Bermuda Fish Chowder with Crab (page 102), where, combined with the other big flavors of bluefish, clove, garlic, tomato, dark rum, and sherry peppers, it makes one of the most exotic and excellent chowders of all. But since the Bermuda Fish Chowder is the only recipe in this book that uses beef stock, and since its flavor is robust, you can use a good-quality canned beef stock or broth. Ordinarily I would recommend homemade over canned, but I don't want to mislead you here—the difference will be minimal in that particular chowder. If you still want to make a fresh beef stock or broth, pick a recipe from one of the classic cookbooks, like the new *Joy of Cooking*. I've noticed that the addition of a few rib bones and/or a bit of shank (with marrow) improves the quality of any beef broth or stock.

Chapter 4

Fish Chowders

Chowder for breakfast, and chowder for dinner,
and chowder for supper, till you began to look for fishbones
coming through your clothes.

—Herman Melville, MOBY-DICK

First there was fish, then came fish chowder—at least that's how it seems! We know it is the most ancient of all chowders, but its origins are as foggy as a sunrise on the coast of Maine. Food historian Sandra L. Oliver, in her book *Saltwater Foodways,* suggests that "chowder making was dispersed by the mixing of French and English fishermen in the early Banks fishing fleets [late 1600s] and possibly in the fishing camps of Newfoundland, Nova Scotia, and Maine." What is known, however, is that the first chowder recipe, a fish chowder, appeared in the *Boston Evening Post* in 1751. Fish remained the primary ingredient in chowder recipes until eighty-six years later, when Eliza Leslie declared, in her *Directions for Cookery* (1837), that "chowder can be made of clams." Early fish chowders were made with fresh fish, salt pork, onions, water, and sea biscuits, the usual provisions on fishing vessels. Sea biscuits, also known as ship's biscuits or hardtack, were made from flour and water kneaded into a smooth paste and then baked in various shapes until completely dry. Cooks aboard ship would shave them into crumbs or powder and simmer them in their chowders. Sea biscuits were essential, because flour was extremely perishable in the damp storage conditions of early fishing vessels. The use of these biscuits in chowder diminished when potatoes became more popular about a century and a half later, but common and Pilot crackers have endured as an accompaniment, a reminder of the humble origins of fish chowder.

As New England became an affluent and influential region, and as New Englanders, especially sailors, traveled to other regions, chowder making spread from Boston to the Caribbean and all the way to the Pacific Northwest. The range of ingredients these Yankees had traditionally used in chowder was enriched and expanded by new locales and by necessity. What started as simply fish chowder in the eighteenth century became a whole category of dishes by the end of the nineteenth century. Clams, lobsters, and other shellfish found their way into the chowder pot, as did corn, beans, parsnips, and even chicken and veal. Nevertheless, fish chowder remained the most popular, especially in the summer, when many New Englanders would prepare chowder on the beach with freshly caught fish. "Chowder parties," as they were called, were held by groups, large and small, who brought the necessary provisions to cook chowder in cauldrons hung from iron tripods over driftwood fires. Some of these parties were even catered! This new role of chowder making, as a social and recreational activity, was well documented in the local newspapers of Mystic, Connecticut, and others in southern New England during the latter half of the nineteenth century.

This chapter starts with three fish chowders: the first is the classic New England Fish Chowder. This is an important recipe because when you make it, you will learn what a true chowder is. It is the chowder I return to whenever I am exploring new possibilities. New England Fish Chowder reminds me what chowder is all about—simplicity and fresh ingredients, especially fish. The next recipe, Church Supper Fish Chowder, looks and tastes similar to the first, but it uses milk instead of cream and demonstrates how to make a milk-based chowder. The flavor of the third recipe, Layered Fish Chowder, is similar to that of the first two recipes, but the cooking technique is radically different. It dates back to the very earliest days of chowder making, before the advent of the stove. The remainder of the recipes are more diverse, with inspirations from Nova Scotia, Bermuda, the Pacific Northwest, and New England's Portuguese community. Some feature shellfish like lobster, crab, and clams, some contain smoked fish, others use exciting seasonal vegetables like spring onions and bold flavors like clove and dark rum. At first glance, you will see the similarities in the recipes—they are all fish chowders, after all—but as you look more closely, you'll notice that each possesses a unique personality and nuance, as well as its own cooking lesson.

For centuries, salt cod was used as a substitute for fresh fish in chowder by those who lived more than a day away from the coast. (In colonial times, it took a day to travel about twenty miles.) I haven't included a salt cod recipe in this chapter, but my Azorean-Style Chowder (page 153) combines salt cod with mussels and squid. In that savory combination, the salt cod adds a pungent flavor that works well. But I just couldn't get excited about a chowder made only with salt cod, because you can't make a stock with it. I like salt cod best in fritters (page 228), in brandade (a creamy puree of salt cod, olive oil, milk, and garlic, a specialty of Provence), and as part of a garlicky salad. Finnan haddie (smoked haddock), on the other hand, makes a delicious stock and is excellent for chowder (Double Haddock Chowder, page 99).

If you have read the chapter on stocks and broths (page 53), you have a sense of how central they are to making chowder. In many of these recipes, I've provided two or three alternatives to choose from for the stock or broth. They are listed in order of preference, with the first being the one I hope you will make and use. All of the stocks and broths are simple and easy to assemble and most take very little time to cook.

Cod and its cousins, haddock, hake, and pollack, are the most frequently used chowder fish. Striped bass and bluefish also produce excellent chowder. Depending on the species, fish fillets are added to chowder whole, in chunks, or in bite-sized pieces. On page 29 you will find a complete review of the types of fish that are good for chowder and the best ways to use them.

Fish chowders are really intended to be served as a main course, as they are appropriately filling and satisfying. These recipes call for 2 to 3 pounds of fish, substantially more than 1 pound of seafood used in most shellfish chowders. If you want to serve chowder as a starter, generally you are better off with a clam, shellfish, or vegetable (farmhouse) chowder, where the ingredients are scaled down in size. Bermuda Fish Chowder with Crab (page 102) is the exception and makes a terrific starter—robust in flavor but low in fat.

Most of the chowders in this chapter yield between 12 and 14 cups, which is enough for 6 to 8 main courses. The recipes can be easily halved or doubled, depending on your requirements (see Stocks and Broths, page 53). More often than not, experienced chowder cooks make substantial pots of chowder—it is part of the karma of this dish, which is perfect for large informal gatherings. Also, keep in mind that chowder tastes good for up to three days after it is made, so that you can prepare these recipes in advance if you like.

The best way to start a fish chowder dinner is with a simple garden salad or a light appetizer of seasonal vegetables such as fresh asparagus, broccoli rabe, tomatoes, eggplant, or beets. (Since chowder provides plenty of protein and carbohydrates, the appetizer should provide the minerals, vitamins, and roughage.) I recommend serving chowder in soup plates or shallow bowls because they are wide enough to make an impressive presentation. Using a slotted spoon, mound the fish, potatoes, and other ingredients in the center of each bowl, then ladle the broth around.

Although each chowder has its own garnishes, I recommend serving toasted common crackers (see page 205) or Pilot crackers (see page 207) with all chowders, because their crunch adds contrasting texture. Toasted Garlic Bread (page 209) can be substituted for crackers for certain chowders, like South Coast Portuguese Fish Chowder (page 90). In chapter 8, Chowder Companions (page 204), I give you recipes for breads, quick breads, biscuits, and fritters that are terrific alongside chowder. In most chowder recipes, I make specific recommendations for side dishes, but please feel free to try whatever appeals to you. I like to serve the extra treats family-style, in baskets placed right on the table. That way, small appetites won't feel intimidated.

Your dessert choice will depend on whether the chowder you served was made with or without cream. My rule is only one dish with cream per meal. Fruit desserts are always appropriate. In keeping with the simplicity of a chowder dinner, you may wish to simply serve the best fresh fruit in season, whole or sliced.

"Curing" Chowder

The term *curing* is used in Cape Cod to describe one of the most consequential (and easiest) steps in chowder making—allowing chowder to rest while the flavors meld. *Do not underestimate the importance of this process.* It is during the resting and cooling-off period that chowder undergoes a metamorphosis, emerging with a deeper flavor and richer texture. Once you cook the chowder and remove it from the heat, you have two options: you can let it sit for up to 1 hour at room temperature to cure, or you can refrigerate it (curing it in the refrigerator) for up to 3 days. A 1-hour resting will improve your chowder immensely, but refrigerating overnight or longer is even better! If you decide to refrigerate your chowder, let it cool at room temperature for 30 minutes, then place it in the refrigerator *uncovered*. Covering can prolong the cooling process, resulting in a warm center that is ideal for bacterial growth. Bacteria ruins the flavor and shortens the shelf life of food. Cover the chowder only after it has chilled completely. I do not recommend freezing chowder, because it destroys the texture of the ingredients, but the stocks and broths in this book, which are often more time-consuming to make than chowder, can be made up to 2 months in advance and kept frozen. Always date the stocks and broths you store in the freezer.

New England Fish Chowder

To me, this is the most authentic and most important recipe in this book. It is the gold standard for chowder: a hearty main course with deep flavors, luxurious texture, and generous chunks of fish, onion, and potato. New England Fish Chowder is easy to make, uses simple ingredients, and doesn't require you to be fussy or exact. After making this chowder a few times, you will begin to understand the Zen of chowder.

In Boston, haddock was always considered a notch above cod, until about ten years ago. More than twenty years ago, I worked as a sous-chef at the Copley Plaza Hotel in Boston under Bob Redmond, a very traditional Yankee chef who would not tolerate any fish other than haddock in his excellent version of fish chowder. At the time cod was sixty-nine cents per pound and haddock was eighty-nine cents. We served cod to the staff and haddock to the guests. I think that the same feeling prevailed in New England homes as well. Cod was fine in chowder for a family dinner, but for company, haddock was what you served.

For several years, commercial fishing on George's Banks (once the world's richest fishing grounds, about a hundred and fifty miles due east of Boston), was restricted, almost completely shut down. More recently, most of the Gulf of Maine has been closed. In both of these areas, cod has always been the premier species targeted by fishermen who, like their prey, are also struggling to survive. But shortages of cod, and sometimes surprisingly good catches of haddock, changed the dynamics of the purely supply-and-demand-driven wholesale fish market and, probably for the first time ever, cod became more expensive than haddock. A few winters ago, during a particularly severe cod shortage, we all took notice when New York chefs didn't flinch at spending twelve dollars per pound for top-quality cod. And all of us in the seafood business gained a little more reverence for this noble fish.

The story isn't over yet. After a long and painful moratorium on cod fishing in Canada that put thousands of people in the Maritime Provinces out of work, cod is showing signs of a comeback. Newfoundland has recently reopened part of its fishery. Supplies seem to be more stable than they have been during the last few years. Haddock and cod are about the same price. So when I say that I still have a personal preference for haddock in fish chowder, I hope you understand that I am grateful to be able to put either of these magnificent fish in my chowder. Wild striped bass, which is also a first-rate fish for chowder during its short season, has made a comeback from near extinction, and we are hoping for a similar success story with cod.

Cook's Notes

Cod and haddock are very similar, but large haddock is just a little firmer and doesn't break up quite as much as cod, making it easier to produce a chowder with large chunks of fish. But even more important than the type of fish is the way you prepare it. Both cod and haddock, and their cousins pollack and hake, all flake apart naturally. Therefore, it isn't necessary to cut them into pieces. Simply add the whole fillets to the chowder, cook it a few minutes longer, and remove it from the heat, without stirring it again. When you reheat the chowder, the fillets will break into lovely big chunks of tender white fish. Most fish can be used for New England Fish Chowder, but if the fish you choose is not native to New England, then your chowder should be called "New England style." Depending on their tendency to break up naturally, some fish need to be cut into pieces. I have listed the various species and how to cut them for chowder on page 29.

Strong Fish Stock made with the heads and bones from the cod or haddock you buy for chowder is by far the best choice for this recipe. I urge you to make it, but if you can't, there are alternatives listed in the recipe.

My favorite accompaniment for this hearty chowder is common crackers, split, buttered, and toasted. They can be arranged around the outside of the soup plate or served in a basket on the side. I also like Skillet Corn Bread (page 219), Anadama Bread (page 217), or Salt Cod Fritters (page 228) with my fish chowder.

For equipment, you will need a 4- to 6-quart heavy pot with a lid, a slotted spoon, a wooden spoon, and a ladle.

4 ounces meaty salt pork, rind removed and cut into ⅓-inch dice

2 tablespoons unsalted butter

2 medium onions (14 ounces), cut into ¾-inch dice

6 to 8 sprigs fresh summer savory or thyme, leaves removed and chopped (1 tablespoon)

2 dried bay leaves

2 pounds Yukon Gold, Maine, PEI, or other all-purpose potatoes, peeled and sliced ⅓ inch thick

5 cups Strong Fish Stock (page 58), Traditional Fish Stock (page 60), Chicken Stock (page 72), or water (as a last resort)

Kosher or sea salt and freshly ground black pepper

3 pounds skinless haddock or cod fillets, preferably over 1 inch thick, pinbones removed

1½ cups heavy cream (or up to 2 cups if desired)

For garnish

2 tablespoons chopped fresh Italian parsley

2 tablespoons minced fresh chives

1. Heat a 4- to 6-quart heavy pot over low heat and add the diced salt pork. Once it has rendered a few tablespoons of fat, increase the heat to medium and cook until the pork is a crisp golden brown. Use a slotted spoon to transfer the cracklings to a small ovenproof dish, leaving the fat in the pot, and reserve until later.

2. Add the butter, onions, savory or thyme, and bay leaves to the pot and sauté, stirring occasionally with a wooden spoon, for about 8 minutes, until the onions are softened but not browned.

3. Add the potatoes and stock. If the stock doesn't cover the potatoes, add just enough water to cover them. Turn up the heat and bring to a boil, cover, and cook the potatoes vigorously for about 10 minutes, until they are soft on the outside but still firm in the center. If the stock hasn't thickened lightly, smash a few of the potato slices against the side of the pot and cook for a minute or two longer to release their starch. Reduce the heat to low and season assertively with salt and pepper (you want to almost overseason the chowder at this point to avoid having to stir it much once the fish is added). Add the fish fillets and cook over low heat for 5 minutes, then remove the pot from the heat and allow the chowder to sit for 10 minutes (the fish will finish cooking during this time).

4. Gently stir in the cream and taste for salt and pepper. If you are not serving the chowder within the hour, let it cool a bit, then refrigerate; cover the chowder *after* it has chilled completely. Otherwise, let it sit for up to an hour at room temperature, allowing the flavors to meld.

5. When ready to serve, reheat the chowder over low heat; don't let it boil. Warm the cracklings in a low oven (200°F) for a few minutes.

6. Use a slotted spoon to mound the chunks of fish, the onions, and potatoes in the center of large soup plates or shallow bowls, and ladle the creamy broth around. Scatter the cracklings over the individual servings and finish each with a sprinkling of chopped parsley and minced chives.

Makes about 14 cups; serves 8 as a main course

Variation: Fish Chowder with Clams

In colonial times, a few clams would sometimes be added to fish chowder to give it a little extra flavor. By the 1830s, clams were so popular—and plentiful—in New England they were cooked separately in their own chowders. This variation pays homage to the original fish chowders with added clams. Scrub 32 to 40 littleneck clams and rinse clean. A few minutes before you serve the chowder, place the clams in a 10- to 12-inch sauté pan that has a tight-fitting lid. Add no more than ¼ cup water, cover the pan tightly, and steam over medium-high heat until the clams open, 6 to 8 minutes. Pour the clam broth into a small bowl or cup. Spoon the fish, onions, and potatoes from the chowder into the soup plates and place 4 or 5 clams around each bowl. Stir about ½ cup of the clam broth into the chowder and ladle the creamy broth over the clams and around the fish. Sprinkle on the warm cracklings, chopped parsley, and minced chives.

Church Supper Fish Chowder

Years ago, I owned a small cottage on Sawyer's Island in the Boothbay region of Maine, an area rich in fish and shellfish of all kinds. I loved fishing on the Sheepscott River in my little boat, and Sunday mornings were valuable fishing time, but I did make it to church once or twice each summer for the Sunday evening chowder suppers. Made by the local church-women, the chowders varied a little but most contained a generous amount of fish (usually cod or pollack), along with potatoes, in a buttery, milky broth. If Maine had a state cracker, it would be Crown Pilot crackers (see page 207). You will rarely see a chowder Down East that isn't served with them. The authentic chowders served at the church supper were handed down from generation to generation; no written recipes were needed.

Most home-style chowders are made with milk, sometimes evaporated milk, but rarely cream. Some chowder makers say that cream covers the true flavor of the seafood in chowder, but I don't agree. When combined with stock in the right proportions, I think cream does everything that milk does, only a little better. Nevertheless, you can make a very fine chowder with milk and I felt obliged to include this one in my book.

This chowder is the milky version of my New England Fish Chowder (page 79) and shares a common heritage. In Maine, cod and pollack are more common than haddock and hake, but you can use any of these or many other fish as well. Pollack is very closely related to cod, and when it is line-caught and fresh, it makes a really fine chowder. Unfortunately, most of the pollack that reaches the market has been caught by commercial gill netters and becomes quite battered because of this harsh fishing technique; Alaskan pollack is no better.

Cook's Notes

I have found that by adding just a little flour, I can stabilize the chowder and avoid the problem of separating that often happens when cooking with milk. Because the broth the potatoes are cooked in is very lightly thickened, I omit the vigorous cooking of the potatoes that I use in most recipes, and the result is a chowder of similar texture (viscosity) as my usual chowders. In order to allow for the milk, which is added after the potatoes are cooked, I use the absolute minimum amount of stock needed to cover the potatoes. Therefore, I advise you to use my Strong Fish Stock if possible. Serve this chowder with Crown Pilot crackers, as they do in Maine.

For equipment, you will need a 4- to 6-quart heavy pot with a lid, a slotted spoon, a wooden spoon, and a ladle.

4 ounces meaty salt pork, rind removed and cut into ⅓-inch dice

4 tablespoons unsalted butter

2 medium onions (14 ounces), cut into ¾-inch dice

6 to 8 sprigs fresh summer savory or thyme, leaves removed and chopped (1 tablespoon)

2 dried bay leaves

2 tablespoons all-purpose flour

3 cups Strong Fish Stock (page 58), Traditional Fish Stock (page 60), Chicken Stock (page 72), or water (as a last resort)

2 pounds Yukon Gold, Maine, PEI, or other all-purpose potatoes, peeled and sliced ¼ inch thick

Kosher or sea salt and freshly ground black pepper

3 cups whole milk (do not use low-fat)

3 pounds skinless cod or pollack fillets, pinbones removed

For garnish

2 tablespoons chopped fresh Italian parsley

2 tablespoons minced fresh chives

1. Heat a 4- to 6-quart heavy pot over low heat and add the diced salt pork. Once it has rendered a few tablespoons of fat, increase the heat to medium and cook until the pork is crisp and golden brown. Use a slotted spoon to transfer the cracklings to a small ovenproof dish, leaving the fat in the pot, and reserve until later.

2. Add the butter, onions, savory or thyme, and bay leaves to the pot and sauté, stirring occasionally with a wooden spoon, for about 8 minutes, until the onions are softened but not browned. Add the flour and cook 1 minute more, stirring constantly. Add 1 cup of the stock and cook, stirring constantly, until the stock has thickened (it will be fairly thick). Add 1 more cup of stock and allow it to come back to a simmer again, stirring all the while. Add the last cup of stock and, when the stock is once again simmering slowly, add the potatoes. If the stock doesn't cover the potatoes, add just enough water to cover them.

3. Slowly simmer the potatoes, partially covered, for about 15 minutes, until tender; stir often to prevent sticking. Season the mixture assertively with salt and pepper (you want to almost overseason the chowder at this point, to avoid having to stir it much once the fish is added). Add the milk. When the milk is hot but not boiling, add the cod or pollack fillets and cook on low heat for 5 minutes, then remove from the heat and allow the chowder to sit for 10 minutes. (The fish will finish cooking during this time.)

4. If you are not serving the chowder within the hour, let it cool a bit, then refrigerate; cover the chowder *after* it has chilled completely. Otherwise, let it sit for up to an hour at room temperature, allowing the flavors to meld.

5. When ready to serve, reheat the chowder over low heat; don't let it boil. Warm the cracklings in a low oven (200°F) for a few minutes.

6. Use a slotted spoon to mound the chunks of fish, the onions, and potatoes in the center of large soup plates or shallow bowls, and ladle the creamy broth around. Scatter the cracklings over the individual servings and finish each with a sprinkling of chopped parsley and minced chives.

Makes about 14 cups; serves 8 as a main course

Layered Fish Chowder

Up in Maine, you still hear people talk about "building a chowder." Long before there were stoves, chowder was baked over open embers in a hearth or a fire in a ship's galley. New England cooks "built" their chowders by layering onions, salt pork, fish (often whole), spices, and crumbled crackers or hardtack. The liquid, usually water or a bit of wine, was poured over, the pot was covered, and the chowder was set over the fire to cook. Judging by the amount of liquid called for in old recipes, the chowder probably looked like a thick fish porridge; it certainly didn't resemble a soup. Modern stoves give us the ability to raise and lower temperatures, to add ingredients as we please, and to use the same pot for sautéing and simmering. There really is no reason to make layered chowder, but I was so intrigued by this technique, used for well over a hundred and fifty years of chowder making, that I decided to build my own.

My goal wasn't to re-create an authentic colonial-style chowder, which would have omitted potatoes and dairy products and would have contained far too large a portion of salt pork for modern palates. What I wanted to rediscover was the technique and the romance of a layered chowder. It took a few tries, but I finally came up with this recipe, which combines the technique and presentation of the old layered chowders with a flavor and texture that is similar to classic New England Fish Chowder (page 79). I used crackers in the layering, but only sparingly. I added potatoes, which I had to slice thin in order for them to cook in the same time as the fish. And I sliced the salt pork, instead of dicing it, keeping the amount at an acceptable level. I used nutmeg and clove as a nod to the past, with the more recent addition of a small amount of cream. I really had a lot of fun putting this culinary puzzle together. At dinnertime, I placed the Dutch oven in the center of the table, surrounded by toasted common crackers and a warm loaf of Anadama Bread (page 217). The table was a picture of rustic charm, and my guests seemed fascinated as I described how this chowder was "built"—and they loved the way it tasted. I do hope you will try it one chilly night!

Cook's Notes

I used a hardware-store variety 5-quart cast-iron Dutch oven, because it is the vessel I think replicates the pot used in the colonial kitchen. In addition, these are easily found and a great bargain compared to "gourmet" imported alternatives. The advantage of a Dutch oven is that it can be heated over a burner first, then transferred to the oven. These pots improve with use. Remember to lightly rub the cast-iron pot with vegetable oil after you wash it. The oil will prevent rusting and help the pot become well seasoned.

The trick to slicing the salt pork is to freeze or partially freeze it, then slice it while still partially frozen and very firm. I prefer salt pork to bacon for this fish chowder, but if you like bacon or do not want to bother slicing salt pork, you can use sliced bacon and cut each strip in half.

In order to have enough fish to make two layers, it is important that you purchase small fillets (no more than ¾ inch thick) of haddock or baby cod (scrod). If all you can find is large thick fillets, you will have to slice them horizontally in half so they resemble fillets from smaller fish.

For equipment, you will need a 10-inch skillet or sauté pan, a wooden spoon, a 5-quart cast-iron Dutch oven or a 4- to 6-quart high-sided braising pan with a tight-fitting lid, a slotted spoon, and a ladle.

4 ounces meaty salt pork, rind removed and thinly sliced, or 4 ounces sliced bacon, each strip cut crosswise in half

4 tablespoons unsalted butter

2 large onions (about 18 ounces), sliced ¼ inch thick

6 to 8 sprigs fresh summer savory or thyme, leaves removed and chopped (1 tablespoon)

2 dried bay leaves

¼ teaspoon ground cloves

¼ teaspoon freshly grated nutmeg

1 pound Yukon Gold, Maine, PEI, or other all-purpose potatoes, peeled and sliced as thin as possible

Kosher or sea salt and freshly ground black pepper

3 pounds skinless baby cod or haddock fillets, no more than ¾ inch thick, pinbones removed

4 Pilot crackers (2 ounces) or 2 ounces oyster crackers, crumbled (1 heaping cup)

5 cups Strong Fish Stock (page 58), Traditional Fish Stock (page 60), Chicken Stock (page 72), or water (as a last resort)

1½ cups heavy cream

For garnish
2 tablespoons chopped fresh Italian parsley

1. Preheat the oven to 400°F.

2. Fry the salt pork in a 10-inch skillet or sauté pan over medium heat until browned and crisp. Remove the meat, leaving the fat in the pan, and set aside until later.

3. Add the butter, onions, savory or thyme, bay leaves, cloves, and nutmeg to the pan and sauté, stirring often with a wooden spoon, for 8 to 10 minutes, until the onions are tender but not browned. Remove from the heat and let cool.

4. To build the chowder, place one third of the onion mixture (including the fat) in the bottom of the Dutch oven or braising pan, lay half of the sliced potatoes over the onions, and season lightly with salt and pepper. Lay half the fish over the potatoes and season lightly with salt and pepper. Crumble half the crackers over the fish. This is the first layer. Repeat the layering, and finish with the remaining onions.

5. Place the Dutch oven over medium heat and pour the fish stock over the layered chowder. Stick the handle of a wooden spoon through to the bottom in three or four places to be sure the stock circulates around the ingredients. Heat the pot until the stock is hot and steam is beginning to appear on the surface.

6. Cover the chowder, place in the oven, and cook for 30 minutes. Check for doneness by taking a potato slice from the top layer: it should be firm and nearly cooked through; if not, cover the pot and return to the oven for 5 to 10 minutes more.

7. Pour the cream into the chowder, then lay the slices of fried salt pork or bacon over the top. Bake, uncovered, for 15 minutes longer, or until the creamy broth is lightly browned around the edges.

8. Present the chowder at the table, before you stir it, then stir it and season with salt and pepper if needed. Use a slotted spoon to place the chunks of fish, the onions, and potatoes in the center of large soup plates or shallow bowls. Put 1 piece of salt pork or bacon on top of each serving, ladle the creamy broth around the fish, and sprinkle with the chopped parsley.

Makes about 14 cups; serves 8 as a main course

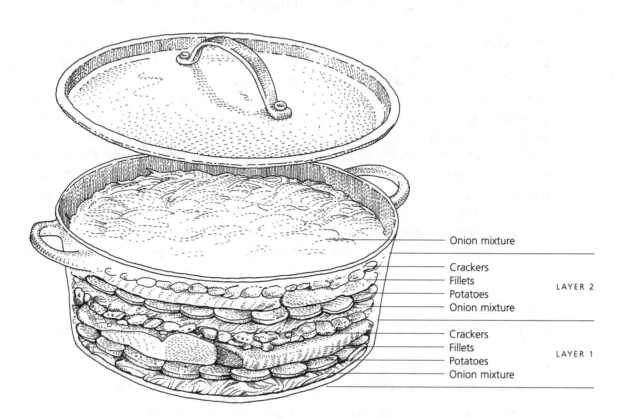

Onion mixture

Crackers
Fillets
Potatoes
Onion mixture

LAYER 2

Crackers
Fillets
Potatoes
Onion mixture

LAYER 1

South Coast Portuguese Fish Chowder

This chowder has a relationship to New Bedford and the area New Englanders call South Coast, which includes that part of southeastern Massachusetts west of Cape Cod and a small piece of eastern Rhode Island. The area is ethnically diverse, with a large Portuguese population, but everyone, even those who aren't Portuguese, loves good food. I served this chowder recently to a group at Sakonnet Vineyards in Little Compton, Rhode Island. As soon as word got out that there was chouriço (a dry, spicy, garlicky Portuguese sausage) in the chowder, the crowd demolished it. Almost everyone in this region loves chouriço, which the locals pronounce "shore-eese." All over New England where the Portuguese have settled, chouriço is included in clambakes, clam boils, and other traditional Yankee fare.

With its translucent reddish broth and colorful pieces of bell pepper, tomato, chouriço, potato, fish, and cilantro, this Portuguese-style chowder is very enticing. It has a splendid aroma and a savory spicy flavor, making it an interesting and exciting alternative to milder creamy chowders.

Cook's Notes

Chouriço has a thick casing, so be sure to remove it before you slice it. Make a small lengthwise slit in the sausage and the casing will peel off easily. The chouriço adds a balanced spiciness to this recipe, but it is not overwhelming. If you want to make the chowder even spicier, sprinkle in ¼ to ½ teaspoon crushed red pepper flakes when you add the onions and bell pepper.

I use canned Italian plum tomatoes packed in juice for this chowder because of their robust flavor. The tomatoes are not added until after the potatoes are fully cooked because otherwise, their acidity causes a reaction that prevents the potatoes from releasing their starch.

Silver hake, a cousin of cod, is smaller and has a slightly more pronounced flavor. It is the hands-down favorite of the Portuguese community but, unlike chouriço, hake has never really caught on in the rest of the region. When it is available, it is quite reasonably priced, and it is excellent panfried as well as braised in fish stews and chowder. A note of caution: do not substitute red hake, which fishermen call mud hake. It is flavorful, but the texture is very soft and it doesn't make good chowder. Cod, haddock, and bass are the best substitutes.

I like to serve this chowder with Toasted Garlic Bread (page 209) or a crusty loaf of Portuguese or Italian bread.

For equipment, you will need a 4- to 6-quart heavy pot with a lid, a wooden spoon, a slotted spoon, and a ladle.

2 tablespoons olive oil

2 dried bay leaves

3 cloves garlic, finely chopped
(1 tablespoon)

2 medium onions (14 ounces), cut into
¾-inch dice

1 green bell pepper (6 ounces), cut into
½-inch dice

¼ teaspoon ground allspice

2 pounds Yukon Gold, Maine, PEI, or other
all-purpose potatoes, peeled and sliced
⅓ inch thick

4 cups Strong Fish Stock (page 58),
Traditional Fish Stock (page 60),
Chicken Stock (page 72), or water
(as a last resort)

2 cups canned whole tomatoes in juice
(from a 28-ounce can), cut into ½-inch
dice (measured with their juice)

6 ounces spicy chouriço or andouille
sausage, casing removed and sliced
¼ inch thick

Kosher or sea salt and freshly ground
black pepper

2 pounds skinless silver hake, cod, haddock, or bass fillets, pinbones removed

10 sprigs fresh cilantro, leaves and tender
stems finely chopped (¼ cup)

For garnish

2 tablespoons coarsely chopped fresh
Italian parsley

1. Heat a 4- to 6-quart heavy pot over medium heat and add the olive oil and bay leaves. As soon as the bay leaves turn brown, add the garlic and cook, stirring constantly with a wooden spoon, for 30 seconds or until it is golden. Add the onions, bell pepper, and allspice and sauté, stirring occasionally, for about 8 minutes, until the onions and peppers are softened but not browned.

2. Add the potatoes and stock; if the stock doesn't cover the potatoes, add just enough water to cover them. Turn up the heat, bring to a boil, cover, and cook the potatoes vigorously for about 10 minutes, until they are soft on the outside but still firm in the center.

3. Reduce the heat to medium, add the tomatoes and sausage, and simmer for 5 minutes. Season the mixture assertively with salt and pepper (you want to almost overseason the chowder at this point, to avoid having to stir it much once the fish is added).

4. Add the whole fillets and cook for 5 minutes, then remove from the heat, gently stir in the cilantro, and allow the chowder to sit for 10 minutes. (The fish will finish cooking during this time.) If you are not serving the chowder within the hour, let it cool a bit, then refrigerate; cover the chowder *after* it has chilled completely. Otherwise, let it sit for up to an hour at room temperature, allowing the flavors to meld.

5. When ready to serve, reheat the chowder over low heat; don't let it boil. Use a slotted spoon to mound the chunks of hake, the chouriço, tomatoes, peppers, and potatoes in the center of large soup plates or shallow bowls, and ladle the savory tomato broth over. Sprinkle with the chopped parsley.

Makes about 14 cups; serves 8 as a main course

Nova Scotia Fish Chowder with Lobster

Chowder is so identified with New England that many people are unaware of the rich tradition of chowder making in Atlantic Canada. Some historians point to Newfoundland and Nova Scotia, where French and English fishermen have crossed paths since the mid-1600s, as the place where chowder may have originated. In this land of friendly people, breathtaking scenery, and some of the world's finest seafood, chowder making is an old custom (as is rum drinking).

The Canadian government, not surprisingly, regulates lobster fishing, but when the season is on, there is a profusion of lobsters in Nova Scotia, and lobster (or scallops) is added as an embellishment to traditional local fish chowders. Haddock is the fish of choice here. This recipe was inspired by my friend David Chernin, a chowder maker from beautiful Cape Breton Island, Nova Scotia. David uses only lobster knuckles and claws in his chowder because he says they hold up better, but since I don't want to leave you with leftover lobster tails, my recipe calls for whole lobsters.

In this harmonious marriage of the flavors of haddock and lobster, chunks of white fish and brilliant red lobster meat are set against a light pink broth that is lovely to look at and even better to eat. Common crackers, split, buttered, and toasted, can be arranged around the rims of the soup plates or served in a basket on the side. In addition to crackers, I also recommend some warm Buttermilk Baking Powder Biscuits (page 210) or Parker House Rolls (page 214).

Cook's Notes

This recipe begins with partially cooking the lobsters; the slightly undercooked meat will finish cooking in the chowder. Shucking the meat from the claws, knuckles, and tails of partially cooked lobster is almost the same process as from fully cooked. Only the claws may be more difficult to remove, but don't worry if the meat tears—it will be diced anyway. If you'd rather not cook whole lobsters, use 8 to 10 ounces of cooked lobster meat. (For more on lobster preparation, see my previous book, *Lobster at Home*.)

The lobster carcasses, tomalley, and shells are used to make a stock that will eventually be combined with fish stock for this chowder. If making two stocks seems unreasonable to you, you can substitute water for the fish stock.

For equipment, you will need an 8-quart stockpot (to par-cook the lobsters), a pair of long tongs, a medium Chinese cleaver or large chef's knife, a 3- to 4-quart pot (to make the stock), a fine-mesh strainer, a 4- to 6-quart heavy pot with a lid (to make the chowder), a slotted spoon, a wooden spoon, and a ladle.

2 live hard-shell lobsters (1¼ pounds each)
Kosher or sea salt
1 teaspoon black peppercorns

For chowder

4 ounces meaty salt pork, rind removed
    (reserve it for the lobster stock) and
    cut into ⅓-inch dice
1 large onion (10 to 12 ounces), cut into
    ¾-inch dice (trimmings reserved for the
    lobster stock)
2 medium stalks celery (4 ounces), cut into
    ⅓-inch dice (trimmings reserved for
    stock)
6 to 8 sprigs fresh thyme, leaves removed
    (reserve the stems for the lobster
    stock) and chopped (1 tablespoon)
2 tablespoons unsalted butter
2 dried bay leaves
2 teaspoons Hungarian paprika

2 pounds Yukon Gold, Maine, PEI, or other
    all-purpose potatoes, peeled and sliced
    ⅓ inch thick
2 cups lobster stock (from above or from
    page 67)
2 cups Strong Fish Stock (page 58),
    Traditional Fish Stock (page 60),
    Chicken Stock (page 72), or water
    (as a last resort)
Kosher or sea salt and freshly ground
    black pepper
2 pounds skinless haddock or cod fillets,
    1 inch thick or more, pinbones removed
1½ cups heavy cream (or up to 2 cups if
    desired)

For garnish

2 tablespoons chopped fresh Italian
    parsley
2 tablespoons minced fresh chives

1. To par-cook the lobsters, fill an 8-quart stockpot with 4 quarts of water, add ⅓ cup salt, cover, and bring to a boil over high heat. One at a time, holding each lobster by the carapace, quickly drop it into the boiling water. Keeping the heat on high, cook for exactly 4½ minutes from the time you put the lobsters into the pot. Using a pair of long tongs, remove the lobsters and let cool to room temperature.

2. When they are cool enough to handle, twist off the claws, with the knuckles attached. Twist off the tails. Remove all the meat and cut into large dice. Be sure to remove the cartilage from the claws and the intestinal tract that runs along the top of the tails. (You should have about 10 ounces [almost 2 cups] of diced lobster meat.) Reserve the shells if you are making the lobster stock. Cover the lobster meat with plastic wrap and refrigerate until later.

3. To make the lobster stock, use a cleaver or large chef's knife to split the lobster carcasses lengthwise in half. Remove the sac from inside the front of each lobster's head. Place the lobster carcasses, along with any tomalley in the carcasses, and the shells from the claws and tail in a 3- to 4-quart pot. Cover with about 4 cups of water, bring to a boil, and skim off the foam from the top. Reduce the heat until the stock is at a brisk simmer, add the peppercorns (along with the rind from the salt pork, any trimmings from the onion or celery, and stems from the thyme) and cook, uncovered, for 1 hour. Strain through a fine-mesh strainer; you should have about 2 cups of strong lobster stock. (The stock can be made a day ahead.)

4. Heat a 4- to 6-quart heavy pot over low heat and add the diced salt pork. Once it has rendered a few tablespoons of fat, increase the heat to medium and cook until the pork is crisp and golden brown. Use a slotted spoon to transfer the cracklings to a small ovenproof dish, leaving the fat in the pot, and reserve until later.

5. Add the butter, onion, celery, thyme, and bay leaves to the pot and sauté, stirring occasionally with a wooden spoon, for about 6 minutes. Add the paprika and cook for 2 minutes longer, or until the onions are softened.

6. Add the potatoes, the reserved lobster stock, and the fish stock. If the stock doesn't cover the potatoes, add just enough water to cover them. Turn up the heat and bring to a boil, cover, and cook the potatoes vigorously for about 10 minutes, until they are soft on the outside but still firm in the center. If the stock hasn't thickened lightly, smash a few of the potato slices against the side of the pot and cook for a minute or two longer to release their starch. Reduce the heat to low and season the mixture assertively with salt and pepper (you want to almost overseason the chowder at this point, to avoid having to stir it much once the fish is added).

7. Add the whole fish fillets and cook for 5 minutes, then remove from the heat and allow the chowder to sit for 10 minutes. (The fish will finish cooking during this time.) Gently stir in the cream and the reserved lobster meat and adjust the seasoning with salt and pepper if needed. If you are not serving the chowder within the hour, let it cool a bit, then refrigerate; cover the chowder *after* it has chilled completely. Otherwise, let it sit at room temperature for up to an hour, allowing the flavors to meld.

8. When ready to serve, reheat the chowder over low heat; don't let it boil. Warm the cracklings in a low oven (200°F) for a few minutes.

9. Use a slotted spoon to mound the chunks of haddock and lobster, the onions, and potatoes in the center of large soup plates or shallow bowls, and ladle the creamy broth around. Scatter the cracklings over the individual servings and finish with a sprinkling of chopped parsley and minced chives.

Makes about 12 cups; serves 6 to 8 as a main course

Savory Summer Fish Chowder

Tourists are not the only visitors to the New England coast in the summer. Bluefish and striped bass hang out there as well, feasting on large schools of pogies (menhadin), alewives, mackerel, squid, and other small fish. I have spent many happy hours fishing for these fish, so my admiration for them both begins at sea. Bluefish are ferocious fighters—pound for pound, as tough as they come. Even when landed, they will bite you if you're not careful! Stripers, as New Englanders call striped bass, travel in schools, and when they're feeding, they will chase small bait fish right up to the shoreline (which is why they are called rockfish in the South). You can catch a big striper in surprisingly shallow water, and when you run into a school, you will more than likely catch a few, but you have to work fast, because they disappear as quickly as they arrive.

As a cook, I love these fish for their rich deep flavor, luscious texture, and versatility. They can be grilled, broiled, roasted, or panfried and are excellent in stews and chowders. You can substitute bluefish or striped bass in any fish chowder recipe and expect splendid results, but I created this recipe especially for them. The chowder bursts with the flavors of summer: fresh wild fish paired with sweet corn, ripe tomato, fresh basil, and a little bite of hot chile. Ignoring the tomato versus cream debate, I've incorporated both, a chowder practice that comes from Connecticut and parts of southern Massachusetts and Rhode Island. I use only fresh tomatoes, because my goal is not to make a "red" chowder, but to produce a creamy fish and corn chowder with tomatoes as an accent.

Cook's Notes

You can use the head and frame (bones) from a bluefish or striped bass to make Strong Fish Stock especially for this recipe. If you do, add the cobs from the corn as well. They will create a perfect stock for this chowder, but not for anything else.

The dark meat (blood line) of the bluefish or bass must be removed and discarded, so be sure to buy extra to allow for trim. To yield 2 pounds of usable fish, you will need to buy about 2½ pounds fillets or a whole fish that weighs 5 to 6 pounds.

Cream adds a pleasant smoothness, but if you want to keep the chowder light, omit it and just add a little more stock. I like to serve this chowder with Skillet Corn Bread (page 219) or Corn Sticks (page 220) or Sweet Corn Fritters (page 222).

For equipment, you will need a 4- to 6-quart heavy pot with a lid, a wooden spoon, a slotted spoon, and a ladle.

3 ears yellow or bicolor corn

4 ounces slab (unsliced) bacon, rind removed and cut into ⅓-inch dice

4 tablespoons unsalted butter

3 cloves garlic, finely chopped (1 table-spoon)

1 large jalapeño chile, seeds removed and very finely diced

1 large onion (10 to 12 ounces), cut into ¾-inch dice

2 medium stalks celery (4 ounces), cut into ⅓-inch dice

1½ pounds Yukon Gold, Maine, PEI, or other all-purpose potatoes, peeled and sliced ⅓ inch thick

4 cups Strong Fish Stock (page 58), Traditional Fish Stock (page 60), Chicken Stock (page 72), or water (as a last resort)

1 pound plum or other ripe red tomatoes, peeled, seeded, and cut into ½-inch dice

Kosher or sea salt and freshly ground black pepper

2½ pounds skinless bluefish or striped bass fillets, pinbones removed, trimmed of all dark meat and cut into 2-inch chunks

1½ cups heavy cream

4 sprigs fresh basil, leaves removed and chopped (¼ cup)

1. Husk the corn. Carefully remove most of the corn silk by hand and then rub the ears with a towel to finish the job. Cut the kernels from the cobs. You should have about 2 cups. Reserve for later.

2. Heat a 4- to 6-quart heavy pot over low heat and add the diced bacon. Once it has rendered a few tablespoons of fat, increase the heat to medium and cook until the bacon is crisp and golden brown. Pour off all but 1 tablespoon of the bacon fat, leaving the bacon in the pot.

3. Add the butter and garlic and cook for 30 seconds, then add the jalapeño, onion, and celery. Sauté, stirring occasionally with a wooden spoon, for about 8 minutes, until the onion and celery are softened but not browned.

4. Add the corn kernels, potatoes, and stock. If the stock doesn't cover the potatoes, add just enough water to cover them. Turn up the heat and bring to a boil, cover, and cook the potatoes vigorously for about 10 minutes, until they are soft on the outside but still firm in the center. If the stock hasn't thickened lightly, smash a few of the potato slices against the side of the pot and cook for a minute or two longer to release their starch. Add the diced tomatoes, reduce the heat to low, and season the mixture assertively with salt and pepper (you want to almost overseason the chowder at this point, to avoid having to stir it much once the fish is added).

5. Add the fish and cook for 5 minutes, then remove from the heat and allow the chowder to sit for 10 minutes. (The fish will finish cooking during this time.) Gently stir in the cream and basil and taste for salt and pepper. If you are not serving the chowder within the hour, let it cool a bit, then refrigerate; cover the chowder *after* it has chilled completely. Otherwise, let it sit at room temperature for up to an hour, allowing the flavors to meld.

6. When ready to serve, reheat the chowder over low heat; don't let it boil. Use a slotted spoon to mound the chunks of fish, the onion, and potatoes, as well as the colorful bits of corn and tomato, in the center of large soup plates or shallow bowls, and ladle the creamy broth around.

Makes about 14 cups; serves 8 as a main course

Double Haddock Chowder

Finnan haddie is haddock with the bone in and the head removed, that has been butterflied, cured, and cold-smoked. The preparation originated in Findon, Scotland, where, many years ago, so the story goes, a fish-drying shed caught fire. Not wanting to be wasteful, the townspeople ate the smoked fish, and discovered they liked it very much. Thus "Findon haddie" (*haddie* is the Scottish term for haddock), eventually known as finnan haddie, was born.

For years, finnan haddie was a favorite of New England cooks, who often poached it in milk and served it with melted butter or sometimes a hard-boiled-egg sauce. It was even popular as a breakfast item, but it was not used for chowder. The broth that results from poaching finnan haddie possesses such a wonderfully deep smoky flavor, I knew it would provide the base for a superb chowder if I could tone it down a little. I have always been intrigued with the Chinese technique of pairing fresh and dried squid in a stir-fry. The concept of using two different preparations of the same ingredient in one dish makes for interesting contrasts—it's really a brilliant idea—and it was the inspiration for this chowder. The combination of fresh and smoked haddock makes a chowder that is smoky but not overwhelmingly so, with distinctly different textures and colors from the meaty, golden brown finnan haddie and the soft, white fresh haddock. Chopped hard-boiled eggs add another flavor dimension, making this one of the most unusual and tasty chowders in my repertoire. Keep the accompaniments simple: toasted common or Pilot crackers are all that is needed.

Cook's Notes
You will find sources for real bone-in smoked haddock on page 232. Finnan haddie is usually made with the small haddock and weighs between 2 and 3 pounds. A 2½-pound fish will yield about 22 ounces of cooked boneless, skinless meat.

Don't substitute bacon for the salt pork—it will make the chowder too smoky.

For equipment, you will need a 12-inch skillet or sauté pan, a slotted spoon, a fine-mesh strainer, a 4- to 6-quart heavy pot with a lid, a wooden spoon, and a ladle.

One 2- to 2½-pound bone-in finnan
    haddie (smoked haddock)
6 cups water
8 sprigs fresh Italian parsley
1 teaspoon black peppercorns
4 ounces meaty salt pork, rind removed
    (reserve it for the stock) and cut into
    ⅓-inch dice
2 medium onions (14 ounces), cut into
    ¾-inch dice (trimmings reserved for
    the stock)
2 medium stalks celery (4 ounces), cut into
    ½-inch dice (trimmings reserved for the
    stock)
2 tablespoons unsalted butter

2 dried bay leaves
2 pounds Yukon Gold, Maine, PEI, or other
    all-purpose potatoes, peeled and sliced
    ⅓ inch thick
Kosher or sea salt and freshly ground
    black pepper
1 pound skinless fresh haddock fillets,
    pinbones removed
1½ cups heavy cream (or up to 2 cups if
    desired)

For garnish
4 hard-boiled eggs, coarsely chopped
    (½-inch pieces)

1. Trim off the tail and cut away the center bone of the finnan haddie, leaving the two halves; reserve the tail and backbone. Cut each half into 3 or 4 pieces about 3 inches across.
2. Place a 12-inch skillet or sauté pan over medium heat and add the water. Bring the water to a steady simmer, add half of the finnan haddie, and simmer for about 10 minutes, until cooked through, turning the pieces of fish halfway through the poaching. Using a slotted spoon, remove the pieces to a large plate and allow to cool. Repeat with the remaining finnan haddie. Add the tail and backbone to the broth and keep it simmering over medium-low heat.
3. As soon as the finnan haddie is cool enough to handle, pull the meat from the bones and remove the skin, taking care to leave the pieces as large as possible. Add the skin and bones to the broth. Remove the leaves from the parsley, coarsely chop, and reserve for garnish. Add the stems to the broth, along with the peppercorns, any trimmings from the onion or celery, and the reserved rind from the salt pork. Simmer for 20 minutes, then remove from the heat and let sit and steep for 10 minutes. Strain the stock through a fine-mesh strainer and reserve for the chowder; you should have about 4 cups of rich stock.
4. Heat a 4- to 6-quart heavy pot over low heat and add the diced salt pork. Once it has rendered a few tablespoons of fat, increase the heat to medium and cook until the pork is crisp and golden brown. Use a slotted spoon to transfer the cracklings to a small ovenproof dish, leaving the fat in the pot, and reserve until later.

5. Add the butter, onions, celery, and bay leaves to the pot and sauté, stirring occasionally with a wooden spoon, for about 8 minutes, until the onions and celery are softened but not browned. Add the potatoes and finnan haddie stock. If the stock doesn't cover the potatoes, add just enough water to cover them. Turn up the heat and bring to a boil, cover, and cook the potatoes vigorously for about 10 minutes, until they are soft on the outside but still firm in the center. If the stock hasn't thickened lightly, smash a few of the potato slices against the side of the pot and cook for a minute or two longer to release their starch. Reduce the heat to low and season the mixture assertively with salt and pepper (you want to almost overseason the chowder at this point, to avoid having to stir it much once the fish is added).

6. Add the whole fresh haddock fillets. Remove from the heat and allow the chowder to sit for 10 minutes. (The fish will finish cooking during this time.) Gently stir in the finnan haddie along with the cream. Taste for salt and pepper. If you are not serving the chowder within the hour, let it cool a bit, then refrigerate; cover the chowder *after* it has chilled completely. Otherwise, let it sit at room temperature for up to an hour, allowing the flavors to meld.

7. When ready to serve, reheat the chowder over low heat; don't let it boil. Warm the cracklings in a low oven (200°F) for a few minutes.

8. Use a slotted spoon to mound the chunks of fresh and smoked haddock, the onions, and potatoes in the center of large soup plates or shallow bowls, and ladle the creamy broth around. Scatter some cracklings along with a heaping spoonful of chopped eggs over each individual serving, and sprinkle on the chopped parsley.

Makes about 14 cups; serves 8 as a main course

Bermuda Fish Chowder with Crab

I first encountered this chowder several years ago, on a weekend getaway to Bermuda with my wife, Nancy. At the café where we had lunch the first day, Nancy ordered the Bermuda chowder. When the waiter brought it to our table, I thought they had perhaps made a mistake: her chowder looked like a bowl of chili, dark and coarse-textured. It was served with two small pitchers, one filled with Gosling's dark rum and the other with a hot sauce called Outerbridge's Sherry Peppers. She poured a few drops of each into her chowder, stirred it, and ate a spoonful. She loved it and offered me a taste. The chowder exploded in my mouth with the unexpected flavors of clove, dark rum, and beef broth. The seafood and vegetable flavors were as powerful and intense as in the French classic *soupe de poisson.* We both became hooked on Bermuda chowder that weekend, ordering it everywhere; the best was the one served at the Elbow Bay Beach Hotel. As soon as I got back to my restaurant in Boston, I began my quest to perfect this amazing chowder. I was thrilled to find another use for bluefish, which is abundant and inexpensive in New England during the summer.

Bermuda chowder could very well have evolved from a recipe called Club Chowder by Elizabeth H. Putnam, in her *Receipt Book,* published in New York in 1869. Her recipe starts with veal or beef broth, is flavored with nutmeg and clove, and is finished with sherry. Although it differs in many ingredients and techniques from Bermuda chowder, the backbone of the two chowders is the same—they are the only known fish chowders that use beef stock. It is fascinating to think that an obscure recipe from the U.S. mainland could somehow end up becoming something akin to the national dish of Bermuda.

Cook's Notes

This chowder begins by cooking the fish (the crab goes in last) for three full hours—the opposite of every chowder in this book. Preparing the recipe is a project, requiring lots of dicing and lots of stirring, but since the fish cooks for an hour before the vegetables are added, I dice them during this time. Because of the time and work involved, I always make a big batch. You can easily cut this recipe in half, but you'll end up wishing you had more.

In Bermuda, bluefish and rockfish (striped bass) are favorites with the local cooks. You can use either one or a combination of the two. Other Southern fish, like snapper, grouper, kingfish, or mahi-mahi are also very good in this chowder.

The dark meat (blood line) of the bluefish or rockfish must be cut away and discarded, so be sure to buy extra to allow for trim. To yield 2 pounds of usable fish, you will need to buy about 2½ pounds fillets.

This chowder makes a stimulating starter. Robust but not fatty, it is more soupy than other chowders. Since its appearance is dark and very plain, serve it in interesting cups or bowls. To be authentic, set small pitchers or cruets of Gosling's dark rum and Outerbridge's Sherry Peppers on the table and let your guests "season" the soup to their liking. If you are serving this as a starter, toasted common or Pilot crackers are all you need. For a main dish, however, I like to pass around Buttermilk Baking Powder Biscuits (page 210) or Toasted Garlic Bread (page 209).

For equipment, you will need a 6- to 8-quart pot with a lid, a ladle, a wooden spoon, and a 10- to 12-inch skillet or sauté pan.

2½ pounds skinless bluefish or striped bass fillets, pinbones removed and trimmed of all dark meat

3 quarts water

2 cans (14.5 ounces each) beef broth

3 dried bay leaves

8 sprigs fresh thyme, leaves removed and finely chopped (1 tablespoon)

1 teaspoon ground cloves

Kosher or sea salt and freshly ground black pepper

¼ cup olive oil or vegetable oil

3 cloves garlic, finely chopped

2 medium onions (14 ounces), cut into ¼- to ⅓-inch dice

2 medium carrots (4 ounces), cut into ¼- to ⅓-inch dice

1 medium green bell pepper (6 ounces), cut into ¼- to ⅓-inch dice

2 medium stalks celery (4 ounces), cut into ¼- to ⅓-inch dice

1½ pounds Yukon Gold, Maine, PEI, or other all-purpose potatoes, peeled and cut into ¼- to ⅓-inch dice

1 can (28 ounces) whole tomatoes in juice, finely chopped (¼ to ½ inch), with their juice

8 ounces crabmeat, picked over for shells and cartilage

1 cup dark rum, preferably Gosling's

Hot sauce, preferably Outerbridge's Original Sherry Peppers Sauce (see sources, page 233)

1. In a 6- to 8-quart pot, combine the fish fillets, water, and beef broth and bring to a boil, skimming off the white foam as it comes to the surface. (Using a ladle and a circular motion, push the foam from the center to the outside of the pot, where it is easy to remove.) Reduce the heat so the liquid remains at a steady simmer and add the bay leaves, thyme, cloves, salt to taste, and a generous amount of black pepper (about 1 teaspoon). Partially cover and let simmer steadily for 1 hour, stirring often with a wooden spoon to help break up the fish and to prevent sticking. (You can dice the vegetables while the fish simmers.)

2. Meanwhile, heat a 10- to 12-inch skillet or sauté pan over medium-high heat. Add the olive oil, garlic, onions, carrots, and peppers and sauté for 10 to 12 minutes, until the vegetables begin to brown lightly. Set aside.

3. After the chowder has cooked for 1 hour, add the sautéed vegetables, along with any oil in the pan, the celery, potatoes, and tomatoes. Partially cover the pot and continue to simmer steadily for 2 more hours, stirring often with a wooden spoon to prevent sticking.

4. Remove the chowder from the heat and stir in the crabmeat. If you are not serving the chowder within the hour, let it cool a bit, then refrigerate; cover the chowder *after* it has chilled completely. (Because of the long cooking time, this chowder is ready to serve anytime after the crab is added.)

5. When ready to serve, reheat over low heat and ladle into cups or bowls. Serve with the dark rum in a small pitcher and the hot sauce. Another option is to add the dark rum to the entire batch and season to taste with the hot sauce.

Makes about 18 cups; serves 18 as a first course or
10 as a main course

Pacific Northwest Salmon Chowder

This recipe is a salute to the West Coast, where salmon is more common in chowders than it is back East. Many of the original settlers in the Pacific Northwest came from New England. These Yankees, who named the new settlements after New England towns like Portland and Salem, also brought their knowledge of chowder making and adapted it to the ingredients they found in the new territory. With salmon available in great abundance, it wasn't long before they made this powerful pink-fleshed fish a regular in the chowder pot. Spring is the season for wild salmon from the Pacific Northwest and Alaska, which I prefer over farmed, so I pair most of my salmon dishes with other spring foods.

I grew spring onions in my garden for the first time last year and have become a big fan of them. They are small young onions, about the size of a big thumb, with leafy green tops. They look like large scallions and have a fresh pungent flavor that is never bitter. The distinctive flavor of salmon combines beautifully with spring onions and here makes a terrific chowder that is wonderful to behold, with its subtle contrasts of white, green, and pink. Serve with toasted common or Pilot crackers, or a crusty loaf of sourdough bread.

Cook's Notes

You can eat the tender green part of spring onions, but for chowder I trim them about 1 inch up from the root, ending up with the bulb and just a bit of green. Spring onions come from small farms, specialty markets, or your own garden; they are not usually available in supermarkets. Pearl onions or trimmed boiling onions make good substitutes.

You can use the head and frame from a salmon to make Strong Fish Stock especially for this recipe. The stock will be perfect for this chowder, but not for others.

For equipment, you will need a 2-quart saucepan, a slotted spoon, a 4- to 6-quart heavy pot with a lid, a wooden spoon, and a ladle.

20 spring onions, 1 pint pearl onions, or 12 ounces small boiling onions

4 ounces slab (unsliced) bacon, rind removed and cut into ⅓-inch dice

4 tablespoons unsalted butter

2 shallots (2 ounces), finely diced

2 dried bay leaves

2 to 3 sprigs fresh summer savory or thyme, leaves removed and chopped (1 teaspoon)

2 to 3 sprigs fresh tarragon, leaves removed and chopped (1 teaspoon)

2 pounds Yukon Gold, Maine, PEI, or other all-purpose potatoes, peeled and sliced ⅓ inch thick

4 cups Strong Fish Stock (page 58), Traditional Fish Stock (page 60), Chicken Stock (page 72), or water (as a last resort)

Kosher or sea salt and freshly ground black pepper

3 pounds skinless salmon fillets, pinbones removed and cut into large chunks (2 to 4 inches)

1½ cups heavy cream (or up to 2 cups if desired)

For garnish

2 tablespoons very coarsely chopped fresh chervil or chopped fresh Italian parsley

1. Remove all the tough outer leaves from the spring onions and trim them to about 1 inch long so they have only a little of the green top attached. Blanch the onions in a 2-quart saucepan of boiling salted water for 3 to 4 minutes. Using a slotted spoon, transfer them to a bowl of ice water to cool, then drain. Cut the larger ones lengthwise in half; reserve until later. If you are using pearl onions, blanch them in their skins for 3 minutes, then transfer to ice water; drain and peel. If you are using small boiling onions, blanch in their skins for 5 minutes, transfer to ice water, drain and peel; trim them down in size if needed.

2. Heat a 4- to 6-quart heavy pot over low heat and add the diced bacon. Once it has rendered a few tablespoons of fat, increase the heat to medium and cook until the bacon is crisp and golden brown. Pour off all but 1 tablespoon of the bacon fat, leaving the bacon in the pot.

3. Add the butter, shallots, and bay leaves and sauté, stirring often with a wooden spoon, for 2 minutes. Stir in the savory or thyme and tarragon and cook 1 minute longer. Add the potatoes and stock. If the stock doesn't cover the potatoes, add just enough water to cover them. Turn up the heat and bring to a boil, cover, and cook the potatoes vigorously for about 10 minutes, until they are soft on the outside but still firm on the inside. If the stock hasn't thickened lightly, smash a few of the potato slices against the side of the pot and cook for a minute or two longer to release their starch. Add the blanched onions, reduce the heat to low, and simmer for 5 minutes. Season the mixture assertively with salt and pepper (you want to almost overseason the chowder at this point, to avoid having to stir it much once the fish is added).

4. Add the salmon and cook for 5 minutes, then remove from the heat and allow the chowder to sit for 10 minutes. (The fish will finish cooking during this time.) Gently stir in the cream and adjust the seasoning if necessary. If you are not serving the chowder within the hour, let it cool a bit, then refrigerate; cover *after* it has completely chilled. Otherwise, let it sit for up to an hour at room temperature, allowing the flavors to meld.

5. When ready to serve, reheat the chowder over low heat; don't let it boil. Use a slotted spoon to place the chunks of salmon, the potatoes, and spring onions in the center of large soup plates or shallow bowls, and ladle the creamy broth around. Sprinkle with the chopped chervil.

`Makes about 13 cups; serves 6 to 8 as a main course`

Variation: Pacific Northwest Salmon Chowder with Peas

Peas and salmon are a classic New England combination, especially for the Fourth of July. The tiny green peas make a dramatic contrast to the pink salmon. I use this variation when I am substituting pearl onions for the spring onions.

1 pound fresh peas, shucked (about 1 cup)	**Kosher or sea salt and freshly ground black pepper**
2 tablespoons unsalted butter	

1. Blanch the shucked peas in boiling salted water for 1 minute. Drain them in a small colander or strainer and rinse them under cold water to stop the cooking.

2. Make the salmon chowder as directed, but reduce the butter by 2 tablespoons. Right before you dish up the chowder, warm the peas with the 2 tablespoons butter in a small sauté pan over low heat. Season the peas with the salt and pepper and spoon them, with the butter, over the individual servings of chowder.

Chapter 5

Clam Chowders

All you need is . . . a pair of pretty tough, bare feet.
Work your toes into the mud or sand as you walk. . . . Quahogs
are round and smooth, so when you feel them with your toes,
all you have to do is to reach down and pick them up.
—Cap'n Phil Schwind, CLAM SHACK COOKERY, 1975

Cap'n Phil Schwind, renowned Cape Cod fisherman, cook, and storyteller, devotes the greater part of his marvelous, one-of-a-kind cookbook, *Clam Shack Cookery,* to explaining techniques for gathering quahogs, soft-shell clams, razor clams, and the other seafood called for in his recipes. "Of course, clams taste better if you catch them yourself," says Cap'n Schwind, and there is much truth to this. Even more important (and this is the historical root of all chowders), chowder made with "found" food is very affordable. Originally, chowder was the everyday food of the working people who lived along the coast and needed little more than a fishing rod or a clam rake to gather their dinner.

Economics has always played a part in chowder making. On Cape Cod, where there is a profusion of both quahogs (pronounced "ko-hog") and soft-shell clams (steamers), the local people prefer quahogs in their chowder. The fact that soft-shell clams have always fetched a higher price than quahogs has a lot to do with this. In Maine, soft-shell clams are preferred for chowder—a good thing, because quahogs are scarce. That being said, Yankees truly do love their clam chowders. If necessity were the only driving force, then mussel chowder (mussels are even easier to gather than clams) would be more famous than clam chowder.

Indeed, most New Englanders—young and old, Yankees and immigrants—have a penchant for clams: raw littlenecks and cherrystones, fried soft-shells, steamers (steamed soft-shell clams), stuffies (stuffed quahogs), clam cakes (clam fritters), clams casino (clams with bacon), *cataplana* (a Portuguese clam dish), *spaghetti con vongole* (pasta with clam sauce), clam hash, clams Cantonese-style (with black bean sauce)—the list is long. But of all the marvelous dishes made from clams, clam chowder most certainly tops the list.

In testing the recipes for this chapter, I cooked littlenecks, cherrystones, quahogs, geoducks, razor clams, mahogany clams, and soft-shell clams. I have always loved the taste of clams, but the experience of seeing and cooking the different types side by side stirred in me a new affection for this humble creature that lives below the sand and mud. With all their different shapes and sizes, all their spectacular flavors, clams are one of nature's great treasures!

Clams can still be taken for free, provided you have a shellfish permit (see How to Dig Clams, page 110). But most of the ones that you see at the market are raised by aquaculturists, who carefully seed (baby clams are called seedlings) and tend their beds (licensed sand and mud flats along bays and estuaries). Unlike farm-raised fish, which are fed an artificial diet, the diet of aquaculture clams is completely natural, so their taste is identical to that of wild clams.

Because several different species of clams are sold in markets on either coast of the United States, I have included descriptions and illustrations of those most commonly cooked in chowder in the corresponding recipe.

Clams were first used as an addition to fish chowder, rather than as the starring player. In the 1829 edition of *The Frugal Housewife,* Lydia Marie Child noted in her fish chowder recipe that "[a] few clams are a pleasant addition." In *American Food, the Gastronomic Story,* author Evan Jones includes the first known published clam chowder recipe from *The Cook's Own Book,* printed in Boston in 1833. I have found several other mentions of clam chowder dating from the 1830s, and it is certain that it was well established by 1851, when, in *Moby-Dick,* Herman Melville described a "surpassingly excellent" chowder that "was made of small juicy clams, scarcely bigger than hazelnuts." By the end of the nineteenth century, clam chowder had taken on many different guises—creamy in northern New England, clear in Rhode Island, and red in Connecticut, New York, and to the south. In Maryland and the Chesapeake region, clam chowder included tomatoes, and it was not unheard of to add chopped chicken breast! There are still pockets of New England, especially in Down East Maine (the northern coastal area of Maine), where fish chowder is as popular as clam, but for many Americans, *chowder* means clam chowder. Forget about lobster and steak—I think the combination of clams and pork (salt pork or bacon) is the ultimate "surf and turf," and this is the foundation of all my clam chowders except Low-Fat Clam Chowder (page 132).

Home-style clam chowders, until recently, were usually made with freshly shucked raw clams. Tradition held that men shucked the clams (sort of like the grilling or barbecue syndrome) and the women made the chowder, but there aren't many men or women these days who can shuck quahogs (though I learned to years ago), and even at the fish market, shucked clams are hard to find. Don't worry. In my recipes, you steam open the clams, making the broth for the chowder in the process. Two exceptions are razor clams and geoducks, which are surprisingly easy to prepare raw.

The first four recipes in this chapter are creamy New England–style chowders made with salt pork or bacon, onions, potatoes, herbs, cream, and clams. However, the clams (quahog, soft-shell, razor, and geoduck) and the procedure for each are so entirely different that they warrant their own recipes. Since geoducks and razor clams are used raw, they cannot be substituted in the remaining four recipes, which call for cooked quahogs or cherrystones. Soft-shell clams, however, can be substituted in Restaurant-Style Thick Clam

Chowder (page 127), Rhode Island Clear Clam Chowder (page 130), Manhattan Red Clam Chowder (page 133), and Clam, White Bean, and Potato Chowder (page 136). Instead of the 8 pounds of quahogs called for in the recipes, use 5 pounds of steamers and follow Steps 1 and 2 in Steamer Clam Chowder (page 114) to prepare them; 8 pounds of quahogs and 5 pounds of steamers yield the same amount of meat (1 pound) and broth (4 cups).

Unlike fish chowder, which is best served as a main course, clam chowder is appropriate as either a starter or a main course. Toasted common crackers or Pilot crackers are always appropriate (almost mandatory) with clam chowder, and they are all you really need for cups of chowder served as a starter. But for main dishes, it is festive to make Clam Fritters (page 225) or other side dishes. You will find other suggestions in the recipes.

Because the chunks or slices of potatoes and other vegetables in clam chowders are scaled down in size to complement the clams, these chowders are not as dramatic-looking as fish chowder can be. Colorful and interesting cups or soup plates with interesting patterns will enhance the presentation. Some chowderheads like to serve clam chowder in coffee mugs, so they can drink their chowders, with or without a spoon.

How to Dig Clams

As a kid growing up on the Jersey shore, I dug soft-shell clams and cherrystones (quahogs) a couple of times, but as an adult, I am far more inclined to eat them than I am to dig for them. When I summered in Maine, I would step right over the soft-shell clams in the cove by my house to get out to my boat so I could fish for stripers and bluefish. I don't pretend to know about razor clams, geoducks, or the other West Coast varieties, but I'm sure in a pinch, I could figure it out—after all, birds and fish don't seem to have much trouble finding clams under the sand and mud.

Before you start thinking about digging for clams, check with the local authorities (usually at the town hall or police station) to find out how to obtain a shellfish license. After you pay for the license and find out where you are allowed to dig for clams legally, you should give a call to the Coast Guard and ask about red tide (an algae bloom that is harmless to shellfish, but toxic to humans). Clams can be harvested year-round in moderate climates. However, when the bays and estuaries freeze solid, during the coldest weeks of the winter, it becomes impossible (not to mention unpleasant) to harvest clams in the Northeast.

continued

Quahogs (including cherrystones and littlenecks) are easy to find because they live only inches under the sand and you can feel them with your bare feet as you walk over them. They feel round and smooth. You can find quahogs anywhere below the high-tide mark, in water as deep as 40 feet (commercial fishermen dredge for these deep-water quahogs). The more popular your spot is, the farther out you will have to look. Bring along a bucket. You can dig, or "scratch" for quahogs with a garden rake or a pitchfork, but a special tool called a quahog scratcher is best of all. You don't always have to feel for quahogs with your feet either. In areas where they are abundant, you can just "scratch" them out, especially when the water is above your ankles. Wash the sand and mud from quahogs in the saltwater before you bring them home.

Quahog scratcher

Soft-Shell Clams are a little more work than quahogs because they live deeper in the sand or mud and are smaller. They live between the high-tide and low-tide marks and will grow in sand, mud, or even grass. They are found in the greatest abundance in protected tidal estuaries. To locate soft-shell clams, look for little holes in the sand or mud; if you step near them, you will see small jets of spray come up from their holes. (This is why they are nicknamed "pisser" clams in some places.) For tools, you need a clam hoe, also called a clam fork, a small shovel or spade, and a bucket or a drain basket. Dig a hole as deep as the clams will be found (no more than 1 foot) about a foot or more away from the clam holes. This hole allows you to loosen the sand around the clams so the pressure doesn't crack their delicate shells. Then stick the clam hoe straight down in the sand or mud and lift the clams up toward the hole you dug. Pick them up and put them in your basket or bucket. Wash them off in the saltwater before you take them home.

Clam hoe

New England Clam (Quahog) Chowder

There are two quintessential New England clam chowders: the first is made with hard-shell quahogs, the second with soft-shell clams (see Steamer Clam Chowder, page 114). Both feature a rich creamy broth with clams, potatoes, onion, celery, and salt pork or bacon. Quahogs and large cherrystones (which are really just smaller quahogs) are plentiful in fish markets and make a powerful and briny clam chowder. The broth quahogs produce is herbaceous, especially briny, and not the least bit delicate. Its unique flavor permeates a chowder, and it needs aggressive flavors like garlic and bacon to complement it. This chowder delivers huge flavor and a true taste of Cape Cod and the Bay State (Massachusetts). Be generous with the parsley and chive garnish, since the colors of the chowder are otherwise neutral.

The word *quahog* comes from the Abnaki (Native American) name for hard-shell clams, *quahaug*. These round hard-shell clams live in sand and mud flats, below the high-tide mark, where they can be dug or raked at low tide. They are found only on the eastern seaboard of North America. However, two similar but smoother-shelled clams from the West Coast, the butter clam and the Pacific littleneck clam, are not quahogs, but they do make a fine chowder. The East Coast littleneck clams, top neck clams, and cherrystone clams are all small quahogs. For some unknown reason, though, we only call the large ones (10 to 16 ounces) quahogs. The term *chowder clam* applies to any quahog that is too large to be eaten raw.

Cook's Notes

This chowder begins with an easy clam broth. Follow the procedure for basic clam broth on page 62, where I also give options for using smaller clams like littlenecks.

Make this chowder with either bacon or salt pork. I like both, but prefer bacon here.

Serve in small cups as a starter with toasted common crackers or Pilot crackers or as a meal in bowls with crackers on the side. If you have extra clams, make Clam Fritters (page 225). Skillet Corn Bread (page 219) or Corn Sticks (page 220) or Anadama Bread (page 217) are good too. In New England, it is traditional to put a dollop of cold butter on top of each serving.

For equipment, you will need an 8-quart pot with a tight-fitting lid (for steaming open the clams), a fine-mesh strainer, a 4- to 6-quart heavy pot with a lid (for the chowder), a wooden spoon, and a ladle.

8 pounds small quahogs or large cherrystone clams

4 ounces slab (unsliced) bacon, rind removed and cut into ⅓-inch dice

4 tablespoons unsalted butter

2 medium onions (12 to 14 ounces), cut into ½-inch dice

2 cloves garlic, finely chopped

2 stalks celery (4 ounces), cut into ⅓-inch dice

5 to 6 sprigs fresh thyme, leaves removed and chopped (2 teaspoons)

2 dried bay leaves

2 pounds Yukon Gold, Maine, PEI, or other all-purpose potatoes, peeled and cut into ½-inch dice

1½ cups heavy cream (or up to 2 cups if desired)

Freshly ground black pepper

Kosher or sea salt if needed

For garnish

2 tablespoons chopped fresh Italian parsley

2 tablespoons minced fresh chives

1. Scrub the clams and rinse clean. Steam them open, following the instructions on page 64. Strain the broth; you should have 4 cups of broth (and 1 pound of clams). Cover the clams with plastic wrap and keep refrigerated. After they have cooled a bit, dice them into ½-inch pieces. Cover again and keep refrigerated until ready to use.

2. Heat a 4- to 6-quart heavy pot over low heat and add the bacon. Once it has rendered a few tablespoons of fat, increase the heat to medium and cook until the bacon is a crisp golden brown. Pour off all but 1 tablespoon of the fat, leaving the bacon in the pot.

3. Add the butter, onions, garlic, celery, thyme, and bay leaves and sauté, stirring occasionally with a wooden spoon, for about 10 minutes, until the onions are softened but not browned.

4. Add the potatoes and the reserved clam broth. The broth should just barely cover the potatoes; if it doesn't, add enough water to cover them. Turn up the heat and bring to a boil, cover, and cook the potatoes vigorously for about 10 minutes, until they are soft on the outside but still firm in the center. If the broth hasn't thickened lightly, smash a few potatoes against the side of the pot and cook a minute or two longer to release the starch.

5. Remove the pot from the heat and stir in the diced clams and the cream. Season to taste with pepper; you will probably not need to add any salt—the clams usually provide enough. If you are not serving the chowder within the hour, let it cool a bit, then refrigerate; cover the chowder *after* it has completely chilled. Otherwise, let it sit at room temperature for up to an hour, allowing the flavors to meld.

6. When ready to serve, reheat the chowder over low heat; don't let it boil. Ladle into cups or bowls, making sure that the clams, potatoes, onions, and bacon are evenly divided. Sprinkle with the chopped parsley and minced chives.

Makes 10 cups; serves 10 as a first course or 6 as a main course

Steamer Clam Chowder

I once owned a summer cottage on Sawyer's Island in Maine. The little cove in front of the house, too small to be named on navigational charts, was called Clam Cove by the locals. I never did any clamming—fishing was my thing—but I have a vivid memory of the muddy flats at low tide, feeling the soft-shell clams under my feet and seeing their tiny sprays coming out of the mud as they burrowed down to get out of my way. Soft-shell clams have two oval shells, about two to three inches long, that gape along the edges. Their most prominent feature is a siphon, about a quarter of the length of the shell, which sticks out of the clam. Whole soft-shell clams are often referred to as "steamers," because that is the way they are most often prepared. When salty old-timers refer to "clams," soft-shells are what they mean. Shucked raw, soft-shell clams may be called "fryers" or "frying clams." Frying clams make a superb chowder, but they are very expensive because of the labor involved in shucking them.

I prefer to steam whole soft-shell clams for chowder. That way, I save a few dollars and get a fantastic broth in the process. The flavor of steamer broth is sweeter and more subtle and round than the pungent broth quahogs (hard-shell clams) yield. The chowder made from steamers may have a little less strength up front, but it is equal to quahog chowder in deep lingering flavor. To celebrate the difference, I use salt pork instead of bacon in steamer chowder, I don't add garlic, and I use fewer herbs and seasoning, letting the luscious little clams provide most of the flavor. And they always rise to the occasion, producing one of the most delicious chowders imaginable.

Soft-shell clam (steamer clam)

Cook's Notes

Soft-shell clams are native to the Atlantic seaboard from Cape Hatteras to the Arctic Ocean, but they have been transplanted to the West Coast and can be found there from San Francisco to Vancouver, Canada. The best steamers are found at lobster or other seafood vendors along the coast, who keep them in tanks. The constant flow of water purges them of most of their sand, making them very easy to clean. You can have fresh soft-shell clams shipped directly to you (see sources, page 232), but they are very delicate—expect to find many with cracked shells. Buy the smallest steamers possible; the very large ones are even more delicate and their bellies break open easily, giving the chowder an undesirable green tinge.

If you have been fortunate enough to find really small steamers, you have the option of leaving the siphon attached, but you will have to peel the skin off it. With large soft-shell clams, the siphon is very chewy and must be removed, but with small ones, it's less noticeable and the little specks of black at the tip give an unusual and interesting appearance to the chowder.

Serve this chowder in small cups as a starter with toasted common crackers or Pilot crackers. For a meal in itself, ladle into bowls, with crackers on the side. Clam Fritters (page 225) or Sweet Corn Fritters (page 222) make a terrific side dish.

For equipment, you will need an 8-quart pot with a tight-fitting lid (for steaming open the clams), a wooden spoon, a fine-mesh strainer, a 4- to 6-quart heavy pot with a lid (for the chowder), a slotted spoon, and a ladle.

5 pounds small to medium soft-shell clams (steamers)

2 cups water

4 ounces meaty salt pork, rind removed and cut into ⅓-inch dice

2 tablespoons unsalted butter

1 large onion (10 to 12 ounces), cut into ½-inch dice

2 stalks celery (4 ounces), cut into ⅓-inch dice

2 to 3 sprigs fresh thyme, leaves removed and chopped (1 teaspoon)

2 dried bay leaves

1½ pounds Yukon Gold, Maine, PEI, or other all-purpose potatoes, peeled and cut into ½-inch dice

1½ cups heavy cream (or up to 2 cups if desired)

Freshly ground black pepper

Kosher or sea salt if needed

For garnish

2 tablespoons chopped fresh Italian parsley

2 tablespoons minced fresh chives

1. Fill two large pots (or two sinks) with cold water. Place the clams in one pot of water, discarding any dead ones or clams with cracked shells. Gently move them around in the water and let them soak for a few minutes, then lift them out and place them in the other pot of cold water. Rinse the first pot and fill it again. Move the clams around again, then transfer them back to the clean pot. Continue to switch the clams back and forth, letting them soak for a few minutes each time, and then lifting them out of the pot, until the water remains crystal clear. The process should take four or five soakings.

2. Put the 2 cups water in an 8-quart pot, cover, and bring to a rolling boil. Quickly but gently place the clams in the pot and cover again. After 4 minutes, remove the lid and quickly stir the clams with a wooden spoon, trying to lift some of the clams from the bottom to the top so they will cook evenly—but be gentle, the shells are very brittle and crack easily. Cover and continue to steam for another 4 to 5 minutes. (The broth will most likely overflow just as the clams have finished cooking.) All the clams should be open; if not, steam them a minute or two longer. Remove the clams and strain the broth; you should have 4 cups.

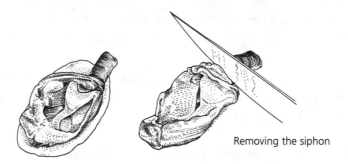

Removing the siphon

3. When the clams are cool, remove them from the shells and cut off the siphons, as well as the protective skin that covers each siphon, and discard. (You should have about 1 pound of clam meat.) Cover and refrigerate until later.

4. Heat a 4- to 6-quart heavy pot over low heat and add the diced salt pork. Once it has rendered a few tablespoons of fat, increase the heat to medium and cook until the pork is crisp and golden brown. With a slotted spoon, transfer the cracklings to a small ovenproof dish, leaving the fat in the pot, and reserve until later.

5. Add the butter, onion, celery, thyme, and bay leaves to the pot and sauté, stirring occasionally with a wooden spoon, for about 10 minutes, until the vegetables are softened but not browned.

6. Add the potatoes and the reserved clam broth. The broth should just barely cover the potatoes; if it doesn't, add enough water to cover them. Turn up the heat and bring to a boil, cover, and cook the potatoes vigorously for about 10 minutes, or until they are soft on the outside but still firm in the center. If the broth hasn't thickened lightly, smash a few potatoes against the side of the pot and cook a minute or two longer to release the starch.

7. Remove the pot from the heat. Stir in the clams and the cream and season to taste with black pepper and possibly a pinch of salt (the saltiness of steamers varies). If you are not serving the chowder within the hour, let it cool a bit, then refrigerate; cover the chowder *after* it has chilled completely. Otherwise, let it sit at room temperature for up to an hour, allowing the flavors to meld.

8. When ready to serve, reheat the chowder over low heat; don't let it boil. Try not to stir too often, because you don't want to break open the clam bellies. Warm the cracklings in a low oven (200°F) for a few minutes.

9. Ladle the chowder into cups or bowls, making sure that the steamers, onions, and potatoes are evenly divided. Scatter the cracklings over the individual servings and sprinkle with the chopped parsley and minced chives.

Makes about 11 cups; serves 10 to 12 as a first course or
6 to 8 as a main course

Razor Clam Chowder

I thought a lot about the legendary James Beard while I was testing this recipe. He was a big fan of the beautiful razor clam, which he first enjoyed as a child in his hometown of Portland, Oregon. (Razor clams are native to both the East and West Coasts.) In his chowder recipes, razor clams were always his first choice, but he did change the basic recipe over time. In his autobiography, *Delights and Prejudices* (1964), he called for clam broth (bottled, I assume, since razors are added raw and have no broth) in his chowder, but in the revised edition of *The James Beard Cookbook* (1980), he used water. I tested razor clam chowders using both broth and water, and although both were delicious (because the clams are so magnificent), I could understand why Beard made the change. Broth made from soft- or hard-shell clams has a more pungent taste than that from razor clams. Adding water, rather than clam broth, in combination with the razor clam's natural juices allows their wonderful sweet taste to shine.

With its long, thin steely, almost ebony shell, the razor clam, named for the old-fashioned straight razor it greatly resembles, is a spectacular sight. Compared to other clams, razor clams are scarce. They are also the most elusive of clams, living in the deepest part of the flats, where they can only be caught during lunar low tides (once or twice a month). They are found in several places in New England, notably on Cape Ann, near Ipswich, Massachusetts, a town famed for its soft-shell clams as well. I have never tried to dig for razor clams, but my friend Kim Marden, a Boston seafood wholesaler, laughed out loud when he told me about trying to dig them with his dad. I guess it is fairly hard, as they are amazingly fast burrowers—it took him over an hour to catch just one!

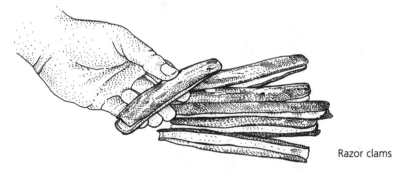

Razor clams

Cook's Notes

Razor clams are hard to find but easy to shuck: all you need is a spoon. And shucked (raw) is the best way to use them in chowder. Other than Seattle Geoduck Chowder (page 123), this is the only chowder recipe in the book that uses raw clams. You can use this recipe as a prototype for making chowder with other raw clams, substituting 2 cups chopped fresh cherrystones or quahogs, or even soft-shell clams (not chopped), for the razor clams.

I'm not sure about availability on the West Coast, but in New England, you should order razor clams from a reputable dealer far in advance and be flexible, because the vendors don't always know when they will be available. When you get razor clams, make the chowder right away—the chowder will be good for three days, but the fresh clams will only be good for a day, or two at the most.

Razor clams weigh only 1½ to 2 ounces each, but they are very strong and can really pinch you, so be careful when you handle them.

Razor clam chowder looks like other clam chowders, but it is very special. Serve it on its own, as a starter or main course, with toasted common crackers, and decorate the table with the cleaned (scrubbed and boiled) shells from the clams.

For equipment, you will need a regular teaspoon, a fine-mesh strainer, a 4- to 6-quart heavy pot with a tight-fitting lid, a slotted spoon, a wooden spoon, and a ladle.

2 pounds razor clams
4 ounces meaty salt pork, rind removed and cut into ⅓-inch dice
4 tablespoons unsalted butter
1 medium onion (7 to 8 ounces), cut into ½-inch dice
2 stalks celery (4 ounces), cut into ⅓-inch dice
2 sprigs fresh thyme, leaves removed and chopped (1 teaspoon)
1½ pounds Yukon Gold, Maine, PEI, or other all-purpose potatoes, peeled and cut into ½-inch dice

About 3 cups water
1½ cups heavy cream (or up to 2 cups if desired)
Freshly ground black pepper
Kosher or sea salt if needed

For garnish
2 tablespoons chopped fresh Italian parsley
2 tablespoons minced fresh chives

1. To shuck the clams, have two small bowls ready, one for the shucked clams and one to catch the juices that drip from the clams as they are shucked. Run a teaspoon (the eating kind, not the measuring kind) lengthwise down the inside of each clam, keeping it pressed against one shell. That will loosen the first shell. Then turn the spoon over and run it back along the

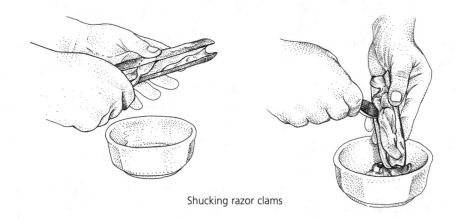
Shucking razor clams

other side, releasing the clam and scooping it out of the shell. To dice the clams, first slice each one lengthwise in half, then cut across into about ⅓-inch pieces to make a small dice. You may wish to chop the area near the siphon (it is darker), a little finer than the rest of the clam, which is more tender. (You should have about 2 cups [1 pound] diced clams.) Place the clams back in the bowl and strain the juice over. Cover and refrigerate until ready to use.

2. Heat a 4- to 6-quart heavy pot over low heat and add the diced salt pork. Once it has rendered a few tablespoons of fat, increase the heat to medium and cook until the pork is crisp and golden brown. With a slotted spoon, transfer the cracklings to a small ovenproof dish, leaving the fat in the pot, and reserve until later.

3. Add the butter, onion, celery, and thyme to the pot and sauté, stirring occasionally with a wooden spoon, for about 8 minutes, until the vegetables are softened but not browned.

4. Add the potatoes and just enough water to barely cover them. Turn up the heat, bring to a boil, cover, and cook the potatoes vigorously for about 10 minutes, stirring every few minutes, until they are soft on the outside but still firm in the center. If the broth hasn't thickened lightly, smash a few potatoes against the side of the pot and cook a minute or two longer to release their starch.

5. Reduce the heat to low and stir in the chopped razor clams. As soon as the chowder comes back to a simmer, remove it from the heat and stir in the cream. Season to taste with pepper and possibly a pinch of salt. (The clams do add their own salt, but since the chowder is made with water instead of clam broth, I have found that it usually benefits from a pinch of salt.) If you are not serving the chowder within the hour, let it cool a bit, then refrigerate; cover the chowder *after* it has chilled completely. Otherwise, let it sit at room temperature for up to an hour, allowing the flavors to meld.

6. When ready to serve, reheat the chowder over low heat; don't let it boil. Warm the cracklings in a low oven (200°F) for a few minutes.

7. Ladle the chowder into cups or bowls, making sure that the clams, onions, and potatoes are evenly divided. Scatter the cracklings over the individual servings and sprinkle with the chopped parsley and minced chives.

Makes 10 cups; serves 10 as a first course or 5 or 6 as a main course

Variation: Abalone Chowder

Since my recipe for razor clam chowder uses only water, not broth, to allow the unique flavor of the very special clams it contains to shine, it is well suited to do the same for abalone, whose taste is also very distinctive. Abalone is not a clam, it is not even a bivalve—it is a univalve, like conches and whelks, with a big foot that helps it move around and can double as a suction cup to hold it steadfast to a rock. The shell is shaped like an ear and the outside looks like a rock, but the inside is spectacular with its opalescent greens and blues and radiant pinks mixed with pearl gray. When I worked in San Francisco, almost twenty-five years ago, I cooked quite a bit of abalone, but it has become very rare and expensive, and these days I prepare it only on very special occasions.

Abalone is native only to the Pacific Ocean. I have special-ordered abalone from Mexico (regulations forbid the exportation of abalone from California), which are not as big as the ones I cooked years ago. Like other mollusks, abalone can be eaten raw. It is quite tough, but its flavor is sugary sweet and heavenly. Like conch (see Bahamian Conch Chowder, page 156), abalone should be pounded and then cooked for either a very short time or long enough to become tender. Abalone, like clams, was originally a "found" food for Native Americans and settlers in California, who only had to walk down to the beach and pry it from the rocks. I'm not sure for how long it had been used in chowder, but I imagine it has been for the better part of the twentieth century. Helen Evans Brown's abalone chowder, published in her *West Coast Cook* (1952), is made in the style of a New England clam chowder, with salt pork, onions, potatoes, and cream. She adds a cup of wine and gives the cook the option of using chicken stock or water. I omit the wine and stock, but if you like, you can squeeze in a few drops of fresh lemon juice at the end of the cooking.

To make abalone chowder, start with about 2½ to 3 pounds of whole abalone. To shuck abalone, use a clam knife. Keeping the knife pressed against the shell, cut the abalone loose with one simple scooping motion. Discard the viscera (the soft belly-like material) and trim off the dark "mantle" around the edges. You will have about 1 pound of meat that resembles large scallops. Scrape the shells clean and reserve them.

Thinly slice the abalone, pound it with the back of a meat cleaver or a meat mallet, and cut it into 1/2- to 3/4-inch dice. Place the abalone meat in a pot with 4 cups of lightly salted water, bring to a simmer, cover, and cook for 30 minutes. Remove from the heat and set the pan aside.

Prepare the chowder as above, starting with Step 2 and adding the cooked abalone with the water they were cooked in, instead of the 3 cups water in the recipe, along with the potatoes. Decorate your table with the abalone shells and serve the chowder simply with toasted common crackers or, for a little taste of California, buttery crisp croutons made from sourdough bread.

Seattle Geoduck Chowder

I'll never forget the first time I saw a geoduck (pronounced "goo-ee-duck). It was more than twenty years ago, and I was helping to open a new French restaurant in Seattle called Annique's. The chef, Alphonse Thomas, and I were both new to the city. On one of our first days together, we ventured down to Pike Place Market on Puget Sound. When we saw the geoducks, we couldn't believe our eyes: clams, bigger than most turtles, with siphons more than a foot long! Recognizing our unfamiliarity with this giant clam, the fish vendor explained, "the siphon's good for chowder, the body's sliced for steaks." We moved on to the other fish stalls, opting for white salmon instead, which was also new to us, but far less intimidating. Alphonse, one of my mentors, didn't know about chowder; it wasn't part of his repertoire (or mine at the time). During the year I lived in Seattle, I ate geoduck chowder a few times, but I never made it. I was too caught up in making consommé and bisque in those days. As strange as geoduck appears, the chowder it makes looks much like any other white chowder. The meat from the siphon is chopped very fine because it is tough, but the body meat is very tender and adds a scallop-like sweetness to the chowder.

Geoducks are found only in tidal areas of the Pacific Northwest and are dug at low tide. Their average weight is about 3 pounds, but they can grow to over 5 pounds, making them by far the largest clam in North America. The body can span 3 feet from end to end, and, with a siphon that accounts for more than half of the length, geoducks are often the subject of lively conversation, not always about chowder.

Geoduck

Cook's Notes
Aside from the amazing clam used to make the chowder, this recipe is typically New England. Making a pot of chowder from one clam (and having leftover meat to boot) felt bizarre to me, especially after needing about sixty steamers to make a batch the same size the day before. The geoduck is a formidable creature, but it is easy to shuck and prepare for chowder. I special-ordered my geoducks from my local seafood market, but they can also be mail-ordered (see sources, page 233). If you live in a city with an Asian seafood market, they just might have geoducks available.

Traditionally, the siphon is ground for chowder, and the body meat is sliced for "clam steaks." In my tests, I preferred the chowder that had some diced body meat added as opposed to all siphon meat. But, in order to use both meats and make a reasonable size batch of chowder without a lot of waste, you will need to purchase the smallest geoduck you can find. One under 2½ pounds works out nicely. A 3-pound geoduck will give you more meat than you need; in that case, trim and weigh the siphon (or chop it and measure it) and make up the difference using body meat. That will leave you with a couple of clam steaks that you can panfry for a snack or appetizer. Use the standard breading procedure (flour, beaten egg with a drop of milk or water, then bread crumbs), fry in hot oil until very crisp, and serve simply with lemon wedges.

The geoduck is used raw and has very little juice of its own, so you will need to buy bottled clam juice, unless you happen to have some of your own clam broth in your freezer.

Serve this chowder as a starter or a main course with toasted common crackers or Pilot crackers. You could also serve Clam Fritters (page 225), substituting some of the geoduck's body meat (diced) for the quahogs and bottled clam broth for the homemade clam broth in the recipe.

For equipment, you will need a sharp paring knife, a food processor, a 4- to 6-quart heavy pot with a lid, a wooden spoon, and a ladle.

1 small geoduck clam (2½ to 3 pounds)
4 ounces slab (unsliced) bacon, rind removed and cut into ⅓-inch dice
4 tablespoons unsalted butter
1 large onion (10 to 12 ounces), cut into ½-inch dice
2 stalks celery (4 ounces), cut into ⅓-inch dice
6 sprigs fresh thyme, leaves removed and chopped (2 teaspoons)
2 dried bay leaves
1½ pounds Yukon Gold, Maine, PEI, or other all-purpose potatoes, peeled and cut into ½-inch dice

4 cups Clam Broth (page 62), bottled clam juice, or water (as a last resort)
2 cups heavy cream
Freshly ground black pepper
Kosher or sea salt if needed

For garnish
2 tablespoons chopped fresh Italian parsley
2 tablespoons minced fresh chives

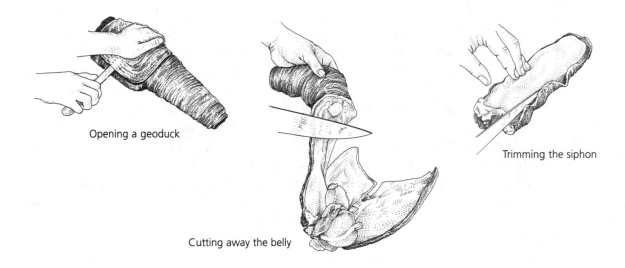

Opening a geoduck

Cutting away the belly

Trimming the siphon

1. To shuck the geoduck, insert a sharp paring knife between the shell and the clam and, keeping your knife pressed against the shell, cut the clam away first from one shell, then the other; it will be easy to cut and fall right out of the shell. Next, cut away the entire soft belly section and discard. Be careful not to puncture the belly, or it will be quite messy. Next, separate the siphon from the body meat with a single cut. With your fingers, peel off as much of the heavy skin as possible, then finish the job by trimming the remaining skin off with the knife. Cut the siphon into ½-inch slices and place in a food processor. Pulse until the meat is chopped into about ¼-inch dice. Weigh or measure the chopped siphon, then cover and refrigerate. Trim off the heavy skin that is attached to the body (where the clam was not covered by its shell). With a knife, dice enough of the tender body meat into ½-inch pieces to give you a total of 12 to 16 ounces, or 1½ to 2 cups; save the remaining meat for clam steaks. Cover and refrigerate until ready to use.

2. Heat a 4- to 6-quart heavy pot over low heat and add the diced bacon. Once it has rendered a few tablespoons of fat, increase the heat to medium and cook until the bacon is crisp and golden brown. Pour off all but 1 tablespoon of the fat, leaving the bacon in the pot.

3. Add the butter, onion, celery, thyme, and bay leaves and sauté, stirring occasionally with a wooden spoon, for about 8 minutes, until the vegetables are softened but not browned.

4. Add the potatoes and clam broth. The broth should just barely cover the potatoes; if it doesn't add just enough water to cover them. Turn up the heat, bring to a boil, and cook the potatoes vigorously for about 10 minutes, until they are soft on the outside but still firm in the center. If the broth hasn't thickened lightly, smash a few potatoes against the side of the pot and cook a minute or two longer to release their starch.

5. Reduce the heat to low and stir in the chopped and diced clam. Cook for 5 minutes, or until the chowder comes back to a full simmer. Remove from the heat, stir in the cream, and season to taste with pepper. Depending on the clam broth or juice that you used, you may need a pinch of salt. If you are not serving the chowder within the hour, let it cool a bit, then refrigerate; cover the chowder *after* it has chilled completely. Otherwise, let it sit at room temperature for up to an hour, allowing the flavors to meld.

6. When ready to serve, reheat the chowder over low heat; don't let it boil. Ladle into cups or bowls, making sure that the pieces of clam, potatoes, onion, and bacon are evenly divided, and sprinkle with the chopped parsley and minced chives.

Makes about 10 cups; serves 10 as a first course or
5 to 6 as a main course

Restaurant-Style Thick Clam Chowder

The origins of restaurant-style roux (flour-and-butter)-thickened clam chowder are vague, but as a professional chef, I feel comfortable speculating how it came about. We professional chefs are trained to memorize flavors and duplicate dishes, but often during the process of translating home-style recipes for restaurant production, we can admittedly change the integrity of a dish. Unlike almost all the chowders in this book, in this recipe, the potatoes do not act as a thickener—they are cooked separately and added as garnish. The chowder is thickened instead with a roux, which changes the texture—and karma—of this dish. My guess is that as New England clam chowder became popular all over the United States, it began showing up on restaurant menus, possibly at the urging of customers. In the hands of professional chefs, many who were French-trained and had never tasted a real chowder, clam chowder became a creamy clam soup (*velouté*) with traditional chowder garnishes. The restaurant chain Howard Johnson's expanded the popularity of roux-thickened chowder, as did many other chains, Red Lobster and Legal Sea Foods, among them. And, because of the volume of business these restaurants have done over the last fifty years, more people have eaten this soup-like chowder than true home-style chowder. This is unfortunate because, at its worst, it is a thick paste, with tough chewy flavorless clams and frozen dehydrated potatoes, and it barely resembles a real chowder. But at its best, which was my goal in this recipe, it can be a silky, suave soup with a true clam chowder flavor and a texture that many will find comforting and familiar. Far be it for me to deny the existence of the most popular style of chowder in America!

Cook's Notes

Because you need extra fat to make the roux that thickens this chowder, all the bacon fat is left in the pot and the bacon is removed, unlike my other recipes. In fact, if you have been making other chowders from this book, you will see the preparation procedure of this one is quite different. Read the recipe carefully.

Since the potatoes are cooked separately and not used as the thickener in this clam chowder, you may substitute low-starch potatoes like red or white new potatoes for the medium-starch potatoes specified in the recipe.

Because it is quite rich, it is probably best to serve small cups of this chowder as a starter (when in Rome . . .). Serve with toasted common crackers or Pilot crackers. Clam Fritters (page 225) are also an appropriate accompaniment.

For equipment, you will need an 8-quart pot with a tight-fitting lid (for steaming open the clams), a fine-mesh strainer, a small pot (for cooking the potatoes), a 4- to 6-quart heavy pot (for the chowder), a slotted spoon, a wooden spoon, and a ladle.

8 pounds small quahogs or large cherry-stone clams

1 pound Yukon Gold, Maine, PEI, or other all-purpose potatoes, peeled and cut into ½-inch dice

4 ounces slab (unsliced) bacon, rind removed and cut into ⅓-inch dice

2 tablespoons unsalted butter

3 cloves garlic, finely chopped (1 tablespoon)

2 medium onions (12 to 14 ounces), cut into ½-inch dice

2 stalks celery (4 ounces), cut into ⅓-inch dice

4 sprigs fresh thyme, leaves removed and chopped (1 teaspoon)

½ teaspoon dried oregano

2 dried bay leaves

⅓ cup all-purpose flour

1 cup Clam Broth (page 62), bottled clam juice, or water (as a last resort)

2 teaspoons Worcestershire sauce

2 dashes Tabasco sauce, or more to taste (optional)

Freshly ground black pepper

Kosher or sea salt if needed

1½ cups heavy cream (or up to 2 cups if desired)

For garnish
2 tablespoons chopped fresh Italian parsley

2 tablespoons minced fresh chives

1. Scrub the clams and rinse clean. Steam them open, following the instructions on page 64. Strain the broth; you should have 4 cups of clam broth (and 1 pound of clams). Cover the clams with plastic wrap and keep refrigerated. After they have cooled a bit, dice them into ½-inch pieces. Cover again and keep refrigerated until ready to use.

2. Put the diced potatoes in a small pot and cover with lightly salted water. Bring to a boil, then reduce the heat and simmer for about 8 minutes, until the potatoes are cooked through but still firm. Drain and rinse under cold water to stop the cooking. Drain again and reserve.

3. Heat a 4- to 6-quart heavy pot over low heat and add the diced bacon. Once it has rendered a few tablespoons of fat, increase the heat to medium and cook until the bacon is crisp and golden brown. Remove the bacon with a slotted spoon, leaving the fat in the pot, and reserve until later.

4. Add the butter and garlic to the pot and cook for 30 seconds, then add the onions, celery, thyme, oregano, and bay leaves. Sauté, stirring occasionally with a wooden spoon, for about 8 minutes, until the onions and celery are soft but not browned.

5. Reduce the heat to low, sprinkle the flour over the vegetables and herbs, and stir constantly for 2 to 3 minutes, until the sticking becomes a problem; do not let the pan scorch. Add 1 cup of the reserved clam broth and stir vigorously with the wooden spoon, loosening any flour that may have stuck to the bottom of the pot. As soon as the broth thickens and bubbles, add another cup of broth. At this point, the mixture will be very thick and pasty. Allow the broth to thicken each time before you add more broth. After you have incorporated all the reserved broth and the additional 1 cup, add the Worcestershire sauce and season to taste with Tabasco and black pepper. (It is unlikely that any salt will be needed.) Let the broth simmer gently for 15 minutes.

6. Add the cooked bacon and potatoes and simmer for another 5 minutes. Remove the pot from the heat and stir in the clams and heavy cream. If you are not serving the chowder within the hour, let it cool a bit, then refrigerate; cover the chowder *after* it has chilled completely. Otherwise, let it sit at room temperature for up to an hour, allowing the flavors to meld.

7. When ready to serve, reheat the chowder over low heat; don't let it boil. Ladle into cups or bowls, making sure that the pieces of clam, potatoes, onions, and bacon are evenly divided. Sprinkle with the chopped parsley and chives.

Makes 10 cups; serves 10 to 12 as a first course

Rhode Island Clear Clam Chowder

When you order chowder in a Rhode Island restaurant, you may get a creamy chowder, a red chowder, or a clear chowder. Although you would think our smallest state might have a consensus on clam chowder, it doesn't. Even jonnycakes, which are unique to Rhode Island, are made in two versions, thick or thin, depending on the cook. Nevertheless, clear chowder made without milk or tomatoes (like the earliest chowders from the 1700s) can still be found in Rhode Island restaurants, and many old-timers claim that it is the true Rhode Island chowder.

Since my wife, Nancy, is from Rhode Island, we spend a good amount of time down there, and I have sampled the local clear chowder many times. It is always served with a small pitcher of warm milk on the side, but I rarely add it. When I make clear chowder, I strive to make it so good in its own right that no one will want to add the warm milk, which I do serve in deference to custom. This chowder is a chowder anatomy lesson. You can see all the parts floating in the broth: clams, bacon, potatoes, onions, celery, and herbs. In my zeal to make the tastiest clear chowder, I add a generous dose of fresh herbs as well as bacon, fennel seeds, and a squeeze of lemon. Certain dyed-in-the-wool Yankees sneer at the idea of lemon in chowder, but I have found lemon in several New England chowder recipes that are far older than they are.

Cook's Notes

I have listed crushed red pepper flakes as an optional ingredient. However, unlike Portuguese and other red chowders, which are intended to be spicy, clear chowder isn't. And since this dish appeals to a wide variety of people, including children, I leave the spicing up to the individual cook. The fennel seeds can be crushed with a mortar and pestle if you have one. Or you can place them on a cutting board and crush them by rubbing them against the board with the side of your knife, then chopping them.

I cook this chowder slowly in order to keep the broth clear, and I don't worry if the potatoes haven't thickened it as much as other chowders; a thinner consistency seems in keeping with the true spirit of this chowder.

The 8 pounds of quahogs in this recipe make 4 cups of clam broth, but you'll need 6 cups of liquid for the chowder. If possible, supplement the quahog broth with fresh or bottled clam broth rather than stock or water.

Serve with toasted common crackers or Pilot crackers. Jonnycakes, although another Rhode Island specialty, don't really go with chowder, but Clam Fritters (page 225) or Sweet Corn

Fritters (page 222) made with jonnycake meal (stone-ground white flint Indian corn) make an authentic and delicious addition.

For equipment, you will need an 8-quart pot with a tight-fitting lid (for steaming open the clams), a fine-mesh strainer, a 4- to 6-quart heavy pot (for the chowder), a wooden spoon, a small pot (to warm the milk), and a ladle.

8 pounds small quahogs or large cherrystone clams
4 ounces slab (unsliced) bacon, rind removed and cut into ⅓-inch dice
4 tablespoons unsalted butter
2 medium onions (12 to 14 ounces), cut into ½-inch dice
3 stalks celery (6 ounces), cut into ⅓-inch dice
6 to 8 sprigs fresh thyme, leaves removed and chopped (1 tablespoon)
2 dried bay leaves
⅛ teaspoon fennel seeds, crushed
½ to 1 teaspoon crushed red pepper flakes (optional)

2 pounds Yukon Gold, Maine, PEI, or other all-purpose potatoes, peeled and cut into ½-inch dice
2 cups Clam Broth (page 62), bottled clam juice, Traditional Fish Stock (page 60), Chicken Stock (page 72), or water (as a last resort)
Freshly ground black pepper
1 tablespoon fresh lemon juice
Kosher or sea salt if needed
2 tablespoons chopped fresh Italian parsley
2 tablespoons minced fresh chives
2 tablespoons chopped fresh chervil (optional)
2 to 3 cups whole milk

1. Scrub the clams and rinse clean. Steam them open, following the instructions on page 64. Strain the broth; you should have 4 cups of broth (and 1 pound of clams). Cover the clams with plastic wrap and keep refrigerated. After they have cooled a bit, dice them into ½-inch pieces. Cover again and keep refrigerated until ready to use.

2. Heat a 4- to 6-quart heavy pot over low heat and add the bacon. Once it has rendered a few tablespoons of fat, increase the heat to medium and cook until the bacon is a crisp golden brown. Pour off all but 1 tablespoon of the fat, leaving the bacon in the pot.

3. Add the butter, onions, celery, thyme, bay leaves, fennel seeds, and red pepper flakes, if using, and sauté, stirring occasionally with a wooden spoon, for 10 to 12 minutes, until the onions are softened but not browned.

4. Add the potatoes, the reserved clam broth, and the additional 2 cups broth, and continue to cook over medium heat until the chowder begins to simmer; if it begins to boil, turn down the heat slightly so that it maintains a steady simmer. Cook for about 15 minutes longer, until the potatoes are very tender.

5. Remove the pot from the heat, stir in the diced clams, and season to taste with black pepper and the lemon juice. (It is unlikely that you will need to add any salt; the clams usually provide enough.) If you are not serving the chowder within the hour, let it cool a bit, then refrigerate; cover the chowder *after* it has chilled completely. Otherwise, let it sit at room temperature for up to an hour, allowing the flavors to meld.

6. When ready to serve, reheat the chowder over low heat; do not let it boil. Stir in the parsley, chives, and chervil. At the same time, heat the milk over low heat; do not let it boil.

7. Ladle the chowder into cups or bowls making sure that the clams, potatoes, onions, and bacon are evenly divided; do not fill the cups or bowls more than three-quarters full. As is customary in Rhode Island, serve the hot milk in a small pitcher so each person can add as much as he or she likes to their chowder, if any.

Makes 12 cups; serves 12 as a first course or
6 to 8 as a main course

Variation: Low-Fat Clam Chowder

Although many chowders can be altered to create low-fat versions, this recipe is particularly well suited for that purpose because it is loaded with savory flavorings. The techniques and substitutions used here can serve as a guideline for reducing fat in other chowder recipes. Since this recipe is based on clam broth, you won't need to add more, but to lower the fat in chowder recipes that are finished with cream, substitute an equal amount of broth, stock, or water. A nonstick pan allows you to use the minimal amount of fat to sauté the vegetables. If you have a nonstick pot that is large enough to make this chowder (4 quarts or more), you can make it in one pot. Otherwise, sauté the vegetables in a nonstick frying pan, then transfer them to a pot and proceed with the recipe.

Prepare the clam broth and diced clams as in Step 1. Omit the bacon and butter; instead, sauté the vegetables in 1 tablespoon of olive or other vegetable oil; if you do not use a nonstick pan, you may have to increase the oil slightly to prevent the ingredients from sticking. Proceed as directed, omitting the milk to be served on the side.

Manhattan Red Clam Chowder

Tomatoes have been added to chowders since the fruit (yes, tomatoes are a fruit) first became popular in America during the early 1800s. An 1851 recipe from Boston that included tomatoes and another Portuguese-inspired chowder from Cape Cod during the same era prove that tomatoes were not always taboo in New England chowders. But old Yankees are very stubborn when it comes to the red versus white chowder debate. Eleanor Early, a born and bred Cape Codder who spent her life writing travel and cooking books about New England, epitomizes the endemic Yankee attitude when she says in her *New England Cookbook* (1954) that "some people make a vegetable soup with a bivalve drawn through it and have the audacity to call it clam chowder." She also looks down her nose at "those parts of Connecticut and Rhode Island where clam chowder is made in the unregenerate fashion of New Yorkers." However, she does give a recipe for a red chowder that she refers to as "Rhode Island"—I guess she couldn't bring herself to publish a recipe with "Manhattan" in the title. I have always thought that this attitude has little to do with chowder and stems from a deeper problem, perhaps a regional inferiority complex.

Some food historians suggest that Manhattan clam chowder may have descended from *zuppa di vongole,* a clam soup served in New York fish houses run by Neapolitans. The flavors do suggest that, but *zuppa di vongole* is usually served with whole clams in their shell. I recently discovered a recipe called Clam Chowder in *The Epicurean,* a twelve-hundred-page tome by Charles Ranhoffer, chef at the famous Delmonico's Restaurant in Manhattan. This turn-of-the-century chowder was made with clams, tomatoes, salt pork, thyme, and potatoes "cut in seven-sixteenth of an inch squares." Maybe this was in fact the origin of Manhattan clam chowder. All the rivalry, history, and speculation are good fun, but what really matters is what's in the pot. With a spicy red briny clam broth and colorful, tasty chunks of green peppers, carrots, tomatoes, celery, onions, potatoes, and clams, my Manhattan clam chowder makes a strong impression.

Cook's Notes
It is tempting to add the tomatoes early on in this recipe, but don't do it. They'll cause the potatoes to form a "skin," for lack of a better description—that prevents them from releasing their starch. As in most chowders, the light thickening from the potato's natural starch helps suspend the overall flavor and gives it a lovely texture. This recipe calls for whole peeled tomatoes cut into ½-inch dice; if you can find good-quality diced canned tomatoes, feel free to substitute them. Toasted common crackers or Pilot crackers are fine with this chowder; Toasted Garlic Bread (page 209) is even better.

For equipment, you will need an 8-quart pot with a tight-fitting lid (for steaming open the clams), a fine-mesh strainer, a 4- to 6-quart heavy pot with a lid (for the chowder), a wooden spoon, and a ladle.

8 pounds small quahogs or large cherry-stone clams

4 ounces slab (unsliced) bacon, rind removed and cut into ⅓-inch dice

2 tablespoons olive oil

3 cloves garlic, finely chopped (1 tablespoon)

1 large onion (10 ounces), cut into ½-inch dice

2 stalks celery (4 ounces), cut into ⅓-inch dice

1 medium green bell pepper (6 ounces), cut into ½-inch dice

2 medium carrots (4 ounces) cut into ½-inch dice

2 dried bay leaves

2 teaspoons dried oregano

½ teaspoon crushed red pepper flakes

1½ pounds Yukon Gold, Maine, PEI, or other all-purpose potatoes, peeled and cut into ½-inch dice

1 cup Clam Broth (page 62), bottled clam juice, Traditional Fish Stock (page 60), Chicken Stock (page 72), or water (as a last resort)

1 can (28 ounces) whole peeled tomatoes in juice, cut into ½-inch dice

¼ cup chopped fresh Italian parsley

Freshly ground black pepper

Kosher or sea salt if needed

1. Scrub the clams and rinse clean. Steam them open, following the instructions on page 64. Strain the broth; you should have 4 cups of broth (and 1 pound of clams). Cover the clams with plastic wrap and keep refrigerated. After they have cooled a bit, dice them into ½-inch pieces. Cover again and keep refrigerated until ready to use.

2. Heat a 4- to 6-quart heavy pot over low heat and add the bacon. Once it has rendered a few tablespoons of fat, increase the heat to medium and cook until the bacon is a crisp golden brown. Pour off all but 1 tablespoon of the fat, leaving the bacon in the pot.

3. Add the olive oil and garlic and cook for 30 seconds, then add the onion, celery, bell pepper, carrots, bay leaves, oregano, and crushed red pepper. Sauté, stirring occasionally with a wooden spoon, for 10 to 12 minutes, until the vegetables are softened but not browned.

4. Add the potatoes, the reserved clam broth, and the additional 1 cup broth. The broth should just barely cover the potatoes; if it doesn't, add enough water to cover. Turn up the heat, bring to a boil, cover, and cook the potatoes vigorously for about 10 minutes, until they are soft on the outside but still firm in the center. If the broth hasn't thickened lightly, smash a few potatoes against the side of the pot and cook a minute or two longer to release their starch.

5. Add the tomatoes and simmer for another 5 minutes. Remove the pot from the heat, stir in the diced clams and chopped parsley, and season to taste with black pepper. (It is unlikely that you will need to add any salt; the clams usually provide enough.) If you are not serving the chowder within the hour, let it cool a bit, then refrigerate; cover the chowder *after* it has chilled completely. Otherwise, let it sit at room temperature for up to an hour, allowing the flavors to meld.

6. When ready to serve, reheat the chowder over low heat; don't let it boil. Ladle into cups or bowls, making sure the clams, vegetables, and bacon are evenly divided.

```
Makes 13 cups; serves 12 as a first course or
6 to 8 as a main course
```

Clam, White Bean, and Potato Chowder

Bean chowders date back to the Shakers in the late 1800s (see Shaker Fresh Cranberry Bean Chowder, page 180), but until I tasted my friend Tony Ambrose's Clam and Fava Bean Chowder at his Boston restaurant, Ambrosia on Huntington, I hadn't been inspired by this combination for chowder. Using traditional chowder techniques and flavor combinations, and incorporating my favorite beans—A-1 jumbo limas from Maine—I came up with this recipe. These fat white dried beans are incredibly creamy and luscious, and I knew they would make a wonderful chowder, because I had used them before in a variety of dishes, including a seafood minestrone.

I have served this chowder several times, and everyone raves about it. It has a familiar clam chowder flavor, pungent and savory, that is mellowed by the beans, half of which I mash to thicken it. The broth is light red from the small amount of tomatoes and translucent enough to make a visual treat of the whole jumbo beans and chunks of potatoes, onion, and clams.

Cook's Notes

I recommend soaking the beans overnight, so plan accordingly. A-1 jumbo lima beans are inexpensive and found in many New England grocery stores. Goya sells a similar dried jumbo lima that is sold in many supermarkets across the country. You can substitute an equal weight of cannellini beans, shell beans, or any other dried good-quality bean, large or small, without noticeably affecting the final results.

In this recipe, the beans are cooked separately, and half of them (the best-looking ones) are added whole to the chowder. The remaining beans are pureed and used to thicken the chowder. I use a food mill because I prefer a puree with a slightly coarse texture, but you can use a food processor, or even a potato masher. Because the beans are used as the primary thickener in this chowder, the potatoes are not cooked as vigorously as in most of my chowder recipes.

Serve with toasted common crackers or Pilot crackers, Skillet Corn Bread (page 219) or Corn Sticks (page 220), or Toasted Garlic Bread (page 209).

For equipment, you will need a medium bowl (to soak the beans), a 2-quart saucepan (for cooking the beans), a small food mill or a food processor, an 8-quart pot with a tight-fitting lid (for steaming open the clams), a fine-mesh strainer, a 4- to 6-quart heavy pot (for the chowder), a slotted spoon, a wooden spoon, and a ladle.

8 ounces large dried white beans, such as large white limas, cannellini, or shell beans, soaked overnight in water to cover generously

8 pounds small quahogs or large cherrystone clams

4 ounces meaty salt pork, rind removed and cut into ⅓-inch dice

2 tablespoons olive oil

3 cloves garlic, finely chopped (1 tablespoon)

1 large onion (10 ounces), cut into ½-inch dice

2 stalks celery (4 ounces), cut into ⅓-inch dice

2 to 3 sprigs fresh thyme, leaves removed and chopped (1 teaspoon)

2 dried bay leaves

½ teaspoon crushed red pepper flakes

8 ounces Yukon Gold, Maine, PEI, or other all-purpose potatoes, peeled and cut into ½-inch dice

1 cup diced (½ inch) peeled tomatoes with their juice (fresh or canned)

2 tablespoons chopped fresh basil

Freshly ground black pepper

Kosher or sea salt if needed

For garnish

2 tablespoons chopped fresh Italian parsley

1. Drain the beans and pick through them, discarding any that are discolored or damaged. Place the beans in a 2-quart saucepan, cover with water, and bring to a boil. Skim off the white foam, reduce the heat, and simmer gently until the beans are very tender. Jumbo white lima beans take about 30 minutes; others may take anywhere from 20 to 40 minutes, depending on the type of bean.

2. Drain the beans and gently rinse them under cold water to stop the cooking. Half of the beans will be used whole in the chowder; pick out the best-looking ones and reserve. Puree the remaining beans with a food mill or in a food processor and reserve.

3. Scrub the clams and rinse clean. Steam them open, following the instructions on page 64. Strain the broth; you should have 4 cups of broth (and 1 pound of clams). Cover the clams with plastic wrap and keep refrigerated. After they have cooled a bit, dice them into ½-inch pieces. Cover again and keep refrigerated until ready to use.

4. Heat a 4- to 6-quart heavy pot over low heat and add the diced salt pork. Once it has rendered a few tablespoons of fat, increase the heat to medium and cook until the pork is crisp and golden brown. Using a slotted spoon, transfer the cracklings to a small ovenproof dish, leaving the fat in the pot, and reserve until later.

5. Add the olive oil and garlic to the pot and cook for 30 seconds. Add the onion, celery, thyme, bay leaves, and crushed red pepper and sauté, stirring occasionally with a wooden spoon, for about 10 minutes, until the onions are softened but not browned.

6. Add the potatoes and the reserved clam broth and simmer until the potatoes are just barely cooked through and are still firm. Add the pureed beans, the whole beans, and the diced tomatoes and simmer for 5 minutes more.

7. Remove the pot from the heat, stir in the diced clams and basil, and season to taste with black pepper. (It is unlikely that you will need to add any salt; the clams usually provide enough.) If you are not serving the chowder within the hour, let it cool a bit, then refrigerate; cover the chowder *after* it has chilled completely. Otherwise, let it sit at room temperature for up to an hour, allowing the flavors to meld.

8. When ready to serve, reheat the chowder over low heat; don't let it boil, and try not to stir too often. Warm the cracklings in a low oven (200°F) for a few minutes.

9. Ladle the chowder into cups or bowls, making sure that the beans, clams, onions, tomatoes, and potatoes are evenly divided. Scatter the cracklings over the individual servings, and sprinkle with the chopped parsley.

```
Makes about 11 cups; serves 10 as a first course or
5 or 6 as a main course
```

Chapter 6

Assorted Shellfish Chowders

Chowders, like stews and other dishes, developed
when cooking was a pleasurable and time-consuming art.
—Louise Tate King and Jean Stewart Wexler, THE MARTHA'S VINEYARD COOKBOOK

For me, cooking still is and always will be a "pleasurable art." Although the nature of chowder making is easygoing and never fussy, some chowders take more time to make than others. Fish and clam chowders are relatively straightforward and, with few exceptions, can be made quickly—relative to chowder making, that is. The shellfish chowders in this chapter are not difficult to make, but I can't promise you "instant gourmet" recipes either.

These recipes are for people who take pleasure in the process of "building" a dish. I find solace in preparations that others might find messy or tedious. I like beating conch, cracking crabs, peeling shrimp, shucking oysters, and removing the meat from lobsters; these are a form of meditation for me. And having done those tasks adds to the satisfaction I feel when I taste the final dish and, even more so, when I see the happiness my efforts bring to others.

Although there is no denying the greatness of clams and the chowder they make, there *is* life after clam chowder. In this chapter, I will show you how to make chowders using other delicious members of the shellfish clan: oysters, scallops, mussels, cockles, prawns, shrimp, squid, conch, crab, and lobster. The flavors of these shellfish are rounder, sweeter, and less complex than the clam's, which is sharp, pungent, and herbaceous. Clams are at their best in basic chowders that feature them exclusively. Other shellfish are more versatile and give us a chance to explore a wider range of flavors. Combinations like oysters with lemon and nutmeg (page 141), scallops with cabbage (page 144), mussels with curry (page 147), and shrimp with fennel (page 160) are exciting, almost provocative, in the context of traditional chowder making. And two of the recipes—Irish Shellfish Chowder (page 150) and Azorean-Style Chowder (page 153)—combine different species of shellfish.

Despite the variety and versatility of shellfish chowders, these chowders remain in relative obscurity. With the exception of crab chowder (common in the Chesapeake Bay region) and conch chowder (the clam chowder of the Caribbean), the dishes in this chapter are not steeped in chowder tradition. I have found a few random recipes for scallop chowder and lobster chowder, but there these splendid creatures are treated merely as a substitute for fish or clams. Until twenty years ago, the primary use of mussels and squid in New England was for fishing bait, so it is no shock that they don't top the charts (actually, they're not even on the chart) of popular chowder ingredients. What I do find surprising, however, is that oysters and shrimp, both wildly popular in America since colonial times, are virtually nonexistent in the folklore of chowder. It seems they were stereotyped early on: oysters for oyster stew, shrimp for bisque and gumbo. Since I am a chef, not a historian, I find this of little consequence. In fact, the lack of any chowder making rituals for oysters, mussels, squid, scallops, and lobster was energizing for me, because I knew they all had potential for excellence. I really had a lot of fun with these shellfish chowders.

My inspirations for the chowders in this chapter cover a lot of water—from the Portuguese Azores to the islands of the Bahamas, from Nova Scotia and the Gulf of Maine to Ireland, from Chesapeake Bay to San Francisco Bay. All these beautiful places are rich in shellfish and fish, and each has a special meaning for me. Being of Irish descent, I'm happy to join the chorus praising the seafood of the Emerald Isle: it is simply outstanding, some of the best in the world. Although I have never visited the Azores, I have spent years working with Azorean cooks (many Azoreans emigrated to New England to work in our fishing industry) and greatly admire their style of seafood cooking. I've also spent plenty of time in the Caribbean (for work and play) and I'm a big fan of *lambi* (conch). In the Caribbean, where necessity rules all cooking, improvisation is a must. There are probably as many versions of conch chowder as there are islands. I used to have a summer home in Maine and I've vacationed in the Chesapeake Bay area—part of my leisure time each year is, inevitably, spent pursuing my passion for eating lobsters and crabs. Finally, San Francisco, where I worked in the early years of my career, is the source for the zany "meatball" chowder. I'm really fond of this chowder: it looks great, it tastes great, and it has a great sense of humor.

Since this chapter covers such a wide range of sea creatures, there are very few general comments that apply to this group of chowders. In chapter 2, you will find information on purchasing shellfish (see page 38). Specific points on choosing the best quality of each species are mentioned in the Cook's Notes that precede the individual recipes. Many of the shellfish included in this chapter have become "high ticket" foods. They weren't always expensive, but the development of our sophisticated worldwide shipping network over the last few decades means most shellfish are now subject to world market prices. And the world holds these foods in very high esteem. (Abalone, one of the rarest and most expensive shellfish in the world, makes a spectacular and sweet chowder. It is used in the same manner as the razor clam, another coveted species of shellfish, so I included it in a variation under that recipe; see page 121.) Chowder makes even the most expensive items, like lobsters, affordable. But the high regard for many of the shellfish in this chapter gives you an opportunity to serve them at more formal dinners. Not that you have to! Whatever the occasion, I hope you have as much fun making and eating these luxurious and delicious chowders as I do.

Oyster and Leek Chowder

It is easy to picture the ancient Romans feasting on oysters by the dozens, as they certainly did. They even devised special transportation systems for oysters and built better roads from Gaul (France), their source for the shelled treasures. And it's no surprise that before the French Revolution, the French aristocracy frequently gorged themselves on oysters, considered mandatory at any festive occasion. But the notion of our staid American fore-fathers (and -mothers) as passionate, sensual food lovers who devoured dozens of oysters daily is contrary to the image in my schoolbooks. Between the Revolutionary War and the Civil War, however, America went through a period that can only be described as oyster mania. Because of the incredible abundance of wild oysters, this mania was more demo-cratic than in Rome or France. In Boston, New York, Philadelphia, Baltimore, in every major city on the East Coast in fact, "oyster parlors" sprang up in great numbers. And inside these establishments, it was not uncommon for a customer to eat four or five dozen raw oysters at a seating.

The oyster craze that swept our nation was responsible for dozens of creative and won-derful dishes, but even after combing through cookbooks from that period, as well as books on culinary history, I came up almost empty-handed in regard to oyster chowder. I found a couple of mentions where some oyster juice or a few oysters were used to finish or flavor a fish chowder. I found only one recipe, from Delmonico's in New York (in *The International Cook Book,* by Alexander Filippini, published in 1906), that used chopped oysters in a tomato-based chowder. I began to doubt the concept of oyster chowder. Oyster stew, a sim-ple dish of shucked oysters warmed in milk with sherry and butter, was wildly popular—obviously the favorite liquid preparation for oysters. It may be possible that the sheer abun-dance of oysters, at least until fifty years ago, precluded the need to extend them in a dish

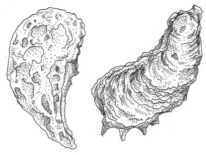

Eastern oyster

such as chowder. In fact, oysters were often used to stretch more precious foods, like chicken! (See Chicken and Oyster Chowder, page 196.) I can't explain the dearth of oyster chowders, but to my delight I was able to make a soothing and subtle oyster chowder with the soft flavor of leeks, lemon zest, and nutmeg. With the high price of oysters these days, maybe this dish has a future!

Cook's Notes

You can buy preshucked oysters, and some are very good, but quality varies. Talk to your fish vendor about them. If you shuck your own, you can be sure of their origin and freshness. (Shuck them over a bowl to catch all their juices.)

Oysters are one of the most delicate of seafoods, so treat them gently. Once they are added to the chowder, stirring should be kept to a minimum.

Serve this chowder in cups as a starter or in soup plates or shallow bowls as a main course, with toasted common crackers or Pilot crackers. If you are serving it as a main course, Anadama Bread (page 217), toasted and buttered, makes a splendid extra offering.

For equipment, you will need a colander, a 3- to 4-quart heavy pot with a lid, a wooden spoon, and a ladle.

2 medium leeks (about 12 ounces)
1 pint shucked oysters with their juice
 (about 30 medium oysters)
4 ounces slab (unsliced) bacon, rind
 removed and cut into ⅓-inch dice
4 tablespoons unsalted butter
1 dried bay leaf
1½ pounds Yukon Gold, Maine, PEI, or
 other all-purpose potatoes, quartered
 and sliced ⅓ inch thick
3 cups Traditional Fish Stock (page 60),
 Chicken Stock (page 72), or water
 (as a last resort)

⅛ teaspoon freshly grated nutmeg
½ teaspoon finely chopped lemon zest
 (yellow part only, no white pith)
2 teaspoons fresh lemon juice
Freshly ground black pepper
2 cups heavy cream
Kosher or sea salt if needed

For garnish

2 tablespoons chopped fresh Italian
 parsley
2 tablespoons minced fresh chives

1. Remove the tough outer leaves from each leek and discard (or reserve for stock). Trim off the roots and the dark green tops of the leaves. Then cut each leek in half where the white meets the green. Split the white part lengthwise in half, then cut across into ⅓-inch slices. Do the same with the green half, removing any darker green parts and slicing only the light green part. Place the leeks in a pot of water and let soak briefly to remove any dirt, then lift them out and drain them in a colander. It is important to drain them well, or they will steam rather than sauté.

2. Shuck the oysters over a bowl to catch all their juices. Check them over and pick out any fragments of shell. Refrigerate them, in their juices, until ready to use.

3. Heat a 3- to 4-quart heavy pot over low heat and add the bacon. Once it has rendered a few tablespoons of fat, increase the heat to medium and cook until the bacon is a crisp golden brown. Pour off all but 1 tablespoon of the fat, leaving the bacon in the pot.

3. Add the butter, leeks, and bay leaf and sauté, stirring occasionally with a wooden spoon, for about 8 minutes, until the leeks are softened but not browned.

4. Add the potatoes and fish stock. The stock should just barely cover the potatoes—if it doesn't, add enough water to cover. Turn up the heat and bring to a boil, cover the pot, and cook the potatoes vigorously for about 8 minutes, until they are soft on the outside but still firm in the center. If the broth hasn't thickened lightly, smash a few potatoes against the side of the pot and cook a minute or two longer to release their starch. Add the nutmeg, lemon zest, lemon juice, and black pepper to taste.

5. Remove the pot from the heat. Gently stir in the oysters and cream and season to taste with a little salt. (Since the oysters are naturally salty, you will need very little, if any.) If you are not serving the chowder within the hour, let it cool a bit, then refrigerate; cover the chowder *after* it has chilled completely. Otherwise, let it sit at room temperature for up to an hour, allowing the flavors to meld.

6. When ready to serve, reheat the chowder over low heat; don't let it boil. Ladle into cups or bowls, making sure that the oysters, potatoes, leeks, and bacon are evenly divided. Sprinkle with the chopped parsley and minced chives.

Makes about 9 cups; serves 8 as a first course or
5 or 6 as a main course

Digby Bay Scallop Chowder
with Cabbage and Bacon

Before we even get started talking about scallops, let's get the pronunciation straight: the *a* in *scallop* is pronounced so it sounds like *dollop,* not *gallop.*

In Nova Scotia, which is blessed with beautiful scallops, as well as lobsters and other seafood, scallops are often added to fish chowders as a bonus ingredient. I wanted to create a chowder just for scallops, celebrating their distinct, sweet flavor. Since winter is the best season for scallops—in some cases, the only season—I thought I would add a little cabbage, which is often the most dependable winter vegetable. The cabbage brought the chowder to life, leaving the flavor of the scallops intact, but also adding a new dimension. We all know wonderful bacon and scallops taste together, so I left all the bacon fat in the pot. My scallop chowder evolved into a hearty, comforting, deeply flavored chowder that is ideal for a cold winter night.

Bay scallop   Sea scallop

Cook's Notes

Scallops from New England and the Atlantic coast of Canada come in various sizes. Small but wonderful "Cape" scallops come from Cape Cod, Martha's Vineyard, and, most notably, Nantucket. A variation using these scallops follows the recipe. Bay scallops are medium-sized, perfect for chowder—those from Digby Bay in Nova Scotia are fabulous. (Do not buy the small "bay scallops" imported from China—they are not the same as bay scallops from the North Atlantic, and they make an inferior chowder.) Large sea scallops are found far offshore and need to be cut down in size for chowder. The term *diver scallop* has recently become popular, used to describe very large sea scallops—many of which are not really harvested by divers. The large sea scallops can be very good in chowder, but don't pay extra for them if bay scallops are available.

The most important consideration when buying scallops is the way they have been treated after being harvested—many scallops are soaked in water (sometimes with preservatives added), which improves their color but destroys their texture. Ask your fish market for "dry" scallops.

If you want to determine if you have real dry scallops, sauté a few in a hot pan: dry scallops will brown up nicely, "soaked" scallops will weep liquid, causing them to steam instead of sear.

Scallops have a small piece of meat attached to their sides, called the strap. Although it has flavor, it is tough. I always remove the strap from scallops and check them over, removing any fragments of shell at the same time.

Savoy cabbage is my first choice here, but you can substitute regular green cabbage, Chinese cabbage, escarole, or even kale. If you use kale, don't dice it—slice it very fine instead and add it during the last minute of cooking.

Serve this chowder as a main course with toasted common crackers or Pilot crackers. Warm Buttermilk Baking Powder Biscuits (page 210) or Cheddar Cheese Biscuits (page 212) are also nice accompaniments.

For equipment, you will need a 4- to 6-quart heavy pot with a lid, a wooden spoon, a slotted spoon, and a ladle.

4 ounces slab (unsliced) bacon, rind removed and cut into ⅓-inch dice

2 tablespoons unsalted butter

1 large onion (10 to 12 ounces), cut into ¾-inch dice

2 to 3 sprigs fresh thyme, leaves removed and chopped (1 teaspoon)

1 dried bay leaf

1½ pounds Yukon Gold, Maine, PEI, or other all-purpose potatoes, peeled and cut into ¾-inch dice

5 cups Traditional Fish Stock (page 60) or Chicken Stock (page 72), or either in combination with water to total 5 cups

8 ounces Savoy cabbage (½ small head or ¼ large head), cut into ¾-inch pieces

Kosher or sea salt and freshly ground black pepper

1½ pounds medium bay scallops, strap removed, or large sea scallops, cut into ¾-inch pieces and strap removed

1½ cups heavy cream (or up to 2 cups if desired)

For garnish
2 to 3 scallions, very thinly sliced

1. Heat a 4- to 6-quart heavy pot over low heat and add the bacon. Once it has rendered a few tablespoons of fat, increase the heat to medium and cook until the bacon is a crisp golden brown.

2. Add the butter, onions, thyme, and bay leaf and sauté, stirring occasionally with a wooden spoon, for about 8 minutes, until the onions are softened but not browned.

3. Add the potatoes and fish stock. The stock should just barely cover the potatoes—if it doesn't, add enough water to cover them. Turn up the heat and bring to a boil, cover the pot, and cook the potatoes vigorously for about 8 minutes. Add the diced cabbage, reduce the heat to medium, and simmer for 5 minutes more, or until the potatoes are soft on the outside but still firm in the center. Season with salt and pepper. If the broth hasn't thickened lightly, smash a few potatoes against the side of the pot and simmer for 1 to 2 minutes longer to release their starch. Remove the pot from the heat.

4. Stir in the scallops and let sit for 5 minutes. Add the cream and let sit for 10 minutes more while the scallops finish their slow cooking. Taste the chowder again and adjust the salt and pepper. If you are not serving the chowder within the hour, let it cool a bit, then refrigerate; cover the chowder *after* it has chilled completely. Otherwise, let it sit at room temperature for up to an hour, allowing the flavors to meld.

5. When ready to serve, reheat the chowder over low heat; don't let it boil. Use a slotted spoon to mound the scallops, potatoes, cabbage, and bacon in the center of large soup plates or shallow bowls, dividing them evenly, then ladle the creamy broth around. Sprinkle generously with the sliced scallions.

Makes about 12 cups; serves 6 to 8 as a main course

Variation: Nantucket Scallop Chowder

In winter only (November through February) the sweetest scallops in the world are harvested off Nantucket, Cape Cod, Martha's Vineyard, and nearby waters. These small scallops (½ to ¾ inch) are delicious raw (I like them with lime, wasabi, and pickled ginger), but they make a fine sweet chowder as well. Cut the onion, potatoes, and cabbage into ½-inch dice instead of larger and shorten the cooking times as necessary. Add the cream as soon as you remove the chowder from the heat and let the chowder sit for about 15 minutes, then add the scallops.

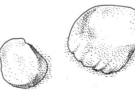

Lightly Curried Mussel Chowder

Mussels are not a typical chowder ingredient, but they should be. They are easy to cook, their texture holds up well, the broth they produce has a lovely enticing fragrance, and they are not expensive. Often, in fact, they're free for the gathering. In addition, mussels have an appealing flavor that goes well with many kinds of seasonings. What else could you ask for? Although you rarely see or hear of a recipe for, or even a mention of, mussel chowder, I'm sure that since necessity often determines the ingredients used in chowder making, mussel chowders do happen, or have happened at some time in the past. They just haven't had their fifteen minutes of fame yet.

This chowder is unrelated to the classic Parisian mussel soup called billi bi, but the use of saffron in billi bi inspired me to investigate how other bold flavors would intermingle with mussels. Adding curry powder to chowder dates back to the clipper ship days in New England, when spices were at the height of their popularity. In the mid-1800s, curry was very trendy and it was called for in several chowder recipes (early fusion cooking). I add a touch of fresh ginger, a few sweet potatoes, and cilantro to this chowder, all of which go superbly with curry. These ingredients may sound peculiar to veteran chowder makers, but the result is still very much a chowder.

Cook's Notes

This recipe calls for 5 pounds of cultivated mussels, which will yield a quart of broth and about a pound of mussel meat. If you use wild mussels, the yield will be a little less, so you may want to start with 6 pounds.

Although in many recipes, salt pork and bacon can be used interchangeably, the smoky flavor of the bacon doesn't work very well with curry. Stay with the salt pork if you can.

I like to serve this chowder as the start to a light meal, but it makes a fine main course as well. Accompany with toasted common crackers or Pilot crackers.

For equipment, you will need an 8-quart pot with a tight-fitting lid (for steaming open the mussels), a fine-mesh strainer, a 4- to 6-quart heavy pot with a lid (for the chowder), a slotted spoon, a wooden spoon, and a ladle.

5 pounds medium PEI mussels or other
    cultivated mussels (or 6 pounds wild)
4 ounces meaty salt pork, rind removed
    and cut into ⅓-inch dice
2 tablespoons unsalted butter
1 teaspoon finely chopped fresh ginger
    (pinky-tip-sized piece)
2 cloves garlic, finely chopped
    (2 teaspoons)
1 small red bell pepper (4 to 6 ounces), cut
    into ½-inch dice
1 medium onion (7 to 8 ounces) cut into
    ½-inch dice
1 tablespoon Madras curry powder

¼ teaspoon cayenne pepper
1 pound Yukon Gold, Maine, PEI, or other
    all-purpose potatoes, peeled and cut
    into ½-inch dice
1 pound small or medium sweet potatoes,
    peeled and cut into ½-inch dice
1½ cups heavy cream (or up to 2 cups if
    desired)
Kosher or sea salt and freshly ground
    black pepper

For garnish
2 tablespoons chopped fresh cilantro
3 scallions, thinly sliced

1. Clean and debeard the mussels. Steam them open following the instructions on page 66. Strain the broth; you should have 4 cups of broth (and 1 pound of mussel meat). Cover the shelled mussels and keep refrigerated until ready to use.

2. Heat a 4- to 6-quart heavy pot over low heat and add the diced salt pork. Once it has rendered a few tablespoons of fat, increase the heat to medium and cook until the salt pork is a crisp golden brown. Using a slotted spoon, transfer the cracklings to a small ovenproof dish, leaving the fat in the pot, and reserve until later.

3. Add the butter, ginger, garlic, bell pepper, onion, curry powder, and cayenne pepper to the pot and sauté, stirring occasionally with a wooden spoon, for about 10 minutes, until the pepper and onion are softened but not browned.

4. Add the white potatoes and the reserved mussel broth, turn up the heat, and bring to a boil. Cover and cook the potatoes vigorously for 5 minutes. Add the sweet potatoes. The broth should just barely cover the potatoes; if it doesn't, add enough water to cover. Lower the heat to medium, cover, and cook for 6 to 8 minutes longer, until the white and sweet potatoes are soft on the outside but still firm in the center. If the broth hasn't thickened lightly, smash a few potatoes and sweet potatoes against the side of the pot and cook a minute or two longer to release their starch.

5. Remove the pot from the heat and stir in the mussels and cream. Mussels are not as salty as clams, but you will still need to exercise a light hand as you season the chowder with salt. Add black pepper to taste. If you are not serving the chowder within the hour, let it cool a bit, then refrigerate; cover the chowder *after* it has chilled completely. Otherwise, let it sit at room temperature for up to an hour, allowing the flavors to meld.

6. When ready to serve, reheat the chowder over low heat; don't let it boil. Warm the cracklings in a low oven (200°F) for a few minutes.

7. Ladle the chowder into cups or bowls, making sure that the mussels, bell pepper, onion, and potatoes are evenly divided. Scatter the cracklings over the individual servings and sprinkle with the chopped cilantro and scallions.

Makes about 9 cups; serves 8 as a first course or
5 or 6 as a main course

How to Gather Mussels

Mussels are so easy to gather, I usually ask my young children to do it. I've never heard of a town or municipality that requires a permit for mussels (possibly because they are found on the rocks, not the beach), but you may want to check with the local authorities. Do check with your local Coast Guard about "red tide," an algae bloom that doesn't affect mussels, but is toxic to humans.

Mussels grow on rocks anywhere below the high-tide mark. Gather your mussels at low tide from as far out as you can go. Mussels that live submerged all the time are usually the plumpest. No special equipment is needed. Just bring along a bucket and, if your hands are sensitive or tender, wear a pair of gardening gloves. Pluck the biggest mussels from the clusters you find and try not to disrupt the smaller ones. Avoid mussels that live near the high-tide line, because they will have been exposed to long periods of sunshine, which may have had adverse effects on them.

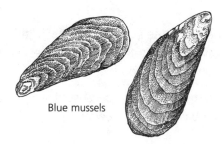

Blue mussels

Irish Shellfish Chowder

Ireland is a land of fantastic ingredients: great dairy products, poultry, lamb, pork, wild game, apples, berries, and vegetables, including the fluffiest potatoes on the planet. The seafood can be exquisite and the variety is extensive, which should hardly be a surprise when you consider that this beautiful green isle lies in the open Atlantic Ocean. This chowder features Dublin Bay prawns, which are famous for their tenderness and sweetness. It also contains cockles (a beautiful shellfish that is related to the clam) and mussels. This combination, of course, has been immortalized in the song about Molly Malone, who sang of "cockles and mussels, alive, alive-o." If you have ever had the chance to walk through the open-air food market on Moore Street in Dublin, you will be amazed at the beautiful seafood, but even more amazed at the women who sell it. They are very aggressive, but still charming, and like Molly Malone, they hawk their wares in a singsong style that they have developed into an art form.

With all the comings and goings between the British Isles and the United States, it was inevitable that North American–style chowder would find its way into the kitchens of Ireland and England. As early as 1763, a "Chouder" recipe was published in London, in Hannah Glasse's *Art of Cookery*. Darina Allen, Ireland's most famous TV chef and cooking teacher (and daughter-in-law of the famous chef Myrtle Allen of Ballymaloe), includes a chowder recipe in her wonderful book *Simply Delicious Fish* (1991). It includes a mixture of monkfish and shellfish. Since the style of her chowder is similar to many from the states and Canada, it is the native species of seafood that make it Irish. But if you're of Irish descent (as, you must have guessed, I am), then, even with a few substitutions, you can still call it Irish chowder!

Cockle

Cook's Notes

Shrimp or langostino can be substituted for the prawns in this recipe; very small littleneck clams or mahogany clams can be substituted for the cockles. Clams will produce a different flavor, but the chowder will still be very good.

Irish bacon can be substituted for slab, but because it is very lean, you will need to add 1 tablespoon of oil to get the bacon to start rendering.

This recipe, like all chowders, removes the meat from the various shellfish. However, if you would like a more elaborate presentation, keep some mussels and cockles whole in their shell, then reheat them separately using some of the liquid from the finished chowder. Garnish each bowl with the whole shellfish.

Serve this as a main course with toasted common crackers or Pilot crackers. Irish soda bread, especially a darker one made with whole wheat, would be supremely appropriate with this chowder. Otherwise, Buttermilk Baking Powder Biscuits (page 210) or Parker House Rolls (page 214) will make a fine accompaniment.

For equipment, you will need a 6- to 8-quart heavy pot with a lid (for steaming open the mussels and making the chowder), a fine-mesh strainer, a 2½- to 3-quart heavy saucepan with a lid (for steaming open the clams), a wooden spoon, and a ladle.

2½ pounds cultivated mussels (3 pounds wild)
3 dozen cockles or littleneck clams (about 3 pounds)
4 ounces slab (unsliced) bacon, cut into ⅓-inch dice
4 tablespoons unsalted butter
2 medium onions (14 ounces), cut into ½-inch dice
2 to 3 sprigs fresh thyme, leaves removed and chopped (1 teaspoon)
1 dried bay leaf
2 pounds Yukon Gold, Maine, PEI, or other all-purpose potatoes, peeled and cut into ½-inch dice

¼ teaspoon freshly grated nutmeg
1 pound prawns, langostino, or shrimp, peeled, deveined, and cut into bite-sized pieces
1½ cups heavy cream (or up to 2 cups if desired)
Kosher or sea salt and freshly ground black pepper

For garnish
2 tablespoons chopped fresh Italian parsley
2 tablespoons minced fresh chives

1. Clean and debeard the mussels. Steam them open following the instructions on page 66, using 1 cup water. Strain the broth; you should have 2 cups of broth (and about 8 ounces of mussel meat). Cover the shelled mussels and keep refrigerated until ready to use. Rinse out the pot and set aside.

2. Scrub the cockles (or clams). Put 1 cup water in a 2½- to 3-quart heavy saucepan and bring to a boil. Add the cockles and cover tightly. After 3 minutes, uncover and stir the cockles. Quickly cover the pan again, and let steam for 3 more minutes, or until most of the cockles have opened (clams will take 2 minutes longer than cockles). Don't wait for them all to open, or they will be overcooked. It should only take a little tug or prying to open the stragglers once they are removed from the heat. As soon as you remove the cockles from the stove, carefully pour as much of the broth as you can into a tall container. Let the broth sit for 10 minutes, then carefully pour through a fine-mesh strainer; you will have about 1½ cups of broth. Remove the meat from the cockles (you should have about 6 ounces), cover, and refrigerate until ready to use. You may want to save their beautiful shells to decorate your table; another option is to leave a few cockles and mussels in their shells and add them to the chowder when reheating for a beautiful presentation.

3. Heat the pot you used for the mussels over low heat and add the bacon. Once it has rendered a few tablespoons of fat, increase the heat to medium and cook until the bacon is a crisp golden brown. Pour off all but 1 tablespoon of the fat, leaving the bacon in the pot.

4. Add the butter, onions, thyme, and bay leaf and sauté, stirring occasionally with a wooden spoon, for about 10 minutes, until the onions are softened but not browned.

5. Add the potatoes and the reserved mussel broth and cockle broth. The broth should just barely cover the potatoes; if it doesn't, add enough water to cover. Turn up the heat and bring to a boil, cover the pot, and cook the potatoes vigorously for about 8 minutes, until they are soft on the outside but still firm in the center. If the broth hasn't thickened lightly, smash a few potatoes against the side of the pot and cook a minute or two longer to release their starch. Lower the heat to medium, add the nutmeg and prawns, and cook for 1 minute.

6. Remove the pot from the heat and stir in the cream, mussels, and cockles. Season to taste with salt and pepper. (Since the mussels and cockles are naturally salty, you will need very little salt.) If you are not serving the chowder within the hour, let it cool a bit, then refrigerate; cover the chowder *after* it has chilled completely. Otherwise, let it sit at room temperature for up to an hour, allowing the flavors to meld.

7. When ready to serve, reheat the chowder over low heat; don't let it boil. Ladle into shallow bowls or soup plates, making sure that the mussels, cockles, prawns, potatoes, onions, and bacon are evenly divided. Sprinkle with the chopped parsley and minced chives.

Makes about 11 cups; serves 6 to 8 as a main course

Azorean-Style Chowder with Mussels, Squid, Mackerel, and Salt Cod

The fish soups from the Portuguese islands of Madeira and the Azores bear such a striking resemblance to our chowders, with their combination of seafood, onions, and potatoes, that Jean Anderson used the word *chowder* to translate two different versions of fish *sopa* (soup) in her book *The Food of Portugal.* My South Coast Portuguese Fish Chowder (page 90) is a North American–style chowder with a strong Portuguese accent: a natural fusion of traditional New England cooking with that of the local Portuguese community. In this recipe, I took a different approach, creating a chowder inspired by the fish *sopas* of the Azores, where a combination of different types of fish and shellfish, often six or more, is the rule. I settled on four types of seafood: two shellfish and two fish. In the Portuguese tradition, I balance fatty fish (mackerel) with lean (salt cod). The broth is flavored with tomatoes, garlic, saffron, and a splash of vinegar—big flavors that harmonize naturally with the equally robust seafood.

Cook's Notes

You can make any or all of the following substitutions in this recipe: clams for the mussels, octopus or conch for the squid, bluefish or eels for the mackerel, and fresh cod or haddock for the salt cod. If you substitute fresh fish for the salt cod, add it at the same time you add the mackerel.

Salt cod was commonly used to make New England chowders in the days before rapid transportation and refrigeration. I have made chowder entirely with salt cod, but find it to be less satisfying than other salt cod dishes and not as good as a fresh cod chowder. In this recipe, however, the salt cod gives a nice kick to the chowder without being overwhelming or, even worse, uninspired. Boneless salt cod comes packed in 1-pound boxes, so you can use half a box for this recipe and store the rest for another time, or make Salt Cod Fritters (page 228) with the remaining ½ pound. You may also be able to buy it by the piece in some ethnic and specialty markets. Let the cod soak in cold water in the refrigerator for at least 8 hours, changing the water a minimum of four times.

The potatoes in this chowder are sliced thicker than in most of my other recipes to allow extra cooking time for the squid to become tender.

Saffron is common in fish soups, but not in chowder, where, in many cases, its flavor might be too dominant (remember, chowder is the sum of its parts). But it is terrific in this chowder; just don't add too much. It is difficult to measure whole strands of saffron, so I chop it a bit before measuring.

If you are not making salt cod fritters to accompany this main-course chowder, serve it with crusty Portuguese or Italian bread or Toasted Garlic Bread (page 209).

For equipment, you will need a 1- to 1½-quart saucepan (for cooking the salt cod), a slotted spoon, a 6- to 8-quart heavy pot with a tight-fitting lid (for steaming open the mussels and making the chowder), a fine-mesh strainer, a wooden spoon, and a ladle.

8 ounces boneless salt cod, soaked
2½ pounds cultivated mussels
    (or 3 pounds wild)
¼ cup olive oil
2 dried bay leaves
3 cloves garlic, finely chopped
    (1 tablespoon)
1 large onion (10 to 12 ounces), thinly
    sliced
½ teaspoon crushed red pepper flakes
1 pound cleaned medium squid, tentacles
    cut into 2 pieces and bodies cut into
    ½-inch-thick rings
1½ pounds Yukon Gold, Maine, PEI, or
    other all-purpose potatoes, peeled,
    quartered, and sliced ½ inch thick
3 cups water

1 cup dry white wine
1 small can (14.5 ounces) peeled whole
    tomatoes in juice, finely chopped
    (⅓ inch), with their juice
½ teaspoon coarsely chopped saffron
    threads
½ pound skinless mackerel fillets, pin-
    bones removed and cut into 1-inch
    pieces
2 tablespoons red wine vinegar
Freshly ground black pepper
Kosher or sea salt

For garnish
2 tablespoons coarsely chopped fresh
    Italian parsley

1. Place the soaked salt cod in a 1- to 1½-quart saucepan, cover with cold water, and bring to a slow simmer over low heat; do not let boil. Using a slotted spoon, remove the salt cod as soon as it has cooked through: you can test by prying it open with a fork—it should be creamy white inside with no translucence. Naturally, the thinner pieces will cook faster than the thicker pieces. After all the salt cod is cooked, break it into ½- to ¾-inch pieces; use a knife for the pieces that don't flake easily. Cover and keep refrigerated until ready to use.
2. Clean and debeard the mussels. Steam them open following the directions on page 66, using 1 cup water. Strain the broth; you should have 2 cups of broth (and about 8 ounces of mussel meat). Cover the shelled mussels and keep refrigerated until ready to use. Rinse out the pot.

3. Heat the pot you used for the mussels over medium heat and add the olive oil and bay leaves. After the bay leaves have begun to brown, add the garlic and cook for 30 seconds. Add the onions and red pepper flakes and sauté, stirring occasionally with a wooden spoon, for about 5 minutes. Add the squid and sauté until the onions are softened and the squid has become very firm.

4. Add the potatoes, the reserved mussel broth, and the water. Turn up the heat, bring to a boil, cover the pot, and cook the potatoes and squid vigorously for about 15 minutes, until the potatoes are soft on the outside but still firm in the center. Lower the heat to medium, add the white wine, tomatoes, and saffron and simmer for another 15 minutes.

5. Add the mackerel and cook for 5 minutes. Remove the pot from the heat and stir in the vinegar, mussels, and salt cod. Season with black pepper. (Do not season with salt yet. You need to give the salt cod a little time before you can tell how much salt it will add to the chowder.) If you are not serving the chowder within the hour, let it cool a bit, then refrigerate; cover the chowder *after* it has chilled completely. Otherwise, let it sit at room temperature for up to an hour, allowing the flavors to meld.

6. When ready to serve, reheat the chowder over low heat; don't let it boil. Taste the chowder and season with salt; most likely, it will need very little. Use a slotted spoon to mound the fish, squid, mussels, onions, and potatoes in the center of large soup plates or shallow bowls, and ladle the savory broth around. Finish each dish with a sprinkling of chopped parsley.

Makes about 12 cups; serves 6 to 8 as a main course

Bahamian Conch Chowder

This is a truly soulful bowl of chowder, with a deep flavor that is sweet from the conch, savory from the vegetables and herbs, and spicy from the hot sauce. It is a rich brown color with colorful specks of red, green, and white. In the Bahamas and throughout the Caribbean, the abundant conch is the food of the people. If you know how to dive, it is free for the taking; otherwise, it is modestly priced at market. Many locals believe that conch, also called *lambi* on some islands, makes you strong and can greatly enhance sexual performance, especially if eaten raw. I have traveled considerably in the Caribbean, for pleasure and business, and have eaten dozens of conch dishes, including several different kinds of chowder. This chowder is based on memories of ones I have tasted in the Bahamas, but similar versions can be found throughout the tropical islands. The variation that follows this recipe resembles the conch chowder I have had in restaurants in Key West and southern Florida, but it is quite likely that it could have originated in the Bahamas as well.

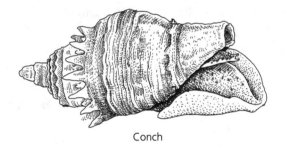

Conch

Cook's Notes

Conch can be very tough unless it is finely chopped or ground up and eaten raw (as in conch salad) or barely cooked (as in fritters). Another method for making conch tender is to pound it with a meat mallet and then simmer it in liquid for a long time, as in this recipe. Don't skimp on the pounding—you really can't beat it too much. It's OK if the pieces look a little ragged, conch lovers are used to it.

Conch can be found in large fish markets and ethnic markets. Most fish purveyors can obtain it with advance notice. You can also purchase conch through mail-order (see sources, page 233).

The potatoes are not boiled vigorously here, unlike most of my recipes, because they are not intended to thicken the chowder.

Serve this chowder as a starter or main course with common crackers or Pilot or other crackers, Skillet Corn Bread (page 219) or Corn Sticks (page 220), or Salt Cod Fritters (page 228).

For equipment, you will need a meat mallet, a 6- to 8-quart heavy pot, a ladle, a 10-inch skillet or sauté pan, and a wooden spoon.

2 pounds conch meat, trimmed of any viscera

4 cups Traditional Fish Stock (page 60), Chicken Stock (page 72), or water

6 cups water

1 dried bay leaf

2 to 3 sprigs fresh thyme, leaves removed and chopped (1 teaspoon)

1 teaspoon dried oregano

½ teaspoon ground cloves

Freshly ground black pepper

1 pound Yukon Gold, Maine, PEI, or other all-purpose potatoes, peeled and cut into ½-inch dice

1 can (28 ounces) peeled whole tomatoes in juice, finely chopped (⅓ inch), with their juice

4 ounces slab (unsliced) bacon, rind removed and cut into ⅓-inch dice

2 tablespoons vegetable oil

1 large onion (10 to 12 ounces), cut into ½-inch dice

1 medium carrot (3 to 4 ounces), cut into ⅓-inch dice

1 large green bell pepper (8 ounces), cut into ½-inch dice

2 stalks celery (4 ounces), cut into ⅓-inch dice

Juice of 1 lime

½ cup dark rum

Kosher or sea salt

Rum peppers (rum-based hot sauce) or other Caribbean hot sauce (see sources, page 233)

For garnish

4 scallions, thinly sliced

1. Slice the conch crosswise about ⅓ inch thick. With a meat mallet, pound the conch very thin. Cut the pounded conch roughly into ½- to ¾-inch squares.

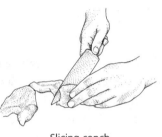

Slicing conch

Pounding conch

2. In a 6- to 8-quart heavy pot, combine the conch, fish stock, and water. Bring to a boil, skimming off the white foam as it appears on the surface. (Using a ladle and a circular motion, push the foam from the center to the sides of the pot, where it is easy to remove.) Lower the heat so the broth is at a slow simmer and add the bay leaf, thyme, oregano, and cloves. Grind some pepper into the pot and simmer, uncovered, for 20 minutes.

3. Add the potatoes and, once the broth has returned to a simmer, cook them for 10 to 12 minutes longer, until they are tender. Add the tomatoes with their juice and keep at a slow simmer.

4. While the conch and potatoes are simmering, heat a 10-inch skillet or sauté pan over low heat and add the bacon. Once it has rendered a few tablespoons of fat, increase the heat to medium and cook until the bacon is a crisp golden brown. Pour off all but 1 tablespoon of the fat, leaving the bacon in the pan. Add the oil, onion, carrot, bell pepper, and celery to the pan and sauté, stirring occasionally with a wooden spoon, for about 15 minutes, until the vegetables are tender.

5. Transfer the vegetables, with the fat they were cooked in, to the chowder pot. Simmer, uncovered, for another 30 minutes.

6. Remove the pot from the heat, add the lime juice and dark rum, and season with salt and more pepper to taste. Season the chowder lightly with hot sauce, then place the hot sauce on the table so each person can finish spicing it to his or her liking. If you are not serving the chowder within the hour, let it cool a bit, then refrigerate; cover the chowder *after* it has chilled completely. Otherwise, let it sit at room temperature for up to an hour, allowing the flavors to meld.

7. When ready to serve, reheat the chowder over low heat. Ladle into cups or bowls, making sure the conch, potatoes, and vegetables are evenly divided. Sprinkle with the chopped scallions.

Makes about 16 cups; serves 16 as a first course or
8 to 10 as a main course

Variation: Key West Conch Chowder

This variation of conch chowder is also outstanding—you may like it even better than the Bahamian version. It is thickened lightly with a brown roux (cooked flour and butter), which is also used for thickening Creole gumbos. I have not been able to find a historical connection, but it seems obvious that this fusion of Caribbean and Creole must be rooted in black culture.

fennel. But larger shrimp are just fine for chowder if you cut them into bite-sized pieces; actually, their texture is a little better than the smaller shrimp. Don't use any shrimp smaller than 40 count.

Serve this chowder in cups as a starter or in soup plates or shallow bowls as a main course with toasted common crackers or Pilot crackers. If you are serving it as a main course, a basket of warm Parker House Rolls (page 214) or Cheddar Cheese Biscuits (page 212) makes a terrific accompaniment. Toasted Garlic Bread (page 209) is nice with the white bean and tomato variation that follows.

For equipment, you will need a 10- to 12-inch high-sided skillet or sauté pan, a fine-mesh strainer, a 4- to 6-quart heavy pot with a lid, a wooden spoon, and a ladle; for the variation, you will also need a food mill or food processor.

1½ pounds small white shrimp (26 to 40 count)	**1 medium onion (8 ounces), thinly sliced**
1 small bulb fennel (8 ounces)	**¼ teaspoon fennel seeds, finely chopped**
3 tablespoons olive oil	**½ teaspoon crushed red pepper flakes (optional)**
5 cloves garlic, 2 crushed and 3 finely chopped (1 tablespoon)	**1½ pounds Yukon Gold, Maine, PEI, or other all-purpose potatoes, peeled, quartered, and sliced ¼ inch thick**
1 cup dry white wine	
4 cups water	**1 cup canned whole peeled tomatoes with their juice, finely chopped**
Kosher or sea salt	**1½ cups heavy cream**
4 ounces slab (unsliced) bacon, rind removed and cut into ⅓-inch dice	**Freshly ground black pepper**

1. Peel the shrimp, reserving the shells. (It is impractical to devein small shrimp, but if you are using larger ones, I recommend that you do.) Split the shrimp lengthwise in half down the back, cover, and refrigerate until needed.

2. Remove the fronds (lacy top) from the fennel, coarsely chop, and reserve for garnish, covered and refrigerated. Trim off the tops and tough outer layers of the fennel and coarsely chop, reserve for the stock. Quarter the fennel bulb lengthwise, cut away the core, and cut very thinly across into ¼- to ⅓-inch slices.

3. Add 2 tablespoons of the olive oil and the 2 crushed garlic cloves to a 10- to 12-inch high-sided skillet or sauté pan and heat over medium-high heat until the garlic begins to brown.

Add the shrimp shells and sauté for 5 minutes, or until the shells turn red and are very aromatic. Add the fennel trimmings, the wine, and water, bring to a simmer, and simmer for 20 minutes. Season lightly with salt. Strain the stock; you should have 3½ cups.

4. Heat a 4- to 6-quart heavy pot over low heat and add the bacon. Once it has rendered a few tablespoons of fat, increase the heat to medium and cook until the bacon is a crisp golden brown. Pour off all the fat except 1 tablespoon, leaving the bacon in the pot.

5. Add the remaining 1 tablespoon olive oil and the chopped garlic and cook for 30 seconds. Add the onion, sliced fennel, fennel seeds, and optional crushed red pepper and sauté, stirring occasionally with a wooden spoon, for about 10 minutes, until the onion and fennel are softened but not browned.

6. Add the potatoes and the reserved shrimp stock. The stock should just barely cover the potatoes; if it doesn't, add enough water to cover. Turn up the heat and bring to a boil. Cover the pot and cook the potatoes vigorously for about 8 minutes, until they are soft on the outside but still firm in the center. If the broth hasn't thickened lightly, smash a few potatoes against the side of the pot and cook a minute or two longer to release their starch.

7. Reduce the heat to medium, add the tomatoes, and simmer for 5 minutes more. Stir in the shrimp and cook for 1 minute, then remove the pot from the heat and stir in the cream. Let sit for 10 minutes while the shrimp finish their slow cooking. Taste the chowder and season with black pepper and more salt if needed. If you are not serving the chowder within the hour, let it cool a bit, then refrigerate; cover the chowder *after* it has chilled completely. Otherwise, let it sit at room temperature for up to an hour, allowing the flavors to meld.

8. When ready to serve, reheat the chowder over low heat; don't let it boil. Ladle into cups or bowls, making sure that the shrimp, fennel, potatoes, and bacon are evenly divided. Sprinkle with the reserved chopped fennel fronds.

Makes about 11 cups; serves 10 as a first course or
6 to 8 as a main course

Variation: Shrimp Chowder with White Beans and Tomatoes

Soak 8 ounces of jumbo lima beans, cannellini beans, or other large dried white beans overnight in cold water to cover generously. Drain the beans and cook in fresh unsalted water until very tender (cooking time will vary with the beans used). Pick out half of the best-looking beans and set aside; puree the remaining beans in a food mill or food processor. Prepare the chowder as instructed through Step 6, but reduce the quantity of potatoes to

8 ounces and simmer the potatoes until they are cooked through but still firm; do not mash any of the potatoes. Add the whole and pureed beans and, instead of the 1 cup finely chopped tomatoes, 2 cups diced (½ inch) tomatoes. Simmer for 5 minutes. Finish the recipe as instructed, but omit the cream.

San Francisco Crab "Meatball" Chowder

If you are looking for a chowder that is deeply flavored and hearty but not overly rich, this is it. It's perfect for a casual occasion, but the "meatballs" deliver an element of surprise, along the lines of an optical illusion, and make it really quite special.

The idea for this chowder came from an old San Francisco recipe for "Force Meatballs" in a cookbook called *Joe Tilden's Recipes for Epicures* (1907), reprinted in Richard Hooker's *Book of Chowders.* The "meatballs" were actually made from crabmeat, a fun idea that I knew had great potential. Tilden, a renowned Bay Area amateur cook, left only these instructions for his meatballs: "Serve in any fish chowder or soup." So I paired my version of his meatballs with a chowder that had flavors similar to cioppino, the famous San Francisco seafood stew flavored with garlic, onions, bell peppers, and tomatoes. I served it to my wife and kids, telling them only that it was "meatball chowder." The well-browned meatballs look like the real thing, so they were all a bit dumbfounded when they tasted them. My son, J.P., said, "Wow, they taste like crab cakes!" Everybody loved the chowder!

Cook's Notes

The chowder can be made up to 2 days in advance, but the crab meatballs should be made the day they are to be served. They are panfried at the last minute as the chowder is reheating.

In addition to the crab meatballs, this chowder contains two whole crabs. Steaming and cracking the crabs is a bit of work, but they add great flavor. If you use the full amount of crab stock called for in the recipe, you can omit the crabs and still have a great chowder, but do not omit them if you make the chowder with fish or chicken stock. Without any crab flavor in the chowder, the meatballs don't connect. Even with crab stock, I recommend the cracked crabs; they add character and rustic charm.

Serve this chowder as a main course with toasted common crackers or Pilot crackers, or with Toasted Garlic Bread (page 209). Crusty sourdough bread is another perfect complement.

For equipment, you will need a 6- to 8-quart pot with a tight-fitting lid (for steaming the crabs), a 4- to 6-quart heavy pot with a lid (for making the chowder), a wooden spoon, an 8- to 9-inch skillet or sauté pan, a slotted spoon, and a ladle.

For the crab "meatballs"

1 pound crabmeat, picked over for shells
   and cartilage
2 large eggs, lightly beaten
¼ cup milk
1 heaping teaspoon Coleman's dry English
   mustard
¼ teaspoon freshly ground black pepper
4 ounces oyster crackers, Pilot crackers, or
   other similar crackers, finely ground
   (about 1 cup)
Kosher or sea salt
Tabasco or other hot sauce
About 1 cup vegetable oil, for cooking
   the meatballs

For the chowder

2 medium blue or rock crabs
   (12 ounces each) or 1 Dungeness
   crab (1½ to 2 pounds)
4 ounces slab (unsliced) bacon, rind
   removed and cut into ⅓-inch dice

3 cloves garlic, finely chopped (1 tablespoon)
2 tablespoons unsalted butter
1 medium onion (8 ounces), cut into
   ¾-inch dice
1 medium green bell pepper (4 to
   6 ounces), cut into ½-inch dice
2 dried bay leaves
1 tablespoon Old Bay Seasoning
1½ pounds Yukon Gold, Maine, PEI, or
   other all-purpose potatoes, peeled and
   cut into ¾-inch dice
4 cups Crab Stock (page 69), Traditional
   Fish Stock (page 60), or Chicken Stock
   (page 72)
1 can (28 ounces) peeled whole tomatoes
   in juice, cut into ½-inch dice
Kosher or sea salt and freshly ground
   black pepper

For garnish

¼ cup coarsely chopped fresh Italian
   parsley

1. To make the meatballs, place the crabmeat in a mixing bowl and shred with a fork. Add the eggs, milk, dry mustard, pepper, and cracker crumbs. Mix well. Season with salt and hot sauce to taste. Moisten your hands and roll the mixture into balls that are about ¾ to 1 inch in diameter (about ½ ounce each); keep your hands slightly wet so the balls are very smooth. Place on a cookie sheet. You should have about 36 balls. Cover and refrigerate while you prepare the chowder.

2. To cook the crabs, fill a 6- to 8-quart pot with ½ inch ocean water or tap water with enough salt added to make it very salty. Bring to a boil, place the crab(s) top shell (carapace) down in the pot, cover, and steam for about 12 minutes for smaller crabs, about 20 minutes for a Dungeness crab. Remove and allow to cool at room temperature.

3. When cool enough to handle, remove the crab legs, break into sections, and neatly crack the large pieces. Pick the meat from the small pieces and reserve. Remove the apron (tail flap) from the bottom of each crab and discard. Remove the top shell, scoop the green stuff (tomalley) out of it, and reserve; discard the shell. Remove the gills from the body and discard. Cut the body into quarters and trim away any extraneous shell or cartilage. Refrigerate all the crabmeat, crab pieces, and tomalley until ready to use.

4. Heat a 4- to 6-quart heavy pot over low heat and add the bacon. Once it has rendered a few tablespoons of fat, increase the heat to medium and cook until the bacon is a crisp golden brown. Pour off all but 1 tablespoon of the fat, leaving the bacon in the pot.

5. Add the garlic and cook for 30 seconds. Add the butter, onion, bell pepper, bay leaves, and the Old Bay Seasoning and cook, stirring occasionally with a wooden spoon, for about 10 minutes, until the onion and pepper are softened but not browned.

6. Add the potatoes and crab stock, turn up the heat, and bring to a boil. Cover the pot and cook the potatoes vigorously for about 10 minutes, until they are soft on the outside but still firm in the center. If the broth hasn't thickened lightly, smash a few potatoes against the side of the pot and cook a minute or two longer to release their starch.

7. Lower the heat to medium, add the tomatoes, and bring back to a simmer. Season with salt and pepper. Remove the pot from the heat and stir in the cracked crab legs, picked leg meat, tomalley, and body sections. If you are not serving the chowder within the hour, let it cool a bit, then refrigerate; cover the chowder *after* it has chilled completely. Otherwise, let it sit at room temperature for up to an hour, allowing the flavors to meld.

8. When ready to serve, reheat the chowder over low heat. While it is reheating, place an 8- or 9-inch skillet or sauté pan over medium-high heat, add about ½ inch vegetable oil, and heat to about 350°F. Carefully but quickly add 8 to 10 meatballs to the hot oil and panfry, turning them as needed, until they are a rich brown color on all sides, so they resemble real meatballs. Using a slotted spoon, remove the meatballs, letting the excess oil drain back into the pan, then place on paper towels to drain. Repeat with the remaining meatballs.

9. Ladle the chowder into shallow bowls or large soup plates, making sure that the crab, onions, peppers, tomatoes, and potatoes are evenly divided. Place 4 meatballs in each bowl and sprinkle generously with the chopped parsley. Serve the remaining meatballs on a plate or platter; your guests can add more, if desired.

Makes about 12 cups; serves 6 to 8 as a main course

Chesapeake Crab Chowder

Down in the Chesapeake Bay area, where blue crabs are king, crab chowder is popular, but it has to compete with many other brothy preparations like crab gumbo, crab chili, she-crab soup, cream of crab soup, and old-fashioned country crab soup (almost a chowder), just to name a few. If there is a common style to these Chesapeake soup-like crab dishes, it would be the use of a great variety of vegetables and other ingredients, a reflection of the abundance of this fertile region. Although this is my recipe and it is not truly authentic, it is inspired by the cooking of the Chesapeake Bay.

I noticed that many of the recipes in John Shields's *Chesapeake Bay Crab Cookbook* call for discarding the salt pork cracklings after they have rendered—I don't understand that, though, so I don't do it. But if you want to cook a real authentic Norfolk, Virginia, crab chowder, discard the pork cracklings and add a small dice of Smithfield ham. I love the powerful aroma of crabs, and it's a good thing, because a pot of crab chowder fills your house with its enticing smell. And it tastes as good as its aroma promises.

Cook's Notes

In New England, blue crabs are found south of Cape Cod and rock crabs are found north of the Cape. Rock crabs are a by-product of lobstering and therefore are more readily available than blue crabs in New England. Rock crab meat is sold as Maine crab; blue crab meat is usually sold as backfin, lump, or claw. If you have a choice, the sweet red claw meat is best for chowder. On the West Coast, the leg and claw meat from Dungeness crab is best for chowder. But you can use virtually any type of crab to make this chowder, the first choice being whatever is freshest. If you opt to buy crabmeat, which is much easier than cooking and picking your own crabs, you will still need to buy a couple of crabs to make a stock. Some seafood markets sell "soup" crabs, which are too small for steaming but add great flavor to soups and stocks.

Serve this chowder in cups as a starter or in soup plates or shallow bowls as a main course, with toasted common crackers or Pilot crackers. Beaten biscuits, a sophisticated and excellent cracker from the mid-Atlantic region, would also be appropriate with this chowder. If you are serving this as a main course, a basket of Skillet Corn Bread (page 219) or Corn Sticks (page 220) makes a terrific accompaniment.

For equipment, you will need a 6- to 8-quart pot with a tight-fitting lid (for steaming the crabs), a fine-mesh strainer, a 4- to 6-quart heavy pot with a lid (for making the chowder), a slotted spoon, a wooden spoon, and a ladle.

1 pound fresh crabmeat plus 2 pounds
   whole crabs, or about 5 pounds live
   crabs, steamed and meat picked (see
   Steps 2 and 3, pages 165 and 166; save
   the shells for stock)
1 pound plum tomatoes
4 ounces meaty salt pork, rind removed
   and cut into ⅓-inch dice
2 tablespoons unsalted butter
1 medium onion (8 ounces), cut into
   ½-inch dice
2 stalks celery (4 ounces), cut into ½-inch
   dice
4 sprigs fresh thyme, leaves removed and
   chopped (2 teaspoons)

1 tablespoon Old Bay Seasoning
2 pounds Yukon Gold, Maine, PEI, or other
   all-purpose potatoes, peeled and cut
   into ½-inch dice
2 teaspoons cornstarch, dissolved in
   2 tablespoons water
2 cups heavy cream
Kosher or sea salt and freshly ground
   black pepper
Tabasco or other hot sauce (optional)

For garnish
4 scallions, very thinly sliced

1. Whether you purchased the crabmeat or picked it yourself, you should double-check it for fragments of shell and cartilage; cover and refrigerate. Using the whole crabs or the reserved crab shells, make a crab stock following the instructions on page 70; allow about 1½ hours for the cooking. Strain the stock; you should have 4 cups of stock.

2. To peel the tomatoes, score an X in the bottom of each one, then drop into a pot of boiling water for about 30 seconds, until the skins loosen. Cool in ice water, drain, and pull off the skin. Quarter the tomatoes and cut out the juicy centers, reserving them for another use. Cut the tomato flesh into ½-inch dice; you should have about 1½ cups.

3. Heat a 4- to 6-quart heavy pot over low heat and add the diced salt pork. Once it has rendered a few tablespoons of fat, increase the heat to medium and cook until the pork is crisp and golden brown. With a slotted spoon, transfer the cracklings to a small ovenproof dish, leaving the fat in the pot, and reserve until later.

4. Add the butter, onion, celery, and thyme to the pot and sauté, stirring occasionally with a wooden spoon, for about 10 minutes, until the onion and celery are softened but not browned. Add the Old Bay Seasoning and cook for 1 minute longer, stirring frequently.

5. Add the potatoes and the reserved crab stock. The stock should just barely cover the potatoes; if it doesn't, add enough water to cover. Turn up the heat and bring to a boil. Cover the pot and cook the potatoes vigorously for about 8 minutes, until they are soft on the outside but still firm in the center.

6. Stir the cornstarch mixture, add it to the chowder, stirring constantly, and cook, stirring, until the chowder lightly thickens and returns to a simmer. Add the tomatoes and simmer for 5 minutes more.

7. Remove the pot from the heat, stir in the crabmeat and cream, and season to taste with salt and pepper and the optional hot sauce. If you are not serving the chowder within the hour, let it cool a bit, then refrigerate; cover the chowder *after* it has chilled completely. Otherwise, let it sit at room temperature for up to an hour, allowing the flavors to meld.

8. When ready to serve, reheat the chowder over low heat; don't let it boil. Warm the cracklings in a low oven (200°F) for a few minutes.

9. Ladle the chowder into cups, large soup plates, or shallow bowls, making sure that the crab, onions, potatoes, and tomatoes are evenly divided. Scatter the cracklings over the individual servings and sprinkle with the sliced scallions.

```
Makes about 12 cups; serves 12 as a first course or
6 to 8 as a main course
```

Variation: Crab and Corn Chowder

Before you make the crab stock, husk 3 ears of yellow or bicolor sweet corn. Carefully remove most of the silk by hand and then rub each ear with a dry towel to finish the job. Cut the kernels from the cobs and reserve. You should have about 2 cups. Break the cobs in half and add them to the stock. Add the corn kernels to the chowder at the same time you add the potatoes and continue with the recipe as instructed.

Variation: Crab Chowder with Cheddar Cheese

Either Chesapeake Crab Chowder or Crab and Corn Chowder can be finished with the rich addition of grated cheddar cheese. The cheese is only added when you reheat the chowder, and the chowder doesn't reheat well a second time; the "formula" is to add about 1/4 cup grated white Cheddar to every 2 cups chowder (or a total of 6 ounces to the whole batch). Stir the cheese in toward the end of reheating and be careful not to boil the chowder.

Lobster and Corn Chowder

Lobster and Corn Chowder is the first chowder recipe I ever wrote. I have been making this chowder for nearly twenty years—it has been a signature dish of mine since I opened the Bostonian Hotel in 1981. Over the years, it has been featured on magazine covers and in many other periodicals, and I included it in my book *Lobster at Home.* As I said there, I think the enormous appeal of this chowder lies in the fact that "for locals and visitors alike, it epitomizes summer in New England, when, up and down the coast, summer lobsters and sweet corn are abundant. It is not chowder. It is a Martha's Vineyard, Boothbay Harbor, Point Judith, Gloucester, and Block Island vacation in a bowl."

Cook's Notes

Lobsters for chowder are only partially cooked because the lobster meat finishes cooking in the chowder, resulting in perfectly cooked meat. Removing the meat from partially cooked lobster is almost the same procedure as for fully cooked, but the claws might be more difficult to remove.

This chowder can be made with soft-shell summer lobsters, but because the yield of meat per pound is less than for hard-shell lobsters, you may wish to use 1 more lobster. You can purchase any size lobster for this recipe as long as the total weight is about 4 pounds.

For more information on the types of corn that are best for chowder, see Corn, page 45.

Serve this chowder as a main course with toasted common crackers or Pilot crackers. For a special treat, serve it with Sweet Corn Fritters (page 222) or Corn Sticks (page 220).

For equipment, you will need an 8- to 10-quart pot (for parboiling the lobsters and making the lobster stock), a pair of long tongs, a fine-mesh strainer, a 4- to 6-quart heavy pot with a lid (for the chowder), a wooden spoon, a slotted spoon, and a ladle.

3 live hard-shell lobsters (1¼ pounds each)
3 medium ears yellow or bicolor corn
4 ounces slab (unsliced) bacon, rind removed and cut into ⅓-inch dice
4 tablespoons unsalted butter

1 large onion (10 ounces), cut into ¾-inch dice
2 to 3 sprigs fresh thyme, leaves removed and chopped (1 teaspoon)
2 teaspoons Hungarian paprika

1½ pounds Yukon Gold, Maine, PEI, or other all-purpose potatoes, peeled and cut into ¾-inch dice

1½ cups heavy cream (or up to 2 cups if desired)

Kosher or sea salt and freshly ground black pepper

For garnish

2 tablespoons chopped fresh Italian parsley

2 tablespoons minced fresh chives

1. Fill an 8- to 10-quart stockpot two-thirds full with ocean water or tap water that is heavily salted. Bring to a rolling boil. One at a time, holding each lobster by the carapace (the protective shell), carefully drop it into the water. Cook for exactly 4 minutes from the time the last lobster went in. Using a pair of long tongs, remove the lobsters from the pot and let them cool to room temperature.

2. Pick all the meat from the tails, knuckles, and claws. Remove the intestinal tract from the tail and the cartilage from the claws. Dice the meat into ¾-inch cubes. Cover and refrigerate until ready to use. (For more on preparing lobsters, see *Lobster at Home.*) Using the carcasses (bodies) and leftover shells, make a lobster stock, following the instructions on page 68; the stock will take about 1½ hours to cook. Strain the stock; you should have 4 cups.

3. Meanwhile, husk the corn. Carefully remove most of the silk by hand and then rub each ear with a dry towel to finish the job. Cut the kernels from the cobs and reserve. You should get about 2 cups. Break the cobs in half and add them to the simmering stock.

4. Heat a 4- to 6-quart heavy pot over low heat and add the bacon. Once it has rendered a few tablespoons of fat, increase the heat to medium and cook until the bacon is a crisp golden brown. Pour off all but 1 tablespoon of the fat, leaving the bacon in the pot.

5. Add the butter, onion, and thyme and sauté, stirring occasionally with a wooden spoon, for about 8 minutes, until the onion is softened but not browned. Add the paprika and cook 1 minute longer, stirring frequently.

6. Add the potatoes, corn kernels, and the reserved lobster stock. The stock should just barely cover the potatoes; if it doesn't, add enough water to cover. Turn up the heat and bring to a boil. Cover the pot and cook the potatoes vigorously for about 12 minutes, until they are soft on the outside but still firm in the center. If the broth hasn't thickened lightly, smash a few potatoes against the side of the pot and cook a minute or two longer to release their starch.

7. Remove the pot from the heat, stir in the lobster meat and cream, and season to taste with salt and pepper. If you are not serving the chowder within the hour, let it cool a bit, then refrigerate; cover the chowder *after* it has chilled completely. Otherwise, let it sit at room temperature for up to an hour, allowing the flavors to meld.

8. When ready to serve, reheat the chowder over low heat; don't let it boil. Use a slotted spoon to mound the lobster, onions, potatoes, and corn in the center of large soup plates or shallow bowls, making sure they are evenly divided, and ladle the creamy broth around. Sprinkle with the chopped parsley and minced chives.

Makes about 10 cups; serves 10 as a first course or
5 or 6 as a main course

Variation: New England–Style Lobster Chowder

For the few winter months when sweet corn is not available, make this recipe omitting the corn (and the cobs in the stock). Winter lobsters can be quite expensive, so chowder, which only uses half a small lobster per portion, is an economical way to serve them during that season.

Variation: Lobster and Cape Scallop Chowder

This variation is also for winter, when Cape scallops (small, sweet native New England scallops) are in season. Cape scallops are named for Cape Cod, but the most famous of this type of scallops comes from Nantucket. Omit the corn and use 8 ounces Cape scallops. Remove the small piece of strap from the side of each scallop and pick out any shell fragments. After you remove the chowder from the heat, add the scallops along with the lobster meat.

Chapter 7

Farmhouse Chowders

A chowder represents the special preparation
of some very ordinary ingredients, while a stew represents an
ordinary preparation of some very special ingredients.
—John Thorne, DOWN EAST CHOWDER

Farmhouse chowders, chowders without seafood, are also true chowders. And like seafood chowders, most of them are made with salt pork or bacon, onions, and potatoes. Using the same techniques as seafood chowders, cooks developed farmhouse chowders to accommodate the foods that were available to them: corn, parsnips, shell beans, eggs, poultry, game birds and veal.

All chowders were born of necessity. They were invented by humble working people, who made them with local, inexpensive ingredients from the sea or the land. My modern interpretations of old-fashioned farmhouse chowders maintain their unpretentious spirit. Nantucket Veal Chowder (page 190) and Pheasant and Cabbage Chowder (page 201) can be made with modest cuts like veal shoulder and pheasant thighs. Leftover turkey (Leftover Turkey Chowder with Sage, page 197), as well as stewing hens (Stewing Chicken Chowder, page 195), are transformed into a special treat that costs pennies per portion. Commonly available seasonal vegetables like sweet corn, parsnips, shell beans, new potatoes, and various mushrooms are celebrated as the main ingredient in their own chowders. Fun and easy to prepare, farmhouse chowders exemplify the true nature of chowder making—creating a special dish with local, everyday ingredients.

The first recipes for farmhouse chowders were printed in an 1874 cookbook, *Nantucket Receipts,* which includes directions for making chicken and veal chowders. Mary Lincoln's 1884 *Boston Cook Book* contains the first-known published recipe for corn chowder. Unlike today, when many of the hundreds of cookbooks published each year report (or even create) the very latest trends, cookbooks from the 1800s usually documented dishes that were fairly well established. No doubt farm cooks, who were familiar with chowder making, had adapted the techniques to farmland ingredients generations before the first recipes for farmhouse chowders were published. In any event, by the end of the nineteenth century, recipes for all sorts of farmhouse chowders, especially corn chowder, were being published in cookbooks and periodicals all across the country.

At first it struck me as strange that the islands of Nantucket and Martha's Vineyard were as well known for chicken and veal chowders as for their seafood chowders. It would be easier to imagine that all farmhouse chowders originated inland, where fresh seafood was unavailable, and indeed a few did. But I have to speculate that chowder was not merely another sea dish in the island cooks' repertoire—it was a method for cooking many types of food, including those from the many farms that blanketed the islands. Egg Chowder with Bacon and New Potatoes (page 188) and Spring-Dug Parsnip Chowder (page 178) can be traced to Vermont and western Massachusetts, respectively. But turkey chowder and pheasant chowder originated in my refrigerator, where necessity, along with some imagination, provided the recipes.

The first five chowders in this chapter, featuring corn, parsnips, cranberry beans, mushrooms, and potatoes, are best served as starters. These vegetable chowders are very tasty, but if you serve more than a cup of one of them, you may change what can be experienced as a special treat into too much of a good everyday thing. Corn chowder, though, may be the exception—some people just can't get enough! Since I think these chowders should be served the way you would a soup, as a starter or a separate course, the yields are smaller than most in this book, about 7 to 8 cups. They can be easily doubled if you wish.

The next five chowders, which feature such proteins as egg, veal, chicken, turkey, and pheasant as the main ingredient, are best presented as main courses. Despite the fact that I serve them as an entrée, though, the egg chowder and veal chowder recipes make only 8 to 9 cups. I thought that cooks unaccustomed to making these novel chowders would like to begin with a smaller batch; you can always double the recipe if you want. The three poultry chowders yield big batches, about 12 cups. Essentially, the size of the whole birds determined the yield. Stewing Chicken Chowder, a variation of Farmer's Chicken Chowder, is an extreme example—it is not possible to make less than 6 quarts of chowder using a whole stewing chicken!

Each of the chowders in this chapter is unique. The flavors vary immensely from one recipe to the next, but each one is delicious. From the pastel yellow corn chowder and the rich brown cranberry bean chowder, to the pale chicken and turkey chowders, this collection of farmhouse chowders demonstrates how you can transform an everyday food into a special dish for family and friends.

Corn Chowder

Corn chowder is the king of farmhouse chowders. Hundreds of recipes for it have been published over the years, but since corn and salt pork were staples of the American farm, it is likely that corn chowder was being made and enjoyed long before any recipe was ever printed. The oldest recipe I have come across is by Mary Lincoln, founder of the famous Boston Cooking School, in her *Boston Cook Book* (1884). Fannie Merritt Farmer, her successor, also published a corn chowder recipe in the original *Boston Cooking School Cookbook* (1896). A crop of corn chowder recipes followed Mary Lincoln's, appearing in cookbooks from Philadelphia to Los Angeles and just about everywhere in between. Some were thickened with flour, others with egg yolks. Some, like Fannie Farmer's, used canned corn (which has been around since the mid-1800s), some used fresh corn. The use of milk, cream, or condensed milk also varies from recipe to recipe. The Shakers, members of the well-known utopian community, are renowned today for their austere yet beautiful furniture, but they were also highly regarded for their cooking skills, especially their farmhouse chowders. My version of corn chowder is made similar to the Shaker style, according to a recipe from the Shakers at Hancock Village in Pittsfield, Massachusetts (1900), using fresh corn, butter, and cream. Its mellow, sweet flavor and lovely pale golden color are very comforting, and it is a big favorite with children as well as adults.

Cook's Notes

Since corn is the heart and soul of this dish, the success of your chowder will rely a great deal on the quality of the corn you use. (For more information on the types of corn that are best for chowder, see Corn, page 45.)

If you are making chicken stock or broth especially for this recipe, add the corn cobs (do not scrape them in this case) to that stock for more corn flavor.

Although potatoes help to thicken this chowder, I also use a bit of cornstarch to give it an extra smooth and creamy consistency. Mix the cornstarch and water to create a smooth paste, called a slurry, before you add it to the chowder.

The ground cumin adds an interesting but subtle contrast to the predominant corn flavor of this chowder. In the Southwestern-style corn chowder variation that follows, the amount of cumin is doubled, letting it stand out even more. The small amount of turmeric brightens the chowder's color, making it a little more yellow.

Serve corn chowder as a starter, with toasted common crackers or Pilot crackers. Or serve with Sweet Corn Fritters (page 222), Skillet Corn Bread (page 219) or Corn Sticks (page 220), or Anadama Bread (page 217) on the side to add a delicious contrasting corn flavor to your meal.

For equipment, you will need a 3- to 4-quart heavy pot with a lid, a wooden spoon, and a ladle.

3 medium ears fresh yellow or bicolor corn

4 ounces slab (unsliced) bacon, rind removed and cut into ⅓-inch dice

2 tablespoons unsalted butter

1 medium onion (7 to 8 ounces), cut into ½-inch dice

½ large red bell pepper (6 to 8 ounces), cut into ½-inch dice

1 to 2 sprigs fresh thyme, leaves removed and chopped (½ teaspoon)

½ teaspoon ground cumin

⅛ teaspoon turmeric

1 pound Yukon Gold, Maine, PEI, or other all-purpose potatoes, peeled and cut into ½-inch dice

3 cups Chicken Stock (page 72) or Chicken Broth (page 74)

Kosher or sea salt and freshly ground black pepper

2 teaspoons cornstarch, dissolved in 2 tablespoons water

1 cup heavy cream

For garnish

2 tablespoons minced fresh chives or thinly sliced scallions

1. Husk the corn. Carefully remove most of the silk by hand and then rub the ears with a towel to finish the job. Cut the kernels from the cobs and place in a bowl. You should have about 2 cups. Using the back of your knife, scrape down the cobs and add the milky substance that oozes out to the corn kernels.

2. Heat a 3- to 4-quart heavy pot over low heat and add the diced bacon. Once it has rendered a few tablespoons of fat, increase the heat to medium and cook until the bacon is crisp and golden brown. Pour off all but 1 tablespoon of the bacon fat, leaving the bacon in the pot.

3. Add the butter, onion, bell pepper, thyme, cumin, and turmeric and sauté, stirring occasionally with a wooden spoon, for about 8 minutes, until the onion and pepper are tender but not browned.

4. Add the corn kernels, potatoes, and stock, turn up the heat, cover, and boil vigorously for about 10 minutes. Some of the potatoes will have broken up, but most should retain their shape. Use the back of your spoon to smash a bit of the corn and potatoes against the side of the pot. Reduce the heat to medium and season the chowder with salt and pepper.

5. Stir the cornstarch mixture and slowly pour it into the pot, stirring constantly. As soon as the chowder has come back to a boil and thickened slightly, remove from the heat and stir in the cream. Adjust the seasoning if necessary. If you are not serving the chowder within the hour, let it cool a bit, then refrigerate; cover the chowder *after* it has chilled completely. Otherwise, let it sit at room temperature for up to an hour, allowing the flavors to meld.

6. When ready to serve, reheat the chowder over low heat; don't let it boil. Ladle into cups or bowls and sprinkle with the chopped chives.

Makes about 7 cups; serves 6 as a first course

Variation: Corn Chowder with Tomato and Basil

Peel ½ pound ripe red tomatoes: Score an X in the bottom of each tomato. Drop into a pot of boiling water for about 30 seconds, until the skins loosen. Cool the tomatoes in ice water, drain, and pull off the skin. Quarter the tomatoes and cut out their juicy centers, reserving them for another use. Cut the tomato flesh into ½-inch dice; you should have about ¾ cup. Add the tomatoes to the chowder right after you add the cornstarch (Step 5). When you remove the chowder from the heat, stir in 2 tablespoons of chopped fresh basil along with the cream.

Variation: Southwestern-Style Corn Chowder

Increase the cumin to 1 teaspoon. Just before you add the cornstarch (Step 5), add 1 small poblano chile, roasted, peeled, seeds removed, and cut into small to medium dice. After you add the cream, stir in 2 or more tablespoons chopped fresh cilantro.

Variation: Corn Chowder with Sweet Potatoes

To make this delectable sweet chowder, substitute 1 pound sweet potatoes, cut into ½-inch dice, for the white potatoes. Sweet potatoes cook a little faster than all-purpose potatoes, so reduce the cooking time to about 8 minutes, then proceed with the recipe as instructed.

Spring-Dug Parsnip Chowder

In New England, the parsnip is held in high esteem, which may surprise Midwesterners, who, so I've heard, sometimes grow parsnips for the sole purpose of fattening pigs. Well, pigs are smart—they love truffles too! Connoisseurs of this humble root know that the tastiest parsnips are "spring dugs," parsnips that are left in the ground through the winter, then dug up as soon as the ground thaws. They are sugary sweet with an earthy flavor that has hints of mace, cinnamon, celery seed, and clove. Westfield, Massachusetts, is to parsnips what Castroville, California, is to artichokes (i.e., America's capital) and Dick Fowler is the premier parsnip farmer in Westfield. He leaves a good portion of his crop in the ground each winter for an early spring harvest, so if you ever see Fowler's Parsnips in your market during spring, you can be sure you are getting authentic New England spring-dug parsnips. In addition to their wonderful taste, parsnips cook into a smooth, creamy texture that makes this chowder velvety and luscious with an off-white color that has a glimmer of yellow.

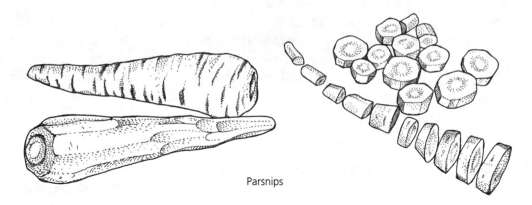

Parsnips

Cook's Notes

Because of their natural spiciness, I avoid combining parsnips with any spice or herb other than pepper and parsley. For the same reason, I use salt pork instead of smoky bacon in this chowder, letting the parsnip do most of the flavoring.

Because parsnips taper from a very fat top to a skinny bottom, you have to slice them thin at the top and thick at the bottom in order for them to cook evenly.

Serve parsnip chowder as a starter with toasted common crackers or Pilot crackers.

For equipment, you will need a 3- to 4-quart heavy pot, a slotted spoon, a wooden spoon, a food mill or food processor, and a ladle.

3 ounces meaty salt pork, rind removed
and cut into ⅓-inch dice
2 tablespoons unsalted butter
1 large onion (10 ounces) cut into
¾-inch dice
1 pound parsnips, peeled and sliced
into rounds (thin—about ⅓ inch—
toward the top and thicker toward
the bottom)
1 pound Yukon Gold, Maine, PEI, or other
all-purpose potatoes, peeled and cut
into ¾-inch dice

3 cups Chicken Stock (page 72) or
Chicken Broth (page 74)
1½ cups heavy cream
Kosher or sea salt and freshly ground
black pepper

For garnish
2 tablespoons chopped fresh Italian
parsley

1. Heat a 3- to 4-quart heavy pot over low heat and add the diced salt pork. Once it has rendered a few tablespoons of fat, increase the heat to medium and cook until the pork is crisp and golden brown. With a slotted spoon, transfer the cracklings to a small ovenproof dish, leaving the fat in the pot, and reserve until later.

2. Add the butter and onion to the pot and sauté, stirring occasionally with a wooden spoon, for 6 to 8 minutes, until the onion is tender but not browned.

3. Add the parsnips, potatoes, and stock, turn up the heat, bring to a boil, and cook vigorously for about 12 minutes. Reduce the heat to low.

4. Remove 2 cups of the chowder from the pot and puree in a food mill held over the pot so it falls directly back into the chowder, or puree in a food processor, then return it to the chowder. Let the chowder simmer slowly for another 5 minutes; the broth should look silky-smooth. Remove from the heat, stir in the cream, and season with salt and pepper. If you are not serving the chowder within the hour, let it cool a bit, then refrigerate; cover the chowder *after* it has chilled completely. Otherwise, let it sit at room temperature for up to an hour, allowing the flavors to meld.

5. When ready to serve, reheat the chowder over low heat; don't let it boil. Warm the cracklings in a low oven (200°F) for a few minutes.

6. Ladle the chowder into cups and scatter the cracklings over the individual servings. Sprinkle with the chopped parsley.

Makes about 8 cups; serves 8 as a first course

Shaker Fresh Cranberry Bean Chowder

"Take the ordinary and make it extraordinary." Those are the words of Eldress Bertha Hudson, who, along with Sister Ethel Hudson, owned and supervised the Creamery, a restaurant at the Shaker Village in Canterbury, New Hampshire, until the early 1990s. Eldress Bertha and Sister Ethel were the last two living Shakers, and with their passing, a marvelous history of more than two hundred years of excellence in the fields of business, philanthropy, invention, furniture making, music, horticulture, herbal medicine, and cooking came to a close. Jeffrey Paige, my friend and a talented chef, worked with the sisters during the last years of their lives, and he documented his experience in his cookbook *The Shaker Kitchen.* According to Jeffrey, the Shakers grew cranberry beans "in quantity" because they could be eaten fresh in the summer and dried for the rest of the year. This chowder, inspired by the Shakers, is made with fresh beans (a variation using dried beans follows this recipe). This simple chowder has a rich brown color that is accented by the deep red of ripe summer tomatoes. The flavor is intense, smoky and savory, with subtle notes of sweet and sour from the molasses and tomatoes: the ordinary made extraordinary.

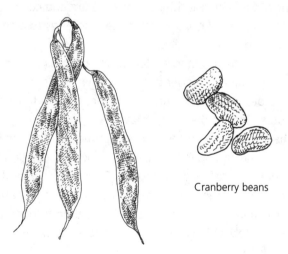

Cranberry beans

Cook's Notes
Cranberry beans are also called shell beans, horticultural beans, and succotash beans. The beans inside the pod are pale beige with wavy pink stripes, which, unfortunately, disappear when they are cooked. Their season in New England coincides with that of the sun-ripened tomatoes of August. If your tomatoes are not truly ripe, the balance of flavor in this chowder will not be right—better to use canned tomatoes.

In this chowder, unlike most chowders in this book, the bacon fat is not removed after the bacon is rendered but is left in to add smokiness. Part of the chowder is pureed and used to thicken the chowder. I prefer the rustic texture of a puree made with a food mill to the super-smooth one a food processor provides.

Serve small cups of this chowder as a starter, with a basket of warm Buttermilk Baking Powder Biscuits (page 210).

For equipment, you will need a 3- to 4-quart heavy pot with a lid, a wooden spoon, a food mill or food processor, and a ladle.

2 pounds fresh cranberry beans (shell beans) in the pod
4 ounce slab (unsliced) bacon, rind removed and cut into ⅓-inch dice
1 clove garlic, finely chopped (1 teaspoon)
1 large onion (12 ounces), cut into ½-inch dice
2 to 3 sprigs fresh thyme, leaves removed and chopped (1 teaspoon)
1 dried bay leaf
5 cups Chicken Stock (page 72), Chicken Broth (page 74), or water

1 pound ripe tomatoes, peeled and cut into ½-inch dice, with their juice, or 1½ cups diced (½ inch) canned tomatoes with their juice
2 tablespoons dark molasses
Kosher or sea salt and freshly ground black pepper

For garnish
3 scallions, thinly sliced

1. Shuck the beans and discard any that are soft or blemished. You should have about 3 cups.
2. Heat a 3- to 4-quart heavy pot over low heat and add the diced bacon. Once it has rendered a few tablespoons of fat, increase the heat to medium and cook until the bacon is crisp and golden brown.
3. Add the garlic and cook for 30 seconds. Add the onion, thyme, and bay leaf and sauté, stirring occasionally with a wooden spoon, for about 8 minutes, until the onion is tender but not browned.
4. Add the beans and stock. Partially cover the pot and bring to a simmer. Cook the beans at a steady simmer over medium heat for 20 to 25 minutes, until they are tender. Reduce the heat to low.

5. Remove 2 cups of the chowder from the pot and puree in a food mill held over the pot so it falls directly back into the chowder, or puree in a food processor and return to the chowder. Add the tomatoes and their juices, along with the molasses, and let the chowder simmer slowly for another 15 minutes. Remove from the heat and season with salt and pepper. If you are not serving the chowder within the hour, let it cool a bit, then refrigerate; cover the chowder *after* it has chilled completely. Otherwise, let it sit at room temperature for up to an hour, allowing the flavors to meld.

6. When ready to serve, reheat the chowder over low heat, stirring occasionally so it doesn't stick. Ladle the chowder into cups and sprinkle with the sliced scallions.

Makes about 7 cups; serves 6 as a first course

Variation: Dried Bean Chowder
Substitute 8 ounces dried shell beans, limas, or other white bean for the fresh shell beans. Soak them overnight in enough water to cover generously; drain. Depending on the bean you choose, the cooking time may be doubled or even longer. Follow the recipe and simmer until the beans are tender, adding water as necessary (about 1 cup) to compensate for the evaporation during the longer cooking time.

Variation: Cider and Bean Chowder
This idea also comes from the Shakers, who used sweet apple cider as the liquid in several of their soups. It adds a new dimension to the sweet-and-sour flavor of this chowder. Cider is pressed from late August through November, so you can try this in either the fresh or dried bean versions. Substitute 3 cups apple cider for 3 cups of the chicken stock (you will still use 2 cups of chicken stock).

Mushroom and Leek Chowder

Mushroom catsup, made from finely chopped mushrooms that are salted, drained, and then boiled down to a paste, predates the making of tomato catsup and was often used as a condiment in early American cooking. I have found a couple of chowder recipes from the 1800s that call for the addition of mushroom catsup, as well as two more recent mushroom chowders, one from 1939 and one from 1972, in Richard J. Hooker's *The Book of Chowder.* Mushroom chowder sounded like a good idea, so I created my own recipe and was pleased. It is a great addition to my mushroom repertoire, a new way to enjoy different varieties of mushrooms, especially chanterelles, as their seasons come and go. I like to imagine that New England chowder makers transplanted to the Pacific Northwest, with its abundance of wonderful wild mushrooms, cooked up a chowder similar to this. Although it is creamy, mushroom chowder is different from the familiar cream of mushroom soup because the mushrooms are sliced, not finely chopped, allowing you to enjoy the shape, color, and texture of the mushrooms.

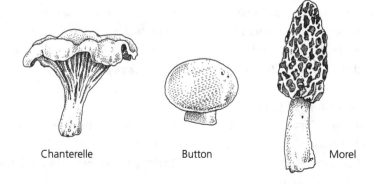

Chanterelle   Button   Morel

Cook's Notes

This chowder can be made with cultivated or wild mushrooms, or a mix. The chowder will take on the flavor of the mushroom or the variety of mushrooms you choose. In most cases, wild mushrooms have a strong flavor and make splendid chowder. Cultivated mushrooms, especially buttons, can be bland, so I add a little curry powder if using them to make the chowder more interesting; see the variation that follows this recipe.

I advise against gathering your own wild mushrooms unless you are an expert mycologist. Specialty grocery stores and farmers' markets often sell chanterelles and other wild mushrooms. Or you can have them shipped to you from the West Coast (see sources, page 233).

Always check over wild mushrooms carefully, as they often have small bugs or grit hiding in them. Wipe mushrooms clean—don't wash them.

It is difficult to give general instructions on cutting mushrooms, because they come in so many shapes and sizes, but I'll try. A good size for chowder is roughly 1 inch square, or round, or wedge-shaped, by ½ inch thick. Leave small mushrooms whole or cut in half; slice medium mushrooms about ½ inch thick; or cut large mushrooms in halves or quarters before slicing ½ inch thick. For flat-topped mushrooms like shiitakes, remove the tough part of the stems and cut the tops into wedges of the appropriate size.

Serve this chowder as a starter with toasted common crackers or Pilot crackers, or with Toasted Garlic Bread (page 209).

For equipment, you will need a colander, a 3- to 4-quart heavy pot with a lid, a wooden spoon, and a ladle.

1 large or 2 medium leeks (12 ounces)	3 cups Chicken Stock (page 72)
1 pound mushrooms (almost any variety)	1 cup heavy cream
3 ounces slab (unsliced) bacon, rind removed and cut into ¼-inch dice	Kosher or sea salt and freshly ground black pepper
2 tablespoons unsalted butter	
1 clove garlic, finely chopped (1 teaspoon)	**For garnish**
2 sprigs fresh tarragon, leaves removed and chopped (1 teaspoon)	2 tablespoons chopped fresh Italian parsley
1 tablespoon fresh lemon juice	2 tablespoons minced fresh chives
1½ pounds Yukon Gold, Maine, PEI, or other all-purpose potatoes, quartered lengthwise and sliced ¼ inch thick (to resemble the size of the mushroom pieces)	

1. Remove the tough outer leaves of the leek(s) and discard (or reserve for stock). Trim off the roots and the dark green tops of the leaves, then cut the leek(s) in half where the white meets the green. Split the white part lengthwise in half, then cut across into ⅓-inch slices. Do the same with the green half, removing any darker green parts and slicing only the light green part. Place the leeks in a pot of water and let soak briefly to remove any dirt, then lift them out and drain them in a colander. It is important to drain them well, or they will steam rather than sauté.

2. Wipe the mushrooms clean. Cut off the tough parts of the stems and discard. Slice the mushrooms as described in the Cook's Notes.

3. Heat a 3- to 4-quart heavy pot over low heat and add the diced bacon. Once it has rendered a few tablespoons of fat, increase the heat to medium and cook until the bacon is crisp and golden brown. Pour off all but 1 tablespoon of the bacon fat, leaving the bacon in the pot.

4. Add the butter and garlic and cook for 30 seconds. Add the leeks, mushrooms, and tarragon and sauté, stirring occasionally with a wooden spoon, for 5 minutes. Add the lemon juice, stir well, and cook for 3 to 4 minutes more, until the mushrooms are very soft.

5. Add the potatoes and stock. Turn up the heat, cover, bring to a boil, and cook vigorously for about 8 minutes, until the potatoes are tender on the outside but still firm in the center. With your spoon, smash a few potato slices against the side of the pot and cook for 2 minutes more to release their starch. Remove from the heat, stir in the cream, and season the chowder with salt and pepper. If you are not serving the chowder within the hour, let it cool a bit, then refrigerate; cover the chowder *after* it has chilled completely. Otherwise, let it sit at room temperature for up to an hour, allowing the flavors to meld.

6. When ready to serve, reheat the chowder over low heat; don't let it boil. Ladle into cups and sprinkle with the chopped parsley and minced chives.

Makes about 7 cups; serves 6 as a first course

Variation: Mushroom Chowder with Curry

If you decide to make this chowder with mild-flavored mushrooms, like white button mushrooms, a little curry powder will both complement the flavor and make the chowder more interesting. Add 2 teaspoons of Madras curry powder with the garlic and cook for 1 to 2 minutes, until the curry starts to stick to the bottom of the pot, then add the leeks and mushrooms and proceed as directed.

Potato Chowder with Cheddar Cheese

Long before the island of Nantucket became a glamorous summer resort, it was an important center for commercial whaling and fishing. In *Moby-Dick,* Herman Melville gives a wonderful description of the fish and clam chowders served at the Try Pots boarding house in Nantucket, where Ishmael and Queequeg were waiting to leave on their whaling voyage. Chowder was a way of life on the island, a method of cooking that could be used for meat as well as seafood (see Nantucket Veal Chowder, page 190) and, with the help of Melville, Nantucket became famous for its chowders. It is credited as the place of origin for potato chowder. Potatoes were not usually added to Nantucket chowders, but in this one exception, they were the main ingredient.

When I was working on the recipes for this book, I thought a potato chowder would demonstrate how good chowder could taste in its most humble form. As it turned out, it was too humble, and novelty was not a reason to include it. But when I added Cheddar cheese to it, potato chowder took on a new life. The soft flavor of the potatoes and the smokiness of the bacon create a nice background for the tangy flavor of a sharp Vermont Cheddar.

Cook's Notes

Serve this chowder as a starter with toasted common crackers or Pilot crackers and, if time allows, with Cheddar Cheese Biscuits (page 212). I think beer or ale is a better match with Cheddar cheese than wine.

For equipment, you will need a 3- to 4-quart heavy pot with a lid, a wooden spoon, a cheese grater, and a ladle.

4 ounces slab (unsliced) bacon, rind removed and cut into ⅓-inch dice

2 tablespoons unsalted butter

1 large onion (10 ounces), cut into ¾-inch dice

3 fresh sage leaves, finely chopped (1 teaspoon)

1 teaspoon Coleman's dry English mustard

1½ pounds Yukon Gold, Maine, PEI, or other all-purpose potatoes, peeled and cut into ¾-inch dice

3 cups Chicken Stock (page 72)

1½ cups heavy cream

Freshly ground black pepper

Kosher or sea salt

6 ounces Vermont or other sharp white Cheddar cheese, grated (1½ cups)

Tabasco sauce (optional)

For garnish

4 scallions, thinly sliced

1. Heat a 3- to 4-quart heavy pot over low heat and add the diced bacon. Once it has rendered a few tablespoons of fat, increase the heat to medium and cook until the bacon is crisp and golden brown. Pour off all but 1 tablespoon of the bacon fat, leaving the bacon in the pot.

2. Add the butter, onion, and sage and sauté, stirring occasionally with a wooden spoon, for 6 to 8 minutes, until the onion is tender but not browned. Stir in the dry mustard and cook for 1 minute more.

3. Add the potatoes and stock. Turn up the heat, cover, bring to a boil, and cook vigorously for about 12 minutes, or until the potatoes are tender on the outside but still firm in the center. With your spoon, smash a few potatoes against the side of the pot and cook for 2 minutes more to release their starch.

4. Remove the chowder from the heat and stir in the cream. Season with pepper, then underseason with a little bit of salt, as the cheese will add more salt when it is added later. If you are not serving the chowder within the hour, let it cool a bit, then refrigerate; cover the chowder *after* it has chilled completely. Otherwise, let it sit at room temperature for up to an hour, allowing the flavors to meld.

5. Reheat the chowder slowly over low heat until it is hot but has not reached a simmer. Gradually stir in the Cheddar cheese and continue to stir constantly until all the cheese has melted into the velvety broth. Taste the chowder and season with the optional hot sauce and more salt if needed. Let it come just to a simmer, then immediately remove it from the heat. Ladle the chowder into cups or small bowls and top each with a generous portion of sliced scallions.

Makes about 7 cups; serves 6 as a first course

Egg Chowder with Bacon and New Potatoes

Eggs are amazing! They are so versatile and at the same time so complete in themselves. But unless you've gone through hard times, it's easy to take the common, ubiquitous, inexpensive egg for granted. My beloved late grandparents, Josephine and Tim Donahue, who lived in Portlaoise, Ireland, loved soft-boiled eggs and ate them for supper (never at breakfast) about twice a week. Watching them slowly eat an egg, waiting for the tiny drops of butter to melt, then carefully salting and peppering each bite, and relishing it as if they were drinking a forty-year-old Château d'Yquem, is a memory that has stayed with me my entire life. I love eggs too, so when I spotted a New Hampshire recipe for egg chowder in *The New England Yankee Cookbook* (1939), I figured it would be easy to make a rustic farmhouse chowder with the combination of eggs, bacon, and potato, which we all know are so good together.

As it turned out, it wasn't so simple. I realized that this classic combination works best when the flavors are somewhat separate (like a plate of eggs and bacon with home fries). But that is not the nature of chowder, where flavors blend to become one. After two attempts, I knew I had to depart from my usual style of chowder making and try something different. New potatoes aren't generally suitable for chowder, because their low starch prevents them from blending with the other ingredients—in this case, though, it was exactly the quality I needed. Keeping the bacon separate was easy. And I let the egg flavor dominate the broth. The result: a surprisingly tasty chowder with colorful slices of red potato, large pieces of golden brown bacon, small cubes of chopped hard-boiled egg, and little specks of green chives.

Cook's Notes

This recipe is too humble for entertaining, and it's too filling to eat as starter, but it makes a nice family dish for lunch or supper.

Serve with toasted common crackers or Pilot crackers and maybe some warm Buttermilk Baking Powder Biscuits (page 210) or Cheddar Cheese Biscuits (page 212).

For equipment, you will need a 1½- to 2-quart saucepan (for boiling the eggs), a 10- to 12-inch skillet or sauté pan (for the chowder), a wooden spoon, a slotted spoon, and a ladle.

6 large eggs
¼ cup distilled white vinegar
8 ounces thick-sliced bacon
4 tablespoons unsalted butter
1 medium onion (8 ounces), cut into
   ¾-inch dice

2 to 3 sprigs fresh thyme, leaves removed
   and chopped (1 teaspoon)
1 teaspoon Coleman's dry English mustard
1½ pounds red or white new potatoes,
   halved and sliced ⅓ inch thick
3 cups Chicken Stock (page 72)

1 cup heavy cream
Kosher or sea salt and freshly ground
    black pepper

For garnish
2 tablespoons minced fresh chives

1. Place the eggs in a 1½- to 2-quart saucepan and add the vinegar and enough water to completely cover them. Bring to a boil, then lower the heat and cook the eggs at a steady simmer for 5 minutes. Remove the eggs from the heat and let sit for 10 minutes.

2. Rinse the eggs under cold running water until cool enough to handle, then peel them. Cut 5 eggs into medium dice: quarter them lengthwise, then cut each quarter into 3 or 4 pieces. Cover and leave at room temperature to add to the chowder. Chop the remaining egg into ⅓-inch dice, cover, and refrigerate for garnish; remove from the refrigerator about 15 minutes before you serve the chowder.

3. In a 10- to 12-inch skillet or sauté pan, gently fry the slices of bacon, in batches, over medium-low heat until crisp and golden brown. Drain on paper towels. Pour off all except 1 tablespoon of the fat from the pan, and set the pan aside. Cut the bacon into large pieces about 1 inch wide. Place in an ovenproof dish, cover, and reserve until later.

4. Return the pan to the stove and turn the heat up to medium. Add the butter, onion, and thyme and sauté, stirring occasionally with a wooden spoon, for 6 to 8 minutes, until the onion is softened but not browned. Stir in the dry mustard and cook for 1 minute more.

5. Add the potatoes and stock. The stock should just barely cover the potatoes; if it doesn't, add enough water to cover them. Bring to a simmer over medium heat and simmer for about 10 to 12 minutes, until the potatoes are fully cooked and tender.

6. Remove the pan from the heat, stir in the medium-dice eggs and the cream, and season to taste with salt and black pepper. If you are not serving the chowder within the hour, let it cool a bit, then refrigerate; cover the chowder *after* it has chilled completely. Otherwise, let it sit at room temperature for up to an hour, allowing the egg flavor to blend into the broth.

7. When ready to serve, reheat the chowder over low heat; don't let it boil. Even though they are hard-boiled, the egg yolks will lightly thicken the chowder. Warm the bacon in a low oven (200°F) for a few minutes.

8. Using a slotted spoon, mound the onions, potatoes, and eggs in the center of large soup plates or bowls, then ladle the broth around. Scatter the bacon over the individual servings and sprinkle with the diced egg and chives.

Makes about 8 cups; serves 5 or 6 as a main course

Nantucket Veal Chowder

"Veal chowder" may sound a little odd—it doesn't have quite the same ring as "clam chowder." But when you behold the creamy white broth with tan chunks of veal and taste the luscious broth and mild, tender meat, you will know that this dish is not an affectation. Veal chowder is the real McCoy. The flavor and texture of veal blend as naturally with traditional chowder ingredients as cod. Veal chowder originated on Nantucket Island, which was famous for its chowders during the heyday of the whaling industry. It makes sense that island cooks would apply their chowder-making skills to some of the foods from the farms that dominated the landscape, if for nothing more than they wanted a change of pace.

Cook's Notes

Veal chowder uses typical chowder techniques, but the cooking time for the veal broth is substantially longer than for a broth used in a seafood chowder. However, it is far less complicated than making the classic French *blanquette de veau,* a creamy veal stew, and it is just as good, although not as refined.

My recipe calls for 2 pounds of veal shoulder cut into 1-inch pieces that are at least ½ inch thick. The shape, however, is unimportant—I'm only looking for bite-sized pieces. You could buy trimmed veal stew meat from the butcher and cut it into smaller pieces, or you could buy a piece of veal shoulder and cut it yourself. If you choose to do it yourself, buy extra meat to allow for the 5 or 6 ounces you will lose in trimming away the fat.

Serve this chowder as a main course with toasted common crackers or Pilot crackers, or with Toasted Garlic Bread (page 209).

For equipment, you will need a 5-quart Dutch oven or heavy pot with a lid (for the broth), a ladle, a slotted spoon, a fine-mesh strainer, a colander, a 3- to 4-quart heavy pot with a lid (for the chowder), and a wooden spoon.

2 pounds lean veal shoulder, cut into 1-inch pieces that are at least ½ inch thick

2 quarts water

2 to 3 sprigs fresh tarragon, leaves removed (stems reserved) and chopped (1 teaspoon)

2 to 3 sprigs fresh thyme, leaves removed (stems reserved) and chopped (1 teaspoon)

2 dried bay leaves

2 whole cloves

1 heaping teaspoon black peppercorns

1 small onion (6 ounces), unpeeled,
    coarsely chopped
4 cloves garlic, 2 crushed and 2 finely
    chopped (2 teaspoons)
Kosher or sea salt
1 medium leek (9 ounces)
4 ounces slab (unsliced) bacon, rind
    removed and cut into ⅓-inch dice
4 tablespoons unsalted butter
2 small Italian frying peppers or
    cubanelle peppers (4 ounces),
    cut into ½-inch dice

1½ pounds Yukon Gold, Maine, PEI, or
    other all-purpose potatoes, peeled
    and cut into ¾-inch dice
1 teaspoon finely chopped or grated lemon
    zest (yellow part only, no white pith)
1½ cups heavy cream
Freshly ground black pepper

For garnish
2 tablespoons chopped fresh Italian parsley
2 tablespoons minced fresh chives

1. Combine the veal and water in a 5-quart Dutch oven or heavy pot and bring to a boil, skimming off the white foam as it rises to the surface. (Using a ladle and a circular motion, push the foam from the center to the sides of the pot, where it is easy to remove.) Reduce the heat so the veal broth is simmering.

2. Add the reserved tarragon and thyme stems, the bay leaves, cloves, peppercorns, onion, and the 2 crushed garlic cloves. Season lightly with salt, partially cover, and simmer for 1½ hours, or until the veal is very tender.

3. Use a slotted spoon to remove the veal and brush off any spices, herbs, and/or vegetables clinging to the meat. Cover and refrigerate until needed. Strain the broth through a fine-mesh strainer. You should have about 4 cups of broth. If you are not making the chowder right away, let the broth cool a bit, then refrigerate; cover *after* the broth has chilled completely. (The veal broth can be prepared a day in advance if you like.)

4. Meanwhile, remove the tough outer leaves from the leek and discard (or add to the simmering stock). Trim off the root and the dark green tops of the leaves, then cut the leek in half where the white meets the green. Split the white part lengthwise in half, then cut into ⅓-inch slices. Do the same with the green half, removing any darker green parts and slicing only the light green part. Place the leek in a pot of water and let soak briefly to remove any dirt, then lift out and drain in a colander. It is important to drain the leek well, or it will steam rather than sauté.

5. Heat a 3- to 4-quart heavy pot over low heat and add the bacon. Once it has rendered a few tablespoons of fat, increase the heat to medium and cook until the bacon is a crisp golden brown. Pour off all but 1 tablespoon of the fat, leaving the bacon in the pot.

6. Add the butter and the chopped garlic and cook for 30 seconds. Add the leek, peppers, tarragon, and thyme and sauté, stirring occasionally with a wooden spoon, for about 8 minutes, until the leek and peppers are softened but not browned.

7. Add the potatoes and the reserved veal broth. The broth should just barely cover the potatoes; if it doesn't, add enough water to cover. Turn up the heat and bring to a boil. Cover and cook the potatoes vigorously for about 12 minutes, until they are soft on the outside but still firm on the inside. Smash a few potatoes against the side of the pot and cook for 2 minutes longer to release their starch.

8. Add the veal and lemon zest and bring back to a simmer. Remove the pot from the heat, stir in the cream, and season to taste with salt and black pepper. If you are not serving the chowder within the hour, let it cool a bit, then refrigerate; cover the chowder *after* it has chilled completely. Otherwise, let it sit at room temperature for up to an hour, allowing the flavors to meld.

9. When ready to serve, reheat the chowder over low heat; don't let it boil. Use a slotted spoon to mound the veal, potatoes, leeks, and peppers in the center of large soup plates or shallow bowls, and ladle the creamy broth around. Sprinkle with the chopped parsley and minced chives.

Makes about 9 cups; serves 4 or 5 as a main course

Farmer's Chicken Chowder

The popularity of corn chowder in the late 1800s spawned a new family of chowders made from common farmland ingredients, such as parsnips, beans, mushrooms, eggs, and chicken. Chicken chowder was made on New England farms, most notably on Martha's Vineyard and Nantucket, and on farms in the Chesapeake Bay region. Chicken is one of the most important ingredients in farmhouse kitchens, and farmwives were well versed in cooking these birds at all stages of their growth, from a 1-pound poussin to 6-pound retired old hens (fowls) and roosters. Brothy chicken dishes like this chowder were usually made with stewing chickens, fowl or rooster. My version uses a small frying chicken, which is tastier and more tender.

Cook's Notes

This recipe begins by making a potent chicken broth from a small chicken; the variation that follows the recipe includes instructions for making broth with a stewing chicken. Because the chicken makes about 2 cups more broth than you will need for the recipe, you have the option of omitting the 2 cups of cream and substituting the extra broth. (Of course, it's always handy to have extra chicken broth in the freezer.) It's good both ways: creamy on cold days, clear on warmer days. The creamy chowder looks similar to a fish chowder, but the clear chowder is more dramatic because you can see the pieces of light and dark chicken, potato, onion, and specks of red pepper floating in the golden broth.

Serve this rustic main-course chowder with toasted common crackers or Pilot crackers, warm Buttermilk Baking Powder Biscuits (page 210), Skillet Corn Bread (page 219), or Cheddar Cheese Biscuits (page 212).

For equipment, you will need a cleaver or heavy chef's knife, an 8-quart stockpot (for the broth), a ladle, a pair of tongs, a fine-mesh strainer, a 4- to 6-quart heavy pot with a lid (for the chowder), a wooden spoon, and a slotted spoon.

1 fryer chicken (about 3 pounds)
About 3 quarts water
6 sprigs fresh thyme
2 large onions (12 to 14 ounces each),
    1 unpeeled, coarsely chopped, 1 peeled
    and cut into ¾-inch dice
2 small carrots (4 ounces), sliced

2 cloves garlic, crushed
2 dried bay leaves
2 whole cloves
1 tablespoon black peppercorns
4 ounces slab (unsliced) bacon, rind
    removed (reserve it for the stock)
    and cut into ⅓-inch dice

2 stalks celery (4 ounces), cut into
⅓-inch dice (reserve any trimmings
for the stock)
Kosher or sea salt
4 tablespoons unsalted butter
1 small red bell pepper (6 ounces), cut into
½-inch dice
2 pounds Yukon Gold, Maine, PEI, or other
all-purpose potatoes, peeled and sliced
⅓ inch thick

2 cups heavy cream (optional)
Freshly ground black pepper
Cayenne pepper (optional)

For garnish
6 scallions, very thinly sliced

1. Remove the giblets and liver from the chicken and reserve for another use; save the neck for the broth. Rinse the chicken under cold running water and, with a cleaver, heavy chef's knife, or poultry shears, split it in half. Place the chicken and neck in an 8-quart stockpot and cover with the water. Bring to a boil, skimming off the white foam as it appears on the surface. (Using a ladle and a circular motion, push the foam from the center to the side of the pot, where it is easy to remove.) Lower the heat so the broth is at a slow simmer.

2. Meanwhile, remove the leaves from 4 sprigs of the thyme and reserve the stems. Chop the leaves and reserve them for later. Add the thyme stems, the remaining 2 whole thyme sprigs, the unpeeled chopped onion, the carrots, garlic, bay leaves, cloves, and peppercorns, along with the reserved bacon rind and celery trimmings. Partially cover the pot and let the broth simmer for 1 hour.

3. Remove the broth from the heat, remove the chicken with tongs, and place on a plate to cool. Set the broth aside. As soon as the chicken is cool enough to handle, pull the meat from the bones and tear into bite-sized pieces (about ½ by 1 inch). (You can cut the meat into pieces with a knife, but I prefer the appearance and texture of hand-picked chicken meat.) Return the bones and skin to the broth as you pick over the chicken. Wrap the meat (you should have about 14 ounces) in plastic wrap and refrigerate.

4. Return the broth to low heat and slowly simmer for 1 hour more. Lightly salt the broth and taste it. It should be very potent; if not, let it cook for another 20 to 30 minutes. Strain through a fine-mesh strainer; you should have 6 cups of broth. If you are not going to make the chowder right away, refrigerate the broth; cover it *after* it has chilled completely. (You can make the broth and prepare the meat a day in advance if you like.)

5. Heat a 4- to 6-quart heavy pot over low heat and add the bacon. Once it has rendered a few tablespoons of fat, increase the heat to medium and cook until the bacon is crisp and golden brown. Pour off all but 1 tablespoon of the fat, leaving the bacon in the pot.

6. Add the butter, the diced onion, celery, bell pepper, and the reserved thyme leaves and sauté, stirring occasionally with a wooden spoon, for about 10 minutes, until the vegetables are softened but not browned.

7. Add the potatoes and 4 cups of the reserved broth; reserve the remaining broth for another use, or set it aside to add later (see Cook's Notes). The broth should just barely cover the potatoes; if it doesn't, add enough water to cover. Turn up the heat and bring to a boil. Cover and cook the potatoes vigorously for about 10 minutes, until they are soft on the out-side but still firm in the center. If the broth hasn't thickened lightly, smash a few potatoes against the side of the pot and cook a minute or two longer to release their starch.

8. Remove the pot from the heat and stir in the chicken meat. Stir in the cream, or add the reserved 2 cups chicken broth. Season to taste with salt, black pepper, and a bit of cayenne pepper if you like. If you are not serving the chowder within the hour, let it cool a bit, then refrigerate; cover the chowder *after* it has chilled completely. Otherwise, let it sit at room temperature for up to an hour, allowing the flavors to meld.

9. When ready to serve, reheat the chowder over low heat; don't let it boil. Use a slotted spoon to mound the chicken, onions, potatoes, celery, bell pepper, and bacon in the center of large soup plates or shallow bowls, and ladle the creamy broth around. Sprinkle each serving with a generous spoonful of sliced scallions.

```
Makes about 12 cups (plus 2 cups extra chicken broth);
serves 6 to 8 as a main course
```

Variation: Stewing Chicken Chowder

Since a stewing chicken weighs double (about 6 pounds) what the fryer does, you will need to double the recipe, which will yield about 6 quarts of chowder. The cost will be about fifty cents for a hearty portion, making this chowder very economical, very Yankee. Instead of halving the chicken, cut it into 4 pieces. Simmer the old bird for 2½ hours, then lightly salt the broth and remove the pot from the heat. Leave the chicken pieces in the broth and let steep for 30 minutes more, then use tongs to pull out the pieces of chicken and let them cool and drain on a plate. When the chicken is cool enough to handle, pull off the now-tender meat and tear it into 2-inch strips about ¾ inch wide. Because you are doubling the recipe, you will need to allow a little extra cooking time in each step.

Variation: Chicken Chowder with Corn

This is a combination of the two most popular farmhouse chowders, a dependable crowd pleaser. Husk 3 ears of sweet yellow or bicolor corn. Carefully remove most of the silk from each ear by hand, then rub the ears with a towel to finish the job. Cut the kernels from the cobs and add the cobs to the broth. You should have 2 cups of corn. Add the corn to the chowder at the same time you add the potatoes, and proceed with the recipe as directed.

Variation: Chicken and Oyster Chowder

Up until about one hundred years ago, chicken was actually more precious than oysters along the eastern seaboard of the United States. Oysters were often used in chicken pies and other casseroles as an extender! I'm not sure if anyone else has ever made chicken and oyster chowder, but I have seen a recipe from Maryland (mid-1800s) in which chopped chicken breast was added to clam chowder. I think oysters pair better with chicken than clams. Their flavor is softer and they combine well with the chicken broth to make a tasty brew. Prepare the chicken chowder through Step 7. Meanwhile, pick over 1 pint shucked oysters for shells. Remove the chowder from the heat and add the oysters with their juices. Let the oysters sit in the chowder for 5 minutes, in which time they will cook and become plump, then gently stir in the chicken and cream. Finish the recipe as instructed, but add a squeeze of fresh lemon juice (1 to 2 teaspoons) just before you ladle it into bowls.

Leftover Turkey Chowder with Sage

It's not much trouble to cook a small turkey at home. A twelve-pounder takes only two and a half hours to roast. You don't always have to make all the trimmings, although I consider mashed potatoes and gravy mandatory. For my family of five, a small turkey gives us a great dinner, meat for sandwiches, a turkey noodle or rice soup, and a turkey chowder—all for under fifteen dollars! Turkey chowder is not a classic American farmhouse chowder, like corn or chicken chowder, but since chowders are often the result of necessity, chances are that turkey chowder has been made many times in the past. This version is one I created, using standard chowder techniques and ingredients and leftover turkey. The distinctive turkey flavor is infused with sage and celery, typical turkey stuffing ingredients, thus giving this unfamiliar chowder a familiar flavor.

Cook's Notes

Since the amount of stock a turkey carcass yields is much more than you will need to make this chowder, I provide a separate stock recipe. (Also, if the ingredients for such an easily put together stock were listed with the chowder ingredients, they would make a straightforward chowder seem overly complex.) This allows those of you who have your own basic turkey stock recipe—or have some stock on hand—to make the chowder directly.

In my other chowder recipes that use celery, I cut it into small dice so it flavors the chowder without becoming one of the featured ingredients. In this chowder, however, celery is a featured ingredient, because it blends so well with the flavor of turkey, so I slice it into its natural U-shape, giving it more importance. You can use from 1 pound to 1½ pounds of leftover turkey meat (light and/or dark) in this chowder; if you use the maximum amount, you will need to add the extra cup of stock. I like to add cream to this chowder because it sets it apart from other turkey soups, but if you wish, you can omit the cream and replace it with additional turkey stock.

Toasted common crackers or Pilot crackers and warm Buttermilk Baking Powder Biscuits (page 210), Parker House Rolls (page 214), or Skillet Corn Bread (page 219) are all good accompaniments for turkey chowder, which is most suitable presented as a main course.

For equipment, you will need a 4- to 6-quart heavy pot with a lid, a wooden spoon, a slotted spoon, and a ladle.

4 ounces slab (unsliced) bacon, rind removed and cut into ⅓-inch dice
4 tablespoons unsalted butter
1 large onion (12 ounces), cut into ¾-inch dice
3 stalks celery (6 ounces), cut into ⅓-inch slices
2 to 3 sprigs fresh thyme, leaves removed and chopped (1 teaspoon)
6 fresh sage leaves, finely chopped (2 teaspoons)
1½ pounds Yukon Gold, Maine, PEI, or other all-purpose potatoes, sliced ⅓ inch thick

About 4 cups Turkey Stock (page 200)
1 to 1½ pounds leftover turkey meat, coarsely shredded or cut into ¾- to 1-inch pieces
1½ cups heavy cream (or up to 2 cups if desired)
Kosher or sea salt and freshly ground black pepper

For garnish
¼ cup chopped fresh Italian parsley

1. Heat a 4- to 6-quart heavy pot over low heat and add the bacon. Once it has rendered a few tablespoons of fat, increase the heat to medium and cook until the bacon is crisp and golden brown. Pour off all but 1 tablespoon of the fat, leaving the bacon in the pot.

2. Add the butter, onion, celery, thyme, and sage and sauté, stirring occasionally with a wooden spoon, for 10 to 12 minutes, until the vegetables are softened but not browned.

3. Add the potatoes and 4 cups of the turkey stock. The stock should barely cover the potatoes; if it doesn't, add more stock or water to cover. Turn up the heat and bring to a boil. Cover and cook the potatoes vigorously for about 10 minutes, until they are soft on the outside but still firm in the center. If the broth hasn't thickened lightly, smash a few potatoes against the side of the pot and cook a minute or two longer to release their starch.

4. Add the turkey and simmer for 5 minutes more. If you have added more than 1 pound of turkey meat, add more stock (up to 1 cup for 1½ pounds of meat). Remove the chowder from the heat, stir in the cream, and season to taste with salt and black pepper. If you are not serving the chowder within the hour, let it cool a bit, then refrigerate; cover the chowder *after* it has chilled completely. Otherwise, let it sit at room temperature for up to an hour, allowing the flavors to meld.

5. When ready to serve, reheat the chowder over low heat; don't let it boil. Use a slotted spoon to mound the turkey, onions, celery, and potatoes in the center of large soup plates or shallow bowls, and ladle the creamy broth around. Sprinkle each serving with chopped parsley.

`Makes 10 to 12 cups; serves 6 to 8 as a main course`

Variation: Smoked Turkey Chowder

As more markets offer smoked turkey and more backyard barbecuers master hot-smoking techniques, smoked turkey leftovers can be substituted for fresh turkey to make a smoky chowder, with only two changes: use only half of the smoked turkey carcass and cut the turkey stock recipe in half, because the smoky stock has no other use.

You may also wish to substitute salt pork for bacon (to avoid making a chowder that is overly smoky).

Turkey Stock

This turkey stock recipe is based on the carcass of a small turkey (12 to 14 pounds). Adjust the amounts as necessary to suit the size of your leftover carcass. Before you start, pick most of the meat off the carcass, but don't strip it completely—a little bit of meat adds extra flavor to the stock. It is important that when you start the stock, the water just barely cover the bones. You can always add more water as the stock simmers, but if you start with too much, your stock will be weak. I don't stuff my turkeys with bread stuffing, but if you do, rinse off any stuffing that is attached to the carcass, or it may make the stock cloudy.

Cook's Note

For equipment, you will need an 8-quart stockpot, a ladle, and a fine-mesh strainer.

1 small turkey carcass, split into 4 or more pieces
About 5 quarts water
1 large or 2 medium onions, unpeeled, coarsely chopped
2 stalks celery, coarsely chopped
1 to 2 carrots, coarsely chopped
2 dried bay leaves
4 sprigs fresh thyme
4 leaves fresh sage
1 tablespoon black peppercorns
Kosher or sea salt

1. Put the turkey pieces in an 8-quart stockpot and cover with the water. Bring to a boil, skimming off the white foam as it appears on the surface. (Using a ladle and a circular motion, push the foam from the center to the sides of the pot, where it is easy to remove.) Lower the heat so the broth is at a slow simmer.

2. Add the onion, celery, carrots, bay leaves, thyme, sage, and peppercorns. Let the broth simmer for 2 hours, stirring once or twice; if necessary, add more water at any time to keep the ingredients covered. After 2 hours, lightly salt the stock and taste it. If it has a nice strong flavor, remove it from the heat; otherwise, let it simmer for another 20 to 30 minutes.

3. Strain the stock through a fine-mesh strainer. If you are not going to use it right away, refrigerate the stock; cover it *after* it has chilled completely. (You can make the stock a day in advance; it can also be frozen for up to 3 months.)

Makes about 3 quarts

Pheasant and Cabbage Chowder

My father has always been an avid hunter. When I was a kid, he and I went hunting together, and although I rarely hunt anymore, I still adore the flavor of freshly killed game, especially game birds. As I created this chowder, I imagined a dark November evening and the welcome warmth and light of an old farmhouse kitchen. In the kitchen, a pot of clear chowder is simmering on a woodstove, filling the room with the spicy scent of game birds, cabbage, thyme, and caraway, mingling with the faint aroma of corn bread baking in the oven. After a few tests, my imaginary chowder became real and tasted really good. I tried using duck, but favored the lighter color and milder flavor of pheasant, which is more in keeping with what I think chowder should look and taste like. You can make this chowder with farm-raised pheasant, available in specialty meat stores, but if you can get a wild bird, it will taste even better.

Cook's Notes

Farm-raised pheasant, which weigh from 2½ to 4 pounds, will work in this recipe, without making any adjustments. Although pheasant breast can be tender and moist when carefully roasted or sautéed, the thighs and drumsticks are hopelessly tough unless they are braised or simmered, as they are in this chowder. If you like, sauté or pan-roast the breasts for more elegant occasions, and freeze the thighs and legs for this recipe; three pheasants are enough for this chowder. You can also substitute two partridges for the pheasant in this recipe.

I prefer to keep this chowder clear, so I simmer the potatoes, rather than cooking them vigorously as in most of my other recipes.

Serve this delicious main-course chowder with Skillet Corn Bread (page 219) or Corn Sticks (page 220) or Anadama Bread (page 217).

For equipment, you will need a cleaver or heavy chef's knife, a 6- to 8-quart stockpot with a lid (for the broth), a ladle, a pair of tongs, a fine-mesh strainer, a 4- to 6-quart heavy pot (for the chowder), a wooden spoon, and a slotted spoon.

1 pheasant (2½ to 3 pounds), or the same weight of pheasant thighs and drum-sticks

About 4 quarts water

4 sprigs fresh thyme

2 large onions (12 ounces each), 1 unpeeled, coarsely chopped, 1 peeled and cut into ¾-inch dice

2 carrots (2 to 3 ounces each), 1 coarsely chopped; 1 sliced into ⅓-inch thick rounds (split the thick end lengthwise and cut into half-moons)

1 large stalk celery, coarsely chopped

1 clove garlic, crushed

2 dried bay leaves

1 heaping teaspoon black peppercorns

2 whole cloves

4 ounces slab (unsliced) bacon, rind removed (reserve it for the stock) and cut into ⅓-inch dice

Kosher or sea salt

4 tablespoons unsalted butter

¼ teaspoon caraway seeds, finely chopped

1 pound Yukon Gold, Maine, PEI, or other all-purpose potatoes, halved and sliced ⅓ inch thick

8 ounces Savoy cabbage (½ small head or ¼ large head), cut into ¾-inch pieces

Freshly ground black pepper

For garnish
¼ cup chopped fresh Italian parsley

1. With a cleaver, heavy chef's knife, or kitchen shears, split the pheasant in half, then cut the thighs and legs from the breasts. Place the 4 pieces of pheasant in a 6- to 8-quart stock-pot and cover with the water. Bring to a boil, skimming off the white foam as it rises to the surface. (Using a ladle and a circular motion, push the foam from the center to the side of the pot, where it is easy to remove.) Lower the heat so the broth is at a slow simmer.

2. Meanwhile, remove the leaves from 3 sprigs of thyme, reserving the stems, chop, and reserve (you should have 1 teaspoon). Add the thyme stems and the remaining thyme sprig to the broth. Also add the coarsely chopped onion and carrot, the celery, garlic, bay leaves, peppercorns, and cloves, along with the reserved bacon rind, to the pot. Season lightly with salt, partially cover, and simmer slowly for 2 hours.

3. Remove the broth from the heat. With tongs, transfer the pheasant pieces to a plate. When they are cool enough to handle, pull the meat off the bones, discarding the bones, and tear the meat into bite-sized pieces. Or cut the meat with a knife into rectangular strips that are approximately ½ by 1 inch. (If you used a whole pheasant, you will have about 12 to 14 ounces of meat; if you used pheasant thighs and legs, you will have about 1 pound of meat.) Cover and refrigerate until needed. Strain the broth through a fine-mesh strainer; you should have about 8 cups. If you are not making the chowder right away, let the broth cool a bit, then refrigerate; cover the broth *after* it has chilled completely. (The broth and meat can be prepared a day in advance if you like.)

4. Heat a 4- to 6-quart heavy pot over low heat and add the bacon. Once it has rendered a few tablespoons of fat, increase the heat to medium and cook until the bacon is crisp and golden brown. Pour off all but 1 tablespoon of the fat, leaving the bacon in the pot.

5. Add the butter, the diced onion, the sliced carrot, the reserved thyme leaves, and the caraway seeds and sauté, stirring occasionally with a wooden spoon, until the onion is softened but not browned.

6. Add the potatoes and the reserved pheasant broth, bring to a simmer, and simmer over medium heat for about 8 minutes, until the potatoes are cooked through but still firm. Add the cabbage and simmer for 5 minutes more, until it just begins to soften (it will continue to cook after the chowder is removed from the stove).

7. Remove the chowder from the heat, stir in the pheasant meat, and season to taste with salt and black pepper. If you are not serving the chowder within the hour, let it cool a bit, then refrigerate; cover the chowder *after* it has chilled completely. Otherwise, let it sit at room temperature for up to an hour, allowing the flavors to meld.

8. When ready to serve, reheat the chowder over low heat; don't let it boil. Use a slotted spoon to mound the pheasant, cabbage, carrots, onions, and potatoes in the center of large soup plates or shallow bowls, and ladle the clear broth around. Sprinkle each serving with a generous spoonful of chopped parsley.

```
Makes about 12 cups; serves 12 as a first course or
6 to 8 as a main course
```

Chapter 8

Chowder Companions

They [common crackers] are difficult to find outside of
New England area, and the recipe has always been
a locked-up secret. Our team decided we would break the
monopoly, and our own determined Kathleen, after thirty-eight
different versions, finally, on October 25, 1994, came up with a
winner. Here it is—a strange method, but a very special cracker.

—Julia Child, IN JULIA'S KITCHEN WITH MASTER CHEFS (1995)

A few years back, I made a traditional fish chowder for Julia Child on her TV series *In Julia's Kitchen with Master Chefs.* She loved the buttery, toasted common crackers that I served with the chowder and wanted to know all about them. I told her that because they have been baked commercially for almost two hundred years, no one really knows the recipe. My reply apparently raised Julia's curiosity. With the help of the Culinary Historians of Boston, and a very patient recipe tester named Kathleen Anino, Julia and her crew worked for weeks before they successfully baked their own common crackers. I never did get to taste them, but I heard they were quite good (like the ones I buy from the Vermont Country Store). The recipe they developed, by the way, takes one and a half days to make from start to finish!

Julia Child's focus on the common cracker underlines the importance of serving something crunchy to complement and balance the soft texture of chowder. Common crackers, Crown Pilot crackers, or other hard crackers should always be offered with chowder. Unless, that is, you are serving my Toasted Garlic Bread (page 209) with a savory chowder, because the toasts are so very dry and crisp that they can be presented in place of crackers.

Crackers are all that is really needed with a cup of chowder served as a starter, but when you're making a meal of chowder, a basket of warm biscuits, bread, quick bread, or fritters is a pleasant addition to—*not* a substitution for—crackers. The recipes in this chapter are some of my tried-and-true favorites, nothing fancy, just good food to make a chowder dinner even more special. In each of the chowder recipes in this book, you will find my suggestion for one or more accompaniments that I typically serve with that chowder. Admittedly, these are only suggestions, meant to help when you're not sure what to serve, but there are a few accompaniments, like Salt Cod Fritters (page 228) and Cheddar Cheese Biscuits (page 212), that are terrific with certain chowders and clash with others. On the other hand, I can't think of any chowder where Sweet Corn Fritters (page 222), Skillet Corn Bread (page 219), Anadama Bread (page 217), Buttermilk Baking Powder Biscuits (page 210), or Parker House Rolls (page 214) would not be in accord.

When chowder is on the menu, you usually have an empty oven, which eliminates the bottlenecks and timing problems that might make you avoid baking close to dinnertime. Quick breads like corn bread, buttermilk biscuits, and cheddar cheese biscuits can be mixed and baked in a very short time, less than thirty minutes once you've made them a few times. I usually make these quick breads while the chowder is resting and developing its full flavor.

Yeast breads take more time but they do not need to be timed so that they're just coming out of the oven for dinner. If you like them warm, you can simply reheat them. But if you like the idea of a loaf warm from the oven, I have found a rhythm for making yeast breads with chowder that works well for me:

Make the dough.

Begin the chowder during the first rising of the dough.

Shape the dough for baking.

Finish the chowder during the second rising of the dough.

Bake the bread while the chowder is resting.

Fritters are best when the batter is made in advance; you can make the batter as much as 6 hours ahead. Because fritters need to be fried very close to mealtime, at which point you are simply reheating the chowder, the logistics are ideal—fritters and chowder go well together in every way.

If you are not a baker, a rustic loaf from a quality bakery will make a fine accompaniment to chowder. Full-flavored whole-grain breads go well with chowder, but avoid breads that are sweetened and made with spices or herbs that may not complement the chowder. In San Francisco, clam chowder is often served inside a scooped-out sourdough loaf (*boule*), and the idea is spreading to other places. Too bad, I think. It is a gimmick that makes poor use of two foods that would otherwise be superb together.

Common Crackers

If there has been a constant in the history of chowder, at least for the last two hundred years, it is the common cracker. A perfect companion for chowder, the common cracker has remained unchanged, while chowder has consistently evolved and taken on new forms. These round puffed, hollow, very hard crackers have been manufactured in New England for so long that almost no home cook knows how to make them. Even those who do know don't bother, because they take almost two days to make and if you do everything just right, they might turn out as good as the ones you can buy at the store. In and around New England, you can find common crackers in many specialty and seafood markets and sometimes in ordinary supermarkets. Bent is a very good brand of common crackers from Vermont that I frequently find at the store. For mail-order, I buy common crackers from the Vermont Country Store (see sources, page 233), whose packaging claims that their crackers have been "made in Vermont since 1828." At its inception, the common cracker was known as the Boston cracker throughout New England, lending plausibility to the belief that Boston was its place of origin. Ironically, it was Bostonians who coined the name "common crackers," and the name stuck—no one calls them Boston crackers anymore, and no one in Boston manufactures them.

Common crackers

The common cracker descended from hardtack, also called ship's biscuit—a very dense, unleavened brick of baked flour. Necessity wrote this recipe, since flour would not keep in the damp and vermin-infested conditions aboard ship. Hardtack was also a staple all along the coast of New England and in the Maritime Provinces of Canada, where villagers faced similar problems with fresh flour. Hardtack had to be shaved or chopped off the baked brick, then soaked in water to soften before it could be used for chowder and other dishes. I imagine that the porridge-like chowders thickened with hardtack were not so much a reflection of any preference for thick chowder as they were a way to add bulk (carbohydrates) to the diets of fishermen and their families. Chowder was a way to make hardtack edible.

When the potato became a popular ingredient in the early 1800s, it put hardtack out of the chowder business. Potatoes became the primary thickener in chowders, producing a version that was more brothy and lighter. But the dry cracker didn't go away completely, it just got moved to the side. The new and improved leavened version, the common cracker, was and still is very dry, with a hard exterior and great storage capabilities. But when you split, butter, and toast them, they strike a perfect balance between being crisp enough to crunch, even after sitting in a hot broth for a few minutes, and having a flaky tenderness. The flavor is plain but quite pleasant, a perfect complement to any style of chowder.

To Prepare Common Crackers for Chowder

Preheat the oven to 375°F. Use a paring knife to split the crackers in half. They will split willingly; some may already have split. Using a pastry brush, dab the inside of each half cracker with very soft (or melted) unsalted butter. Use enough butter to coat the surface evenly; you will need about 2 tablespoons for every 12 crackers. Line them up on a cookie sheet or baking sheet, buttered side up, and bake for 10 to 12 minutes, until the crackers are golden brown. Serve warm or at room temperature.

Crown Pilot Crackers

I always keep a box of Crown Pilot crackers on hand for times when preparing common crackers is impractical, as when I'm reheating a small amount of chowder for a quick lunch or my oven is tied up with other foods. Crown Pilot crackers are very crisp, large rectangular crackers that are made with very little salt or leavening, very similar to the hardtack used in the original fish chowders. They were first produced in 1792 by John Pearson, a baker from Newburyport, Massachusetts, who sold his "Pilot Bread" primarily to sailors, because they kept well during long sea voyages. Mr. Pearson's bakery grew into a prosperous family business, which, in 1898, joined with an association of bakeries to form the National Biscuit Company—known today as Nabisco (an $8.8-billion multinational food business marketing in eighty-five countries). Pilot Bread became known as Crown Pilot crackers and has the distinction of being Nabisco's oldest product. Crown Pilot crackers are sold only in the Northeast, but they can be mail-ordered from Nabisco (see sources, page 233).

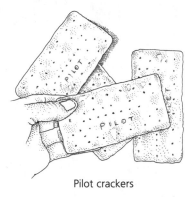

Pilot crackers

For reasons unknown, in May 1996, Nabisco stopped producing Crown Pilot crackers. Up in Maine, where some old-fashioned chowder makers still layer their chowders with crackers, Pilots, as they are called, have an almost cult-like following, and all throughout New England, people who grew up with Crown Pilot crackers as a staple were heartbroken. The response was passionate and overwhelming. Nabisco received more than thirty-five hundred calls and letters from loyal fans. (A spokesperson for Nabisco commented that they had discontinued 300 products at the same time, "and 299 of them passed quietly into the night.") After nine months, Nabisco reversed its decision and, in a symbolic gesture, loaded the first batch of reintroduced Pilot crackers onto a ship in Boston that made stops in Newburyport and Gloucester, Massachusetts, before sailing on to its final destination, Portland, Maine. When the ship arrived in Portland, it was greeted by hundreds of people for whom this was a joyous occasion. It may seem corny that the citizenry could care so much about a cracker, but this was not just any cracker: it was hardtack. For many people, it was an irreplaceable component of their chowders and an integral part of their seafaring heritage.

Other Crackers

In addition to common crackers and Crown Pilot crackers, there are many other crackers that are suitable to serve with chowder. Crackers for chowder should be crisp and hard so they don't get soggy too quickly. Tender crackers, which usually have a high fat content, are not very good in chowder, nor are salty crackers, because chowder should be well seasoned before it is set on the table—salty crackers could ruin a good chowder. The shape of the cracker doesn't really matter. Small soup crackers can be put whole into chowder, large crackers can be crumbled. Chowder is a rustic dish, so, when possible, choose a cracker that has a simple, even homemade, appearance. With the wide variety of crackers available, I'm sure you won't have any trouble finding one that meets my criteria for chowder.

Toasted Garlic Bread

Crisp slices of toasted baguette spread with garlic butter and sprinkled with a touch of coarse salt and pepper pair beautifully with several of the more bold-flavored chowders in this book, such as South Coast Portuguese Fish Chowder (page 90), Manhattan Red Clam Chowder (page 133), and San Francisco Crab "Meatball" Chowder (page 164). Although there is nothing wrong with serving crackers or mild-flavored bread with these assertive chowders, I don't like to miss the chance to serve these toasts when appropriate. I do love soft, chewy American-style garlic bread, but with chowder I prefer a drier, crisper version. Instead of crumbling these toasts into the chowder, as I do with crackers, I like to dunk them in the chowder, a little bit at a time. If you're inclined to, you can also serve them in the French style, placing them in the bottom of the bowl and ladling the chowder over them.

Cook's Notes

In this recipe, I sauté the garlic in olive oil, which softens the flavor of the garlic as it infuses the oil with garlic flavor. After the garlic oil cools, I mix it with butter, creating a garlic butter with a smooth, even flavor.

For equipment, you will need a serrated knife, a large baking sheet, a 5- to 6-inch skillet or sauté pan, a small mixing bowl, and a pastry brush.

1 rustic baguette (French bread)
2 tablespoons olive oil
6 cloves garlic, finely chopped
**   (2 tablespoons)**

6 tablespoons unsalted butter, softened
Kosher or coarse sea salt and freshly
**   ground black pepper**

1. Preheat the oven to 350°F.

2. Using a serrated knife, slice the baguette on a bias into pieces that are ⅔ inch thick and about 5 inches from end to end. Lay the slices of bread on a baking sheet and bake in the oven for 20 minutes, or until golden brown. Remove from the oven and let cool. (Leave the oven on.)

3. Combine the oil and garlic in a 5- to 6-inch skillet or sauté pan and sauté over medium heat for about 4 minutes, until the garlic is softened but has not colored. Pour the garlic and olive oil into a small mixing bowl. When it has cooled down a bit, add the softened butter and stir to make a smooth paste. Brush the garlic butter evenly over the toasted baguette slices, season with salt and pepper, and return to the oven for another 15 minutes, or until the garlic is browned and the toasts are a deep golden brown. Serve warm or at room temperature.

Makes 14 to 16 toasts

Christopher Kimball's Buttermilk Baking Powder Biscuits

The summer of 1999 will remain vivid in my memory because of two meals. The first was a striped bass chowder I prepared from fish that I caught on vacation in Rhode Island. The second was a hearty down-home dinner cooked by my friend Chris Kimball when my family and I visited the Kimballs on their farm in West Sandgate, Vermont. Overlooking the cornfield, we dined on braised veal shanks and sweet corn picked minutes earlier from that same field. Buttermilk biscuits, still warm from the oven, were in high demand. We had to fend off our combined seven children, who intended to eat every one of the biscuits as quickly as possible. I couldn't blame them: they were the best biscuits I've ever put in my mouth—a perfect combination of rich flavor and light, flaky texture. The secret: a combination of butter and shortening. Chris, publisher and editor of *Cook's Illustrated,* has long been one of the staunchest champions of American cooking, and the testing and precision involved in his recipes, even the simplest, is legendary.

I like to eat buttermilk biscuits with chowders, and I originally intended to include my recipe in this book, but after one bite of Chris's biscuits, I retired it. Chris was gracious enough to let me print his recipe, which was published in his marvelous *Yellow Farmhouse Cookbook.*

Cook's Notes
This recipe requires a food processor. If you do not have one, make instead Cheddar Cheese Biscuits (page 212), which can be made quickly and easily by hand, with or without cheese.

For equipment, you will need a food processor, a rubber spatula, a rolling pin, a biscuit cutter (2- to 2¾-inch), and a baking sheet.

2 cups all-purpose flour	**4 tablespoons chilled unsalted butter, cut**
½ teaspoon salt	**into 1-tablespoon pieces**
2 teaspoons baking powder	**3 tablespoons chilled vegetable shortening**
½ teaspoon baking soda	**⅔ to ¾ cup buttermilk**

1. Preheat the oven to 425°F.

2. Combine the flour, salt, baking powder, and baking soda in the bowl of a food processor. Process for 2 seconds to mix. Add the butter to the flour and pulse 7 times, 1 second each time. Add the shortening and pulse another 6 times, or until the mixture looks like coarse meal (the flour should take on a slightly yellowish hue from the butter).

3. Transfer the mixture to a large bowl. Using a rubber spatula, fold the mixture together while adding the buttermilk in a very thin stream. When the dough starts to hold together, press it with the side of the spatula into one mass; note that you may use a little more or less than the buttermilk called for.

4. Turn the dough onto a floured surface and use a rolling pin to roll it out very gently to a thickness of ½ inch. (You can also simply flatten the dough with your outstretched hands.) Use a biscuit cutter to cut out rounds, pushing the cutter straight down without twisting, and arrange the biscuits at least 1 inch apart on a baking sheet. Bake for about 10 minutes, until golden brown, turning the sheet from front to back after 5 minutes. Serve hot.

Makes 10 thick 2³/₄-inch biscuits or 16 thicker 2-inch biscuits

Cheddar Cheese Biscuits

These rich yet fluffy biscuits are a cheesy version of old-fashioned cream biscuits. The cream does double duty as liquid and fat, making them quick and easy to prepare. Served hot from the oven, cheddar cheese biscuits are terrific with many different chowders, especially the farmhouse (non-seafood) varieties. This recipe makes a dozen medium-sized biscuits; they are so good you will probably want to double it!

Cook's Notes

You can make the unbaked biscuits up to 6 hours in advance, cover, and store in the refrigerator. Pull them out of the refrigerator about an hour before dinner and pop them into the oven right before you begin to reheat the chowder. They will bake in 15 minutes, so you can serve them right out of the oven.

Plain cream biscuits, although not quite as good as Buttermilk Baking Powder Biscuits (page 210), are a snap to make and are good with almost any chowder. Simply omit the Cheddar cheese, without any other adjustments to the recipe.

For equipment, you will need a baking sheet, a medium mixing bowl, a rubber spatula, a rolling pin, and a pastry brush.

4 tablespoons unsalted butter, melted
2 cups pastry flour
2 teaspoons baking powder
1 teaspoon sugar
1 teaspoon salt

6 ounces Vermont or other sharp
white Cheddar cheese, finely
grated (1½ cups)
About 1 cup heavy cream

1. Preheat the oven to 375°F. Lightly grease a baking sheet (approximately 10 by 15 inches) with 1 tablespoon of the melted butter.
2. Combine the flour, baking powder, sugar, and salt in a medium mixing bowl and stir well to mix. Add 1 cup of the Cheddar cheese and gently stir until the cheese is evenly mixed into the flour. Slowly add the cream, mixing gently with a rubber spatula, until a soft dough begins to form; you may need slightly more or less than 1 cup cream. Transfer the dough to a lightly floured surface and gently knead until smooth. Try not to overwork the dough.
3. Roll the dough out into a rectangle about 10 by 6 inches and about ¾ inch thick. Dust the work surface lightly with additional flour if needed. Cut the dough crosswise in half and brush one half with half of the remaining melted butter. Place the other half on top of the

buttered half and gently roll your pin over the top so the pieces stick to each other. Sprinkle the top of the dough with the remaining ½ cup grated Cheddar and press it gently into the dough so it stays put. Using your hands, even the sides of the rectangle, and brush the top with the remaining butter. Cut the dough into approximately 1½-inch squares by cutting it lengthwise into 3 strips and then cutting each strip into 4 pieces. Place about 1 inch apart on the buttered baking sheet and bake for about 15 minutes, until golden brown, turning the pan around halfway through the baking. Serve hot.

Makes 12 medium biscuits

Parker House Rolls

Having worked for more than a year in the kitchen of the famous Parker House in Boston, I can speak with some authority about these legendary rolls, the most buttery of America's traditional yeast breads. Owned and operated by Harvey D. Parker, the Parker House opened in 1856 and was the first hotel in America to abandon the rigid custom of a set time for each meal. Parker was a true innovator. The environment he created spawned many original dishes that have become classics: Boston Scrod, Boston Cream Pie, Parker House Tripe, and Parker House Rolls. One story about how this folded (almost dented) dinner roll came about credits an angry baker, whose lover, a chambermaid at the hotel, was falsely accused of stealing jewelry from a guest. The baker went postal, taking out his rage on the unbaked dinner rolls, smashing every one of them with his fist. When he calmed down, he brushed them with butter, folded them back together, and baked them. The guests raved about them, and Parker House Rolls have been folded ever since.

Parker House Rolls are not difficult to make at home, they just require a little time and patience: the dough has to be shaped and given time to rise three times. The result is a unique elegant, slightly sweet, buttery, soft, and tender roll that is hard not to like. This recipe makes two dozen; at the Parker House, we made about twelve hundred every day. Although we portioned the dough in a Duchess Divider (a press that cuts dough into equal portions), everything else was done by hand. It took hours on end to make the rolls each morning, and the bakery was always cluttered with trays of rolls waiting to finish rising. The bakers rarely smiled until the last pan of rolls went into the oven.

Cook's Notes

Like all breads, you can make these rolls by hand, but if you have a KitchenAid or other heavy-duty mixer with a dough hook, it makes the job much easier. I enjoy the process of kneading bread, so I use the mixer until the dough is well formed (that's the messy part), then I finish kneading it by hand. Parker House Rolls do not require as much kneading as other breads, because they are intended to be soft and tender, not overly chewy.

Because of their high butter content, these rolls are best served warm. You can time them for dinner, or simply reheat them before you serve them.

For equipment, you will need a small saucepan (for scalding the milk and for melting the butter), a heavy-duty mixer, a large mixing bowl, a wooden spoon, a pastry brush, and a large baking sheet (14 by 16 inches is perfect).

1 cup whole milk

1½ teaspoons kosher salt or 1 teaspoon table salt or fine sea salt

1 tablespoon unsalted butter, plus 5 to 6 tablespoons unsalted butter, melted

1 package (¼ ounce) active dry yeast

1 tablespoon sugar

¼ cup warm water (110° to 115°F)

3 cups all-purpose flour, or a little more if needed

2 teaspoons vegetable oil

1. In a small saucepan, combine the milk, salt, and 1 tablespoon butter and scald the milk (heat just until a few bubbles appear around the edges) over medium heat. Immediately remove from the heat. Let the milk cool slightly—it should be warm, not hot, when you add it to the dough.

2. Combine the yeast, sugar, and warm water in the bowl of your mixer or in a large mixing bowl and give it a stir. Let sit for about 10 minutes, while the yeast "blooms." When the yeast is frothy, add the warm milk and flour. Using the dough hook, jog the mixer (turn it on and off quickly), to prevent the flour from flying out of the bowl, and mix until the dough comes together and the sides of the bowl are clean; or mix it with a wooden spoon. If the dough is sticky, add another tablespoon of flour. Knead the dough by machine for about 5 minutes, or by hand for 8 to 10 minutes, until smooth and elastic.

3. Grease a large bowl with the vegetable oil. Shape the dough into a ball, place it in the bowl, and turn it once so it is lightly greased all over. Cover with plastic wrap or a damp cloth and place in a warm, draft-free spot. (An oven that has been heated to 200°F and then turned off is a perfect spot.) Let the dough rise for about 30 minutes, until it doubles in size.

4. Punch down the dough. Divide it into 24 equal pieces, weighing about 1 ounce each. (I shape the dough into a rectangle, then cut it lengthwise into 4 strips and crosswise into 6 pieces each.) Using a pastry brush, generously brush melted butter on the baking sheet (use at least 1½ tablespoons). Roll each piece of dough into a ball and arrange them about 1 inch apart on the baking sheet. Place the pan back in the warm, draft-free spot and let the balls rise for about 20 minutes, until they double in size. (There is no need to cover them for this step.)

5. After the balls have doubled in size, press the handle of a wooden spoon down across the center of each ball, without cutting the balls in half. The balls will deflate a little. Generously brush one side of each ball with melted butter, using about 1½ tablespoons in all. Fold the unbuttered side of each roll over the buttered side and press together. The rolls will look like half-moon-shaped pillows. Place the pan back in the warm spot and let the rolls rise until they have doubled in size.

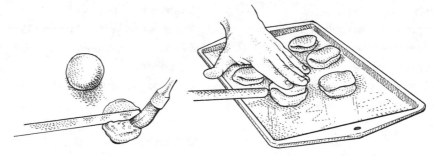

Folding Parker House Rolls

6. While the dough is rising for the last time, preheat the oven to 400°F.

7. Place the rolls in the oven and bake for 15 minutes, until the tops are evenly browned, turning the pan front to back halfway through the baking. Remove the rolls from the oven and, while they are still piping hot, brush the tops generously with the remaining melted butter. Serve warm.

Makes 24 medium rolls

Anadama Bread

The story of Anna and her angry husband who cursed her ("Anna, damn her") has become a cliché in New England cookbooks, but the bread that resulted from her misfortune (this part of the story has a few versions) is truly delicious, and anadama is definitely one of New England's best traditional breads. So the story (which I am trying to avoid repeating here once more) does have a happy ending . . . especially for those who love baking and eating home-baked bread.

Cook's Notes

There are many recipes for anadama bread, all made with a mixture of flour and a small amount of yellow cornmeal. Most versions are pretty similar, although some use milk and others don't, and some use maple syrup while others use molasses. I don't use milk; I use a little more corn than usual; and I do use molasses, but only half as much as most. My version of anadama bread is less sweet, with a little more corn flavor than most, making it more suitable as an accompaniment to savory foods like chowder. This bread is especially well suited to serve alongside any of the chowders that include corn.

In this recipe, I call for bread flour. You can substitute all-purpose flour with good results, but the bread will not be quite as chewy. If two loaves are too many, you can freeze the second loaf for another day.

For equipment, you will need a heavy-duty mixer, a large mixing bowl, a wooden spoon (if making the dough by hand), two 9½- by 5-inch loaf pans, and a pastry brush.

1 package (¼ ounce) active dry yeast	**3½ cups bread flour**
1 tablespoon sugar	**1 cup yellow cornmeal**
About 1¼ cups warm water (110° to 115°F)	**Butter or vegetable oil for greasing the bowl and loaf pans**
2 tablespoons unsalted butter, melted	**1 large egg, beaten with 2 tablespoons water for egg wash**
2 tablespoons dark molasses	
2 teaspoons salt	

1. Combine the yeast, sugar, and ¼ cup of the warm water in the mixer bowl or in a large mixing bowl and mix well. Set aside for about 10 minutes, while the yeast "blooms." When the yeast looks frothy, add the melted butter, molasses, salt, flour, and cornmeal. Slowly add up to 1 cup more warm water, mixing with the dough hook or a wooden spoon. The amount of liquid may vary, depending on the flour, so add just enough water to form a soft, but not sticky dough. Knead by machine for about 10 minutes, or by hand for about 15 minutes, until the dough is smooth and elastic.

3. Lightly oil or butter a large bowl. Shape the dough into a ball, place it in the bowl, and turn it once so it is lightly greased all over. Cover with plastic wrap or a damp cloth and place in a warm, draft-free spot. (An oven that has been heated to 200°F and then turned off is a perfect spot.) Let the dough rise until doubled in volume, about 1 hour.

4. Grease two 9½- by 5-inch loaf pans. Turn the dough out onto a lightly floured surface. Cut it in half and shape each half into a loaf. Place each in a greased 9½- by 5-inch loaf pan, return to the warm spot, and let the loaves rise until they are about doubled in size, 20 to 30 minutes.

5. Meanwhile, preheat the oven to 350°F.

6. Brush the top of the loaves with the egg wash and bake for 1 hour, or until deep golden brown. To test for doneness, remove the hot bread from one pan and knock on the bottom of the loaf: you will hear a hollow sound if the bread is done. If necessary, return to the oven for 5 to 10 minutes. Turn both loaves out of the pans and cool on a rack for at least 20 minutes before serving.

Makes 2 loaves

Skillet Corn Bread

I love the smell of corn bread hot out of the oven. It's my idea of what a home kitchen ought to smell like. Skillet corn bread takes only five minutes to mix and twenty minutes to bake, and it costs less than a dollar for a thick eight-inch round—a good deal, no matter how you slice it. Skillet corn bread makes a good companion for creamy fish or clam chowder. It's also right at home with any of the farmhouse chowders.

There are hundreds of recipes for corn bread, all very similar. The proportions of corn and flour vary, but the rest of the ingredients are basically the same. I like to use a fifty-fifty cornmeal-flour ratio. Once you make this recipe a few times, you won't even need a recipe— you can just eyeball it—that's how I make it, and I never have a problem.

Corn bread is not just a south of the Mason-Dixon Line dish; almost every one of my old New England cookbooks has a recipe for it. The most common version was called "spider" corn bread (named after the round pot it was baked in, a spider) and it was usually made with a cup of milk poured over the batter to create more moistness. For chowder, I prefer a skillet corn bread, which is crisper and drier. You can make very good corn bread with butter or corn oil, but for great corn bread you need bacon drippings. In my chowder recipes, most of the bacon fat is removed—instead of discarding it, I save it to make this corn bread!

Cook's Notes

An 8- or 9-inch round cake pan, well greased, can be substituted for the skillet. The timing is about the same, but the corn bread will not be as crisp or browned on the bottom and sides.

For equipment, you will need a large mixing bowl, a wire whisk, a rubber spatula, and a well-seasoned 8- to 9-inch cast-iron skillet; for corn sticks, you will also need a standard corn stick pan (or pans) and a pastry brush.

1 cup yellow cornmeal

1 cup all-purpose flour

1 teaspoon kosher salt or scant
   ¾ teaspoon table salt or fine sea salt

2 tablespoons sugar

1 tablespoon baking powder

2 large eggs, beaten

1 cup plus 2 tablespoons whole milk

4 tablespoons bacon fat, unsalted butter, or corn oil (3 tablespoons for the batter, 1 tablespoon for the skillet)

1. Preheat the oven to 425°F.

2. Combine the cornmeal, flour, salt, sugar, and baking powder in a large mixing bowl and whisk together to mix well. Add the eggs and milk and mix well until you have a smooth batter.

3. Heat an 8- to 9-inch cast-iron skillet over low heat and add the bacon fat or butter. (If you are using corn oil, just add 3 tablespoons directly to the batter.) When the fat is melted, pour 3 tablespoons into the corn bread batter and mix well. Leave the remaining 1 tablespoon of fat in the skillet and turn the heat up to medium-high. When the pan is hot (but not scorching hot), scrape in the batter; you will hear it sizzle. Immediately place the skillet in the oven and bake for about 20 minutes, until the corn bread is golden brown on top. To test, stick a skewer into the center of the corn bread; if it comes out clean, the bread is done. Use a spatula to remove the corn bread to a wire rack and let it cool for 10 minutes, then cut into wedges and serve warm.

Makes one 8-inch round corn bread

Variation: Corn Sticks

I adore everything about these miniature corn-shaped breads—their appearance, aroma, taste, and texture. Bread doesn't get more all-American than corn sticks, even though the corn stick mold I bought recently was made in China! Follow the skillet corn bread recipe to make corn sticks, but make these few changes:

Increase the oven temperature to 450°F.

Substitute 1 cup heavy cream for the milk.

Add the cooked kernels (see Step 1, page 223, for cooking instructions) from 1 ear of corn (½ cup) along with the cream.

Separate the eggs, and whip the egg whites until stiff. Mix the batter as instructed, adding only the yolks, then fold in the egg whites.

Increase the bacon fat to about 6 tablespoons and use about 3 tablespoons to brush the corn stick molds.

Preheat the oven and place the corn stick mold on the middle oven rack, close to the front of the oven, to preheat for at least 10 minutes. Melt the bacon fat or butter. Open the oven door, pull out the rack, and quickly brush the inside of the molds with bacon fat; you will hear it sizzle. Immediately spoon enough batter into each indentation to fill it completely. Gently push the rack back into the oven, close the door, and bake the sticks for about 10 minutes, until they are light golden brown. (They taste great when they are well browned, but you can see the corn kernel design more clearly when they are golden brown.) Leave the mold on the oven rack and use a fork to lift the sticks from the indentations. (I use my fingers, but they are very heat-resistant.) If you work quickly, you can grease and fill the mold again for the next batch as soon as you've removed the first one; if you want to play it safe, heat the empty mold for 5 minutes, then start again. Repeat until all the batter is used up.

Makes about 24 corn sticks

Sweet Corn Fritters

These crisp golden fritters, made with fresh sweet corn and cornmeal, are a great summer treat and a terrific side dish for chowder. Everybody loves them! I first started serving these with Lobster and Corn Chowder (page 170). It may seem redundant, but because the corn is stewed in chowder and quick-cooked in fritters, the combination offers an interesting contrast. These fritters go well with many other chowders in this book as well, from fish to clam to all of the farmhouse chowders.

Cook's Notes

Use any variety of fresh sweet corn, although the yellow and bicolor varieties will make the fritters more colorful.

You can make great fritters with yellow cornmeal, but for authentic New England flavor, use real "jonnycake flour," a stone-ground meal made from white flint Indian corn (see sources, page 233).

A little ham or bacon makes a tasty addition to the fritters. Add 2 to 3 ounces cooked ham, cut into ¼-inch dice, or 3 ounces bacon fried crisp and finely chopped. You could also substitute 3 tablespoons of the rendered bacon fat for the butter in this recipe.

Your batter should be tight enough so that the fritters hold together easily when dropped in the hot fat, but not so tight that they retain a perfect round shape when cooking. Fritters should take on their own funny imperfect shapes—when I see a perfectly round fritter, I know it will be dense and heavy. Step 4 in the recipe explains how to test and adjust the batter to the perfect consistency.

Cooked fritters do not make very tasty leftovers, but you can keep leftover batter in the refrigerator for an extra day. Before cooking, test one fritter first, and if it seems dense, add a few drops of milk and a pinch of baking powder to lighten the batter.

It will take you about 20 minutes to fry the entire batch, so have a warm oven (200°F) ready to keep the cooked fritters warm. (The recipe can be halved, but even with just my wife and three kids, half a batch left us wanting more.)

For equipment, you will need a 4-quart pot (for cooking the corn); a pair of tongs; a 5- to 6-inch skillet or sauté pan (for sautéing the bell pepper); a large mixing bowl; a wooden spoon; a heavy saucepan that is 8 to 10 inches in diameter and 6 inches deep (the deep pan makes frying safer) and a deep-frying thermometer, or a Fry Daddy or other deep fryer (for frying the fritters); two ordinary tablespoons or soupspoons or, even better, a small ice cream scoop (for dropping the fritters); and a wire-mesh or slotted spoon.

2 large or 3 small ears corn, husked	1 teaspoon kosher or sea salt
1 small red bell pepper (4 ounces), cut into ¼-inch dice	½ teaspoon freshly ground black pepper
	¼ teaspoon cayenne pepper
3 tablespoons unsalted butter	5 scallions, thinly sliced
1½ cups all-purpose flour	3 large eggs, beaten
½ cup jonnycake meal or yellow cornmeal	1 cup whole milk
1 tablespoon baking powder	Corn oil for deep-frying

1. Fill a 4-quart pot two-thirds full with lightly salted water and bring to a boil. Husk the corn and wipe away any corn silk sticking to the ears of corn. Drop the ears into the boiling water and cook until the corn is tender, 1 to 5 minutes, depending on the corn. Generally, the younger and fresher the corn, the more quickly it will cook; I always take a little nibble to test for doneness. Use a pair of tongs to remove the corn and let cool to room temperature. With a knife, cut the kernels from the cobs. Using the back of the knife, scrape out any of the milky remains and add to the kernels. You should have 1½ cups.

2. Combine the bell pepper and butter in a 5- to 6-inch skillet or sauté pan and simmer over low heat for about 5 minutes, until the pepper is tender. (This may seem like a lot of butter for the pepper, but the butter will also serve as the fat in the batter.) Remove from the heat.

3. In a large mixing bowl, combine the flour, jonnycake meal, baking powder, salt, black pepper, and cayenne and stir to mix well. Add the corn, the bell pepper with the butter, the scallions, eggs, and milk. Mix thoroughly, but do not overmix, or the fritters will be tough. Cover and refrigerate the batter for at least 1 hour. (The batter can be made as far as 6 hours in advance.)

4. Preheat the oven to 200°F. Before you fry, check the consistency of the batter: it should be thick enough to hold its shape on a spoon. It will be thicker than most batters (such as muffin batter) and have a gritty texture. If necessary, the batter can be thickened by sprinkling in a bit more flour, or thinned with a few drops of milk (see Cook's Notes). In a deep heavy 8- to 10-inch saucepan, heat 3 inches of oil to 350°F. Using one spoon to scoop out some batter and another to release the batter from the spoon, or using an ice cream scoop, drop one fritter (3 to 4 tablespoons batter) in the hot oil and fry, turning it with tongs or a spoon so it cooks evenly, for about 2 minutes, until it is a deep golden brown. Remove it with a mesh or slotted spoon, giving it a little shake over the pan of oil to drain, and place it on a plate lined with paper towels to absorb the excess oil. Check the size: it should be about the size of a golf ball, no larger. Then taste this test fritter, and adjust the seasoning and consistency of the batter if necessary. (Salt especially plays an important roll in cornmeal-based breads, here enhancing the flavor of the corn and the cornmeal.)

5. Drop 5 to 6 fritters into the pan, leaving enough space for them to move freely. Cook for 2 to 3 minutes, until golden brown, turning them frequently, then remove, drain, and place on the plate lined with paper towels. Transfer to a baking sheet lined with paper towels and keep warm in the oven while you continue to fry the remaining batter; allow the oil to reheat to 350°F between batches. Serve hot.

Makes about 24 small fritters (about 1½ inches in diameter)

Clam Fritters

Clam fritters, also called clam cakes in New England, go well with other clam dishes, especially clam chowder and steamers. This deep-fried quick bread is served in clam shacks and local restaurants up and down the New England coast. Each place has its own style and size; unfortunately, many don't use enough clams in them. I add a generous portion of chopped clams, and the broth from steaming the clams for even more flavor.

Cook's Notes

You can make great clam fritters with yellow cornmeal, but for authentic New England flavor, use real "jonnycake flour," a stone-ground meal made from white flint Indian corn (see sources, page 233).

I don't usually add bacon to clam fritters, but if I have any extra bacon fat left over from chowder making, I substitute that for the butter in this recipe. It adds terrific flavor.

In this recipe, the butter (or bacon fat) is warmed with the clam juice and milk (Step 3) until melted. Although not completely necessary, warming the liquid softens the cornmeal and makes the fritters a bit more tender.

Your batter should be tight enough so that the fritters hold together easily when dropped in the hot fat, but not so tight that they retain a perfect round shape when cooking. Fritters should take on their own imperfect shape—when I see a perfectly round fritter, I know it will be dense and heavy. Step 4 in the recipe explains how to test and adjust the batter to the perfect consistency.

This recipe makes 24 large fritters, enough to accompany a full batch of chowder. If that is too many, you can cut the recipe in half. Cooked fritters do not make very good leftovers, but you can keep leftover batter in the refrigerator for an extra day. Before cooking, test one fritter first; if it seems dense, add a few drops of milk or clam broth and a pinch of baking powder to the batter to lighten it up.

It will take you about 20 minutes to fry the entire batch, so have a warm oven (200°F) ready to keep the cooked fritters warm.

For equipment, you will need a 4-quart pot with a tight-fitting lid (for steaming open the clams); a fine-mesh strainer; a large mixing bowl; a wooden spoon; a 1-quart saucepan; a heavy saucepan that is 8 to 10 inches in diameter and 6 inches deep (the deep pan makes frying safer) and a deep-frying thermometer, or a Fry Daddy or other deep fryer (for frying the fritters); two large soup spoons or small serving spoons, or even better, a small ice cream scoop (for dropping the fritters); and a wire-mesh or slotted spoon.

4 pounds small quahogs or large cherry-stone clams	**1 cup whole milk**
½ cup water	**4 tablespoons unsalted butter**
2 cups all-purpose flour	**4 large eggs, lightly beaten**
1 cup jonnycake meal or yellow cornmeal	**6 scallions, thinly sliced**
1 tablespoon baking powder	**Corn oil for deep-frying**
1 teaspoon freshly ground black pepper	**Kosher or sea salt**

1. Scrub the clams thoroughly and rinse clean. Add the water to a 4-quart pot, cover, and bring to a boil over medium-high heat. As soon as the water boils, quickly add the clams and cover tightly. After 5 minutes, uncover and stir the clams. Quickly cover the pot again and let steam for 5 minutes more, or until most of the clams have opened; don't wait for all of them to open, or they will be overcooked. It should only take a little tug or prying to open the stragglers once they are removed from the heat. The total cooking time for large cherry-stones is about 10 minutes; quahogs will need as much as 5 minutes longer. As soon as you remove the clams from the heat, carefully pour as much of the broth as you can into a small container. Let the broth sit for 10 minutes, then carefully pour through a fine-mesh strainer; you should have about 1 cup of broth (you may have more, but you only need 1 cup). Remove the clams from their shells and dice into ⅓- to ½-inch pieces (you will have about 1 cup [8 ounces] of diced clams.)

2. In a large mixing bowl, combine the flour, jonnycake meal, baking powder, and pepper, and stir to mix well.

3. In a 1-quart saucepan, combine the milk, the reserved clam broth, and the butter and heat over low heat until the butter has melted and the mixture is almost hot, but not boiling. Stir the liquid into the flour mixture and, as soon as it is fairly well blended, add the eggs. Continue to mix until the batter is almost smooth, then add the clams and scallions and mix thoroughly; do not overmix, or the fritters will be too tough. Cover and refrigerate the batter for at least 1 hour. (The batter can be made as far as 6 hours in advance.)

4. Preheat the oven to 200°F. Before you fry, check the consistency of the batter; it should be thick enough to hold its shape on a spoon. It will be thicker than most batters (such as muffin batter) and have a gritty texture. If necessary, the batter can be thickened by sprinkling in a bit more flour, or thinned with a few drops of milk. In a deep heavy 8- to 10-inch saucepan, heat 3 inches of oil to 350°F. Using one spoon to scoop out some batter and another to release the batter from the spoon, or using an ice cream scoop, drop one fritter in the hot oil and fry, turning it with tongs or a spoon so it cooks evenly, for about 3 minutes, until it is a deep golden brown. Remove it with a mesh or slotted spoon, giving it a little shake over the pot of oil to drain, and place it on a plate lined with paper towels to absorb the excess oil. Check the size: it should be about 2 inches in diameter, no larger. Then taste this test fritter and, if necessary, add salt and adjust the consistency. (Salt plays an important roll in cornmeal-based breads, enhancing the flavor of the cornmeal.)

5. Drop 4 or 5 fritters into the pan, leaving enough space for them to move freely. Cook for 3 to 4 minutes, until golden brown, turning them frequently, then remove, drain, and place on the plate lined with paper towels. Transfer to a baking sheet lined with paper towels and keep warm in the oven while you continue to fry the remaining batter; allow the oil to reheat to 350°F between batches. Serve as soon as possible.

Makes about 24 medium fritters (about 2 inches in diameter)

Salt Cod Fritters

I love salt cod, but I seldom use it in chowder. The only chowder I make with salt cod is the Azorean-Style Chowder (page 153) where, mixed with other fish and shellfish, it adds depth and contrast. Otherwise, I like it better for brandade, salad, fish cakes, or these fritters, which are a very special treat, well worth the trouble to make. Serve these fritters alongside a New England Fish Chowder (page 79) made with fresh cod, or with the Bahamian Conch Chowder (page 156) or the Azorean-Style Chowder. In New England, salt cod fritters are traditionally made with a lot of potatoes in the mix. In this recipe, I use some potatoes, but I also add in flour and baking powder, like the Caribbean salt cod fritters known as acra or "stamp and go." The result is light, puffy balls that are crisp, tangy, salty, and delicious.

Cook's Notes

Let the salt cod soak in fresh water for at least 8 hours, changing the water a minimum of four times; keep it refrigerated during the soaking. My directions should leave you with salty, but not overly salty, cod; you will adjust the final seasoning at the end.

Your batter should be tight enough so that the fritters hold together easily when dropped in the hot fat, but not so tight that they retain a perfect round shape when cooking. Fritters should take on their own funny imperfect shapes—when I see a perfectly round fritter, I know it will be dense and heavy. Step 5 in this recipe explains how to test and adjust the batter to the perfect consistency.

Cooked fritters do not make very good leftovers, but you can keep leftover batter in the refrigerator for an extra day. Before cooking, test one fritter first and if it seems dense, add a few drops of milk or clam broth and a pinch of baking powder to the batter to lighten it.

It will take you about 20 minutes to fry the entire batch, so have a warm oven (200°F) ready to keep the cooked fritters warm.

For equipment, you will need two 1-quart saucepans (for simmering the salt cod and boiling the potatoes); a food mill (for ricing the potatoes; optional); a 6- to 7-inch skillet or sauté pan (for frying the garlic and onions); a large mixing bowl; a wooden spoon; a heavy saucepan that is 8 to 10 inches in diameter and 6 inches deep (the deep pan makes frying safer) and a deep-frying thermometer, or a Fry Daddy or other deep fryer (for frying the fritters); two ordinary tablespoons or soupspoons or, even better, a small ice cream scoop (for dropping the fritters); and a wire-mesh or slotted spoon.

½ pound boneless salt cod, soaked in cold
water
10 ounces Yukon Gold, Maine, PEI, or
other all-purpose potatoes, peeled and
cut into 1-inch pieces
4 tablespoons unsalted butter
½ small onion (2 ounces), finely minced
1 clove garlic, finely minced (1 teaspoon)
1 cup all-purpose flour

2 teaspoons baking powder
1 teaspoon Coleman's dry English mustard
½ teaspoon freshly ground black pepper
3 large eggs, lightly beaten
½ cup whole milk
5 large sprigs fresh Italian parsley, leaves
removed and coarsely chopped (¼ cup)
Vegetable or corn oil for frying
Kosher or sea salt

1. Place the soaked salt cod in a 1-quart saucepan, cover with cold water, and bring to a simmer over low heat; do not let it boil. Using a slotted spoon, remove the salt cod as soon as it has cooked through. You can tell if it's cooked by prying it open with a fork—it should be creamy white, with no translucence. Naturally, the thinner pieces will cook faster than the thicker pieces. After all the salt cod is cooked, place it on a cutting board and finely chop. Cover and keep refrigerated until ready to use.

2. Meanwhile, place the potatoes in another 1-quart saucepan, cover with lightly salted water, and bring to a boil. Turn down the heat to a simmer and cook the potatoes until tender, about 15 minutes, then drain well. Mash them very fine or rice them in a food mill.

3. Place the butter, onion, and garlic in a 6- to 7-inch skillet or sauté pan and sauté over medium heat for 5 minutes, or until the onion is very soft and beginning to brown. Remove from the heat and let cool to room temperature.

4. In a large mixing bowl, combine the flour, baking powder, dry mustard, and pepper and stir to mix well. Add the salt cod, mashed potatoes, the sautéed onions and garlic with the butter, the eggs, milk, and parsley. Mix thoroughly, but do not overmix, or the fritters will be too tough. Cover and refrigerate the batter for at least 1 hour. (The batter can be made as far as 6 hours in advance.)

5. Preheat the oven to 200°F. Before you fry, check the consistency of the batter: it should be thick enough to hold its shape on a spoon. It will be thicker than most batters (such as muffin batter). If necessary, the batter can be thickened by sprinkling in more flour, or thinned with a few drops of milk. In a deep heavy 8- to 10-inch saucepan, heat 3 inches of oil to 350°F. Using one spoon to scoop out some batter and another to release the batter from the spoon, or using an ice cream scoop, drop one fritter into the hot oil and fry, turning it with tongs or a spoon so it cooks evenly, for about 3 minutes, until it is a deep golden brown. Remove it with a mesh or slotted spoon, giving it a little shake over the pot of oil to drain, and place it on a plate lined with paper towels to absorb the excess oil. Check the size; it should be about the size of a golf ball, no larger. Taste this test fritter and adjust the seasoning (you haven't added any salt yet, but the salt cod adds a lot); also check the consistency and adjust if necessary.

6. Drop 5 or 6 fritters into the pot, leaving enough space for them to move freely. Cook for 2 to 3 minutes, until golden brown, turning them frequently, then remove, drain, and place on the plate lined with paper towels. Transfer to a baking sheet lined with paper towels and keep warm in the oven while you continue to fry the remaining batter; allow the oil to reheat to 350°F between batches. Serve as soon as possible.

Makes about 24 small fritters (about 1½ inches in diameter)

Sources

Most of the ingredients I include in my chowders are common, everyday foods—nothing fancy or exotic. However, in this day and age, when it is easier to find balsamic vinegar than good salt pork, I thought a list of a few sources might be useful. Some items, like jonnycake meal, Pilot crackers, and common crackers, are readily available in parts of New England but unheard of elsewhere. If you live away from the Atlantic or Pacific coasts, mail-ordering seafood is a great way to get fresh ocean fish and shellfish. Prices are better than you may think, although the overnight shipping charges are expensive and unavoidable. There are hundreds of seafood vendors who ship fresh seafood; I don't pretend to know them all. These are sources that I have used and have been happy with; it is for your convenience and is not meant to reflect, in any way, on those sources not included.

Salt Pork, Bacon, and Other Meat

Basse's Choice
P.O. Box 1
Smithfield, VA 23430
(800) 292-2773
Gwaltney salt pork, slab bacon, Smithfield ham

The Harrington Ham Company
Main Street
Richmond, VT 05477
(800) 487-9549
smoked bacon and hams and Vermont cheeses

D'Artagnan
280 Wilson Avenue
Newark, NJ 07105
(800) DARTAGNAN
pheasant, specialty meats and foods

Hormel Foods
1 Hormel Place
Austin, MN 55912
Kansas City, MO
(800) 533-2000
Homeland salt pork (no mail-order, but will direct you to a store in your region)

Gaspar's Sausage Company
384 Faunce Corner Road
North Dartmouth, MA 02747
(800) 542-2038
Portuguese chouriço

Cavendish Game Birds
396 Woodbury Road
Springfield, VT 05156
(800) 805-2251
pheasant and game birds

Cheese and Dairy

Kate's Homemade Butter
P.O. Box 79
Old Orchard Beach, ME
(207) 934-5134
terrific butter

Shelburne Farms
Harbor Road
Shelburne VT 05482
(802) 985-8686
farmhouse Cheddar cheese

Cabot Creamery
P.O. Box 128
Cabot, VT 05647
(800) 639-3198
*Vermont Cheddar cheese and other
dairy products*

Fish and Shellfish

Maine Lobster Promotional Council
382 Harlow Street
Bangor, ME 04401
(207) 947-2966
*complete list of mail-order specialists for
Maine lobster and other seafood*

Captain Marden's Seafoods, Inc.
279 Linden Street
Wellesley, MA 02482
(781) 235-0860
*fresh cod, haddock, bluefish, clams,
and other New England fish and shellfish;
also salt cod and finnan haddie*

Browne Trading
260 Commercial Street
Portland, ME 04101
(800) 944-7848
*fresh cod, haddock, oysters, and other
New England fish and shellfish; also
specialty seafood like diver scallops*

Cotuit Oyster Company
P.O. Box 563
Cotuit, MA 02635
(508) 428-6747
quahogs and oysters

Mill Cove Lobster Pound
P.O. Box 280
Boothbay Harbor, ME 04538
(207) 633-3340
lobsters and other Maine seafood

Constitution Seafoods
1 Fish Pier Road
Boston, MA 02210
(888) 767-1776
*cod, haddock, lobster, and other
New England seafood*

Faidley's Seafood
Lexington Market
200 N. Paca Street
Baltimore, MD 21202
(410) 727-4898
*steamed blue crabs and other
Chesapeake region seafood*

Waterfront Market
201 Williams Street
Key West, FL
(305) 294-8418
conch and other tropical seafood

Mutual Fish
2335 Rainier Avenue South
Seattle, WA 98144
(206) 328-5889
geoduck clams and other West Coast fish and shellfish

Crackers and Grains

The Vermont Country Store
RR1, P.O. Box 231
North Clarendon, VT 05759
(802) 775-4111
common crackers and other New England specialties

Gray's Grist Mill
P.O. Box 422
Adamsville, RI 02801
(508) 636-6075
authentic jonnycake meal (white cornmeal), yellow cornmeal

Nabisco
7 Campus Drive
Parsippany, NJ 07054
(800) NABISCO
Crown Pilot crackers (one-case minimum)

Kenyon Corn Meal Company
21 Glenn Rock Road
West Kingston, RI 02892
(800) 753-6966
authentic jonnycake meal (white cornmeal) and other stone-ground meals

Odds and Ends

Mo Hotta Mo Betta
P.O. Box 4136
San Luis Obispo, CA 93403
(800) 462-3220
Outerbridge's Original Sherry Peppers Sauce, Full Hot Rum Peppers Sauce, and other hot sauces

Somerset Bean Company
RFD 1, P.O. Box 1575
Skowhegan, ME 04976
(207) 474-8865
cranberry beans and other dried beans

Gourmet Mushrooms
P.O. Box 391
Sebastopol, CA 95472
(707) 823-1743
wild mushrooms

Bibliography

Allen, Darina. *Simply Delicious Fish.* Dublin: Gill and Macmillan, 1991.

Anderson, Jean. *The Food of Portugal.* New York: William Morrow, 1986.

Beard, James. *Delights and Prejudices.* New York: Atheneum, 1964.

———. *The James Beard Cookbook.* rev. ed. New York: Dell, 1980.

Bowles, Ella Shannon, and Dorothy S. Towle. *Secrets of New England Cooking.* New York: M. Barrows, 1947.

Child, Julia. *In Julia's Kitchen with Master Chefs.* New York: Alfred A. Knopf, 1995.

Child, Lydia Maria. *The American Frugal Housewife.* 1833. Facsimile edition. New York: Applewood Books, 1984.

Davidson, Alan. *North Atlantic Seafood.* New York: Harper & Row, 1979.

Early, Eleanor, *New England Cookbook.* New York: Random House, 1954.

Farmer, Fannie Merritt. *The Boston Cooking School Cookbook.* Boston: Little, Brown, 1930.

———. *The Original Boston Cooking School Cookbook.* Facsimile edition. New York: Hugh Lauter Levin Associates, 1986.

Hibler, Janie. *Dungeness Crabs and Blackberry Cobblers.* New York: Alfred A. Knopf, 1991.

Hooker, Richard J. *The Book of Chowder.* Boston: Harvard Common Press, 1978.

Jones, Evan. *American Food: The Gastronomic Story.* New York: Dutton, 1974.

Jones, Evan, and Judith Jones. *The L.L. Bean Book of New New England Cookery.* New York: Random House, 1987.

Kimball, Christopher. *The Yellow Farmhouse Cookbook.* Boston: Little, Brown, 1998.

King, Louise Tate, and Jean Stewart Wexler. *The Martha's Vineyard Cookbook.* Boston: Globe Pequot Press, 1971.

Kurlansky, Mark. *Cod: A Biography of the Fish That Changed the World.* New York: Walker, 1997.

McClane, A. J. *The Encyclopedia of Fish Cookery.* New York: Holt, Rinehart and Winston, 1977.

Melville, Herman. *Moby-Dick.* 1851. New York: Mead and Company, 1942.

Nabisco Public Relations. News release. February 4, 1997.

Oliver, Sandra L. *Saltwater Foodways.* Mystic, CT: Mystic Seaport Museum, 1995.

Paige, Jeffrey S. *The Shaker Kitchen.* New York: Clarkson N. Potter, 1984.

Platt, June. *June Platt's New England Cookbook.* New York: Atheneum, 1971.

Ranhoffer, Charles. *The Epicurean.* Chicago: Hotel Monthly Press (John Wiley), 1920.

Root, Waverly, and Richard de Rochemont. *Eating in America: A History.* 1976. Reprint. Hopewell, NJ: Ecco Press, 1981.

Shields, John. *The Chesapeake Bay Crab Cookbook.* Reading, MA: Addison-Wesley, 1992.

Schwind, Cap'n Phil. *Clam Shack Cookery.* Camden, ME: International Marine Publishing, 1975.

Thorne, John. *Down East Chowder.* In *Serious Pig,* by Thorne, John, with Matt Lewis Thorne. New York: Farrar, Straus and Giroux, 1996. (Originally published by Jackdaw Press, Boston, 1982.)

Wakefield, Ruth Graves. *Toll House Tried and True Recipes.* New York: M. Barrows, 1941.

Wolcott, Imogene. *The New England Yankee Cook Book.* New York: Coward-McMann, 1939.

Index

When a recipe has more than one reference, the page number in **boldface** refers to the recipe itself; other page numbers refer to additional information. Page numbers in *italics* refer to illustrations.

breads:

anadama, 205, **217–18**

Pilot Bread, 21, 207

quick, 205

skillet corn, 205, **219–21**

toasted garlic, 77, 204, **209**

yeast, 205

broths, 53–74

chilling and freezing of, 56–57

composition of, 53

cooking time for, 56

liquid in, 55

making of, 54–57

mussel, 55, **65–66**

store-bought, 53

substituting of, 54

see also beef broth; chicken broth; clam broth

Brown, Helen Evans, 121

butter:

in early chowder recipes, 23

as salt pork or bacon substitute, 40

sweet vs. salted, 50

buttermilk baking powder biscuits, Christopher Kimball's, 205, **210–11**

button mushrooms, 183, 183

C

cabbage:

Digby Bay scallop chowder with bacon and, 139, **144–46**

and pheasant chowder, 41, **201–3**

Canada, chowder-making tradition in, 15–16, 19–20, 25, 93

cannellini:

in clam, white bean, and potato chowder, 136–38

in shrimp chowder with white beans and tomatoes, 162–63

Cape scallop and lobster chowder, 172

caraway seeds, in pheasant and cabbage chowder, 201–3

carrots:

in Bermuda fish chowder with crab, 102–4

in chicken stock, 72–73

in farmer's chicken chowder, 193–95

in lobster stock, 67–68

in Manhattan red clam chowder, 133–35

in pheasant and cabbage chowder, 201–3

in strong fish stock, 58–59

in traditional fish stock, 60–61

in turkey stock, 200

Castroville, Calif., 178

cayenne pepper:

in farmer's chicken chowder, 193–95

in lightly curried mussel chowder, 147–49

in sweet corn fritters, 222–24

celery:

in Bahamian conch chowder, 156–59

celery (cont.)

in Bermuda fish chowder with crab, 102–4

in Chesapeake crab chowder, 167–69

in chicken stock, 72–73

in clam, white bean, and potato chowder, 136–38

in crab stock, 69–71

in double haddock chowder, 99–101

in farmer's chicken chowder, 193–95

in leftover turkey chowder with sage, 197–99

in lobster stock, 67–68

in Manhattan red clam chowder, 133–35

in New England clam (quahog) chowder, 112–13

in Nova Scotia lobster chowder, 93–95

in pheasant and cabbage chowder, 201–3

preparation of, 45

in razor clam chowder, 118–21

in restaurant-style thick clam chowder, 127–29

in Rhode Island clear clam chowder, 130–32

in savory summer fish chowder, 96–98

in Seattle geoduck chowder, 123–26

in steamer clam chowder, 114–17

herbs (*cont.*)

Hooker, Richard J., 19, 164, 183

hot sauce:

    in Bermuda fish chowder with
      crab, 102–4

    in Chesapeake crab chowder,
      167–69

    rum-based, in Bahamian
      conch chowder, 156–59

    see also Tabasco sauce

Howard Johnson's restaurants,
    127

Hudson, Bertha, 180

Hudson, Ethel, 180

I

ingredients, chowder, *see* chow-
    der ingredients

*In Julia's Kitchen with Master
    Chefs* (Child), 58, 204

*In Julia's Kitchen with Master
    Chefs* (TV series), 58, 204

International Cook Book, The
    (Filippini), 141

Irish shellfish chowder, 63, 139,
    150–52

Irving, John, 27

J

jalapeño chile, in savory summer
    fish chowder, 96–98

James Beard Cookbook (Beard),
    118

Joe Tilden's Recipes for Epicures
    (Tilden), 164

Jones, Evan, 25, 109

jonnycake meal:

    in clam fitters, 225–27

    in sweet corn fritters,
      222–24

jowter, 19

K

ketchup:

    mushroom, 21, 183

    in nineteenth-century chow-
      der recipes, 21, 22, 183

    tomato, 22

Key West conch chowder, 158

Kimball, Christopher, 210

King, Louise Tate, 139

L

lambi, 156

    see also conch

langostino, in Irish shellfish
    chowder, 150–52

layered fish chowder, 38, 76,
    86–88, *89*

leek(s):

    and mushroom chowder, 44,
      183–85

    in Nantucket veal chowder,
      190–92

    and oyster chowder, 44, 139,
      141–43

leftover turkey chowder with
    sage, 41, 173, **197–99**

Legal Sea Foods restaurants, 127

Leslie, Eliza, 22, 75

lightly curried mussel chowder,
    51, 65, 139, **147–49**

lima beans:

    in clam, white bean, and
      potato chowder, 136–38

    in dried bean chowder, 182

    in shrimp chowder with white
      beans and tomatoes,
      162–63

lime juice, in Bahamian conch
    chowder, 156–59

Lincoln, Mary J., 23, 24, 173, 175

Little Compton, R.I., 17, 210

littleneck clams, *see* clams, little-
    neck

Lobster at Home (White), 170

lobster carcasses and shells:

    in crab stock, 69–71

    in lobster stock, 67–68

lobster chowder:

    Cape scallop and, 172

    corn and, 26, 40, 45, 51, 67,
      170–72, 222

    New England–style, 172

    Nova Scotia, 93–95

lobsters, 38, *67*

    flavor and storage of, 39

lobster stock, 67–68

    in Nova Scotia lobster chow-
      der, 93–95

low-fat clam chowder, 109, **132**

Lucas, Dione, 25

Lynde, Benjamin, 20, 28

M

mackerel, Azorean-style chowder
    with mussels, squid, salt fish
    and, 76, 139, **153–55**, 228

turkey stock, 200
	in leftover turkey chowder
		with sage, 197–99
turmeric, in corn chowder,
	175–77
turnips, 25

V

veal chowder:
	early recipes for, 23
	Nantucket, 41, 173, **190–92**
vegetable oil, as salt pork or veg-
	etable substitute, 40
Vermont Country Store, 22, 204,
	206
vinegar, red wine, in Azorean-
	style chowder with mussels,
	squid, mackerel, and salt fish,
	153–55
vinegar, white, in egg chowder
	with bacon and new pota-
	toes, 188–89
Virginia Housewife, The
	(Randolph), 21–22

W

Webster, Daniel, 22
Webster's New World Dictionary,
	15
West Coast Cook (Brown), 121
Westfield, Mass., 178
Wexler, Jean Stewart, 139
White, Hayley, 17
White, Jasper, 25–26, 170
White, J. P., 17, 164
White, Mariel, 17
White, Nancy, 17, 72, 102, 130
white bean(s):
	clam, and potato chowder,
		110, **136–38**
	shrimp chowder with toma-
		toes and, 162–63
whiting, *see* hake
wine, in eighteenth-century
	chowders, 20, 21, 28
wine, white:
	in Azorean-style chowder
		with mussels, squid, mack-
		erel, and salt fish, 153–55

in lobster stock, 67–68
in shrimp chowder with fen-
	nel, 160–62
in strong fish stock, 59
in traditional fish stock, 60–61
wolffish, *37*
	cutting fillets of, 30, 37
Worcestershire sauce, in restau-
	rant-style thick clam chowder,
	127–29
World According to Garp, The
	(Irving), 27

Y

yeast breads, timing of, 205
Yellow Farmhouse Cookbook
	(Kimball), 210

Z

zuppa di vongole, 24, 133